Homes for the Third Age

A Design Guide for Extra Care Sheltered Housing

Homes for the Third Age

A Design Guide for Extra Care Sheltered Housing

David Robson   Anne-Marie Nicholson   Neil Barker

E & FN SPON

Published by E & FN Spon, an imprint of Chapman & Hall,
2-6 Boundary Row, London SE1 8HN, UK

Chapman & Hall, 2-6 Boundary Row, London SE1 8HN, UK

Chapman & Hall, GmbH, Pappelallee 3, 69469 Weinheim,
Germany

Chapman & Hall USA, 115 Fifth Avenue, New York, NY 10003,
USA

Chapman & Hall Japan, ITP-Japan, Kyowa Building, 3F,
2-2-1 Hirakawacho, Chiyoda-ku, Tokyo 102, Japan

Chapman & Hall Australia, 102 Dodds Street, South Melbourne,
Victoria 3205, Australia

Chapman & Hall India, R. Seshadri, 32 Second Main Road,
CIT East, Madras 600 035, India

First edition 1997

© 1997 University of Brighton, School of Architecture and
Interior Design, and Hanover Housing Association

Desk-top publishing by Neil Barker

Printed in Great Britain by George Over Ltd, Rugby

ISBN 0 419 23120 X

This book is based on original research conducted by

The Housing Research Unit
of
The University of Brighton
School of Architecture and Interior Design
Mithras House, Lewes Road, Brighton BN2 4AT

in collaboration with

Jim Bagley, Michèle Hollywood and Peter Shearer
of
The Hanover Housing Association

Material on environmental engineering was supplied by
Dr Andrew Miller and Dr. Kenneth Ip
of
The University of Brighton
Department of Construction, Geography and Surveying

The research project was supported by

The Housing Corporation
149 Tottenham Court Road, London W1P OBN

and

The Hanover Housing Association
Hanover House, 18 The Avenue, Egham TW20 9AB

Acknowledgements

The authors would like to acknowledge help received from:

Staff and residents in schemes run by:

Hanover Housing Association
Hanover Property Management Ltd
Anchor Housing Association
Bovis Retirement Homes
Brighton Borough Council
Ealing Family Housing Association
CCHA Extra Care
London and Quadrant Housing Association
McCarthy and Stone plc
Notting Hill Housing Trust
Peverell Services Ltd, New Milton
Retirement Security Ltd
Servite Houses Ltd
South Downs Health Trust
West Lambeth Community Care Trust

and the following individuals and organisations:

Professor Peter Lloyd of the University of Sussex
Heather Burnley and Kester Merrington,
  Ealing Family Housing Association
Biba Hanson and Malcom Wilson,
  Peter Lyell Court, Ruislip
Mr & Mrs Graham Woodman
Ursula Robson-Schuster
Paul Tanner
The East Sussex Disability Association, Lewes
Paul Trofimov, McCarthy & Stone plc, Bournemouth
Peter Phippen, Roger Battersby and Maurice Heather,
  PRP Architects, Hampton Court
Jim Monahan of CGHP Achitects, London .
Andrew Farrell,
  Purvis & Purvis Architects, Greenwich
The Charter Partnership, Bedford
Fielden Clegg Architects, Bath
The University of the Third Age
Jeremy Porteus of the RNIB
Manchester Fire Brigade
DOE Fire and Stuctures Branch
Tim Knowles, Pressalit Ltd, Ilkley

Contents

Foreword

As we age chronologically, so our bodies grow frail; we lose mobility and our senses become impaired. We need support but we struggle to maintain our independence.

Most of us would prefer to continue living in our own homes - places which we know - surrounded by memories and mementoes. But for some retirement or sheltered housing is an attractive option. It offers security from street violence; a manager maintains a watchful eye over us; we no longer have to cope with unused rooms, awkward stairs, an unruly garden or with fixing the broken tiles on the roof. The companionship of others, though often not considered initially as a high priority, later becomes a valued resource.

So we have a new home, new neighbours; and here we hope to spend the rest of our days. Retirement housing is not just a staging post on the last lap of our journey. Care packages - whether facilitated by the manager or provided by an in-house team - can be provided more efficiently within the context of grouped housing.

But our efforts to maintain a good quality of life are often frustrated by the poor design of our own home. For most of us 'design' suggests those corners which the wheelchair or frame cannot navigate, the cupboards and window catches which we cannot reach, taps which we cannot turn - all prevalent faults in homes built for older people but designed by strapping younger men and women. There is however much more to 'design' than this. We must be able to enjoy and control our living environment; we need to express our own individuality; we should be able to distinguish public from private space. For those who cannot move outside of their housing complex the corridors and foyers are their outside world and the 'kiosk' takes on the role of a village shop and meeting place.

Far too many retirement housing schemes have been poorly designed; now with this manual there should be no excuse for deficiencies. The authors would not claim to have touched upon every eventuality, but they do raise the important issues. Their brief was to deal with a very specific form of housing - 'extra care' sheltered housing. However, their prescriptions are no less valid for any housing which might be occupied by older people and they thus concern us all, for we will all grow older, hoping to stay in our homes for as long as possible.

Congratulations, therefore, both to the authors and their colleagues in the University of Brighton, to the Hanover Housing Association and to the Housing Corporation for their respective contributions to this exciting enterprise.

Peter Lloyd

Emeritus Professor of Social Anthropology in the University of Sussex

Introduction

This guide is intended to serve as a design primer. It focuses on the requirements of a particular type of housing for the elderly known as 'Extra Care Sheltered Housing' which fills a gap between sheltered housing and residential care accommodation.

Sheltered housing first appeared in Britain in the early 1960s and exists today under a number of different guises run by a bewildering array of sometimes competing agencies. Although local authorities are still the main providers of sheltered housing for rent, the role of housing associations in the voluntary sector has been growing for some time. An estimated 700 separate housing associations now manage over 150,000 dwellings between them (NFHA, 1991). For this reason there is often confusion about terminology with different associations applying different names to the same category or giving the same name to different categories.

The term 'Extra Care Sheltered Housing' refers to a particular concept of sheltered housing which provides fully independent housing units to which a range of care services can be delivered, and to which a variety of communal facilities can be added. Being something of a hybrid this concept has already attracted a confusing clutch of names, among them 'Category 2.5 Sheltered Housing', 'Frail Elderly Sheltered Housing', 'Very Sheltered Housing' and 'Assisted Sheltered Housing'. A further confusion results from the fact that in the past some organisations have used the term 'Extra Care Sheltered Housing' to describe what are in fact versions of registered residential care accommodation.

In this report the term is applied to a specific concept in which the key elements are:

- fully independent dwelling units
- comprehensive communal facilities
- a separation of housing management from care delivery
- a cost-effective and flexible method to mobilise public subsidies and individual savings

The guide has evolved as a direct response to a particular concept of Sheltered-Housing-With-Care which is currently being developed by the Hanover Housing Association. This concept is aimed primarily at frail elderly people of slender means who rent their homes, and whose housing and care costs are met, at least in part, from a complex cocktail of housing benefit, income support, attendance allowances and state pension. However, the Hanover Housing Association is now working together with McCarthy & Stone plc, a leading developer of retirement homes for owner occupiers, to extend the concept of Sheltered-Housing-With-Care into the private sector, and the way is open for new initiatives which cross over the normal tenure boundaries.

As local authorities gradually withdraw from their role as providers of sheltered housing, it seems likely that the housing needs of a substantial group of the frail elderly will be met in the future by housing associations and by private house builders, working either separately or in tandem, and collaborating with social services departments. It is hoped therefore that much of what is contained in this report will be applicable to both sectors.

The guide is mainly concerned with those planning, spatial, environmental and constructional issues which have a direct bearing on the design and development of a sheltered housing scheme. These issues are considered primarily from the point of view of the two main groups of people who would inhabit such a scheme: the residents and the various support professionals who serve them. It is not a book about management, about finance or about the detailed issues of care provision. Nor does it stray into general technical areas which are not specific to sheltered housing.

The report has been written for all those who are involved with the commissioning, the building and the running of sheltered housing schemes: development managers, scheme managers, social workers, carers, architects and planners. Every effort has been made to avoid the use of technical jargon or complicated drawings. It has been prepared by the Housing Research Unit in the University of Brighton in collaboration with the Hanover Housing Association and with the support of the Housing Corporation.

In preparing this report members of the unit have visited a large number of sheltered housing schemes of every category and have interviewed a large cross section of people including residents, scheme managers, carers, and development managers.

Homes for the Third Age

Chapter 1
Background

1.1
The Third Age

'...............................It is ten o'clock:
Thus may we see......how the world wags
'Tis but an hour ago since it was nine;
And after one hour more 'twill be eleven;
And so, from hour to hour, we ripe and ripe,
And then, from hour to hour, we rot and rot;
And thereby hangs a tale.'

Touchstone/Jacques in 'As You Like It'
by William Shakespeare

1.1.1
Old Age

When does old age begin? Age can be defined in physiological, chronological or socio-economic terms. Our bodies change as we pass from childhood to adolescence, from adolescence to maturity and from maturity into old age, though these changes affect us all at different chronological points in time. But society marks or acknowledges these changes with precise chronological definitions and celebrates them with 'rites of passage'. In Britain people start their formal education at five, are given the vote at eighteen, and are considered officially to have reached 'retirement age' at sixty if they are women and sixty-five if they are men.

A number of important social and economic changes occur for many people as they approach old age: those who have brought up children suddenly find themselves alone, those in active employment are confronted with retirement and life on a pension; for some the change is signalled by the loss of a partner, for others by loss of employment or income. Sooner or later everybody must come to terms with the fact that they 'are not getting any younger' and so there comes a moment which can never be defined precisely when they enter the 'Third Age'.

1.1.2
A Demographic Time Bomb

The population of Britain has recently stabilised and only a modest growth is predicted for the coming decades. However, this relative stability in the total population disguises some enormous changes which are taking place in its composition: in particular the number of older people is set to increase rapidly during the early decades of the next century.

The 1991 census recorded that, during the previous decade, the population of Britain had remained almost static at around 54 million. There were 10 million people of pensionable age (i.e. women over 60 and men over 65). Of these about 4 million were over the age of 75 and almost a million over the age of 85. Because women were living on average 5 years longer than men, their relative proportion increase in ascending age bands. In the group aged over 75 women outnumbered men by almost two to one.

A comparison of age structure profiles over the past hundred years reveals the extent to which the composition of the British population has changed. The steep pyramid structure which characterised the final decades of the 19th century has given way to a

beehive shape as the proportion of middle-aged people increased and the proportion of younger people decreased.

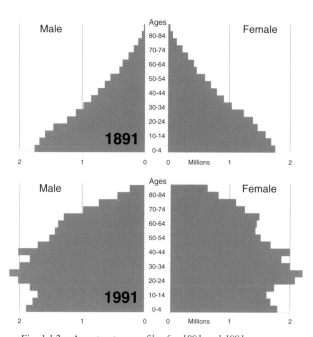

Fig. 1.1.2a: Age structure profiles for 1891 and 1991

Future numbers of older people can be predicted with some accuracy because those cohorts which will form the elderly of the next six decades are already with us. If current trends continue, the combination of declining birth rates and increased longevity will lead to a substantial increase in the number of older people.

During the present decade the proportion of people over retirement age will grow by less than 2%. This is because an increase in the number of old elderly which results from high birth rates following the end of the First World War is neutralised by a smaller number of young elderly which results from falling birth rates during the late 1920s.

After 2001 dramatic changes are predicted. In England and Wales between 2001 and 2031 the total population will increase from 50 million to 53 million, while the number of pensionable people will rise from 9.4 million to 14.8 million. More dramatically still, the number of people over 75 will rise to 4.5 million, and over 85 to nearly 2 million.

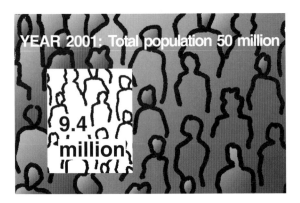

Fig. 1.1.2b: People of pensionable age in 2001

Fig. 1.1.2c: People of pensionable age in 2031

The predicted increase in the number of pensionable people, a result of the post-Second World War baby boom, will coincide with a drop in the number of people of working age as the effects of the lower fertility rates of the 1970s and 1980s are felt. The proportion of retired to employed people is expected to rise steeply during the first decades of the twenty-first century: a growing number of non-working people will then have to be supported by a shrinking work force. The situation in Britain will be less serious, however, than in other European countries.

Minority ethnic groups at present account for about 6% of the general population. Their age structure is younger as a result of migration patterns and different rates of fertility and mortality. However, the number of elderly people of West Indian origin will start to increase rapidly during the next decade, while changes in the age structure of other communities will occur after 2011.

Source: Housing Corporation, 1996

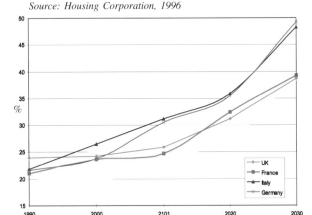

Fig. 1.1.2d: Population aged 65+ as a % of working age population

1.1.3
Summary

The number and proportion of older people in Britain's population will remain fairly static during the present decade. However, substantial increases are predicted during the following three decades. This growth will impact on many aspects of life and is bound to increase the demand for more small homes which can meet the needs of elderly and very elderly people.

1.2
The Effects of Ageing

'...........................The sixth age slips
Into the lean and slipper'd pantaloon,
With spectacles on nose and pouch on side;
His youthful hose, well sav'd, a world too wide
For his shrunk shank; and his big manly voice,
Turning again toward childish treble, pipes
And whistles in his sound. Last scene of all,
That ends this strange eventful history,
Is second childishness and mere oblivion;
Sans teeth, sans eyes, sans taste, sans
everything.'

Jacques in 'As You Like It'
by William Shakespeare

1.2.1
Frailty

Elderly people become more frail as they grow older, though they do so at different rates and in different ways. The effects of ageing are classified under five general headings: musculo-skeletal, cardio-vascular, respiratory, psychiatric and sensory. Deterioration can be rapid or it can be slow and progressive. Often a period of decline can be followed by a period of respite or improvement. Nor do these changes affect every individual to the same degree or in the same way. Some people remain physically strong but suffer mental or sensory deterioration, others remain mentally alert but suffer from physical decline. As these changes overtake people their independence is threatened, their quality of life is seriously affected, and their vulnerability to accident and illness is increased.

Frail elderly people can be thought of as those who have already suffered a degree of physical or mental deterioration, but who are still able to lead fairly independent lives. They are likely to be single, having perhaps already lost a partner, and a large proportion of them are women. They face the frustration of not being able to do all those things which they have been accustomed to do: they have been forced to alter their social habits and as a result they often suffer from isolation, boredom and depression.

Advances in medicine and improvements in medical care have been in part responsible for increased longevity and can help to mitigate the effects of ageing and age-related illnesses. But this does not alter the fact that people become more vulnerable to illness as they grow older. It has been estimated that 40% of people of pensionable age, 4 million people in Britain, suffer from a disabling impairment or long-standing illness. Amongst the 85+ age group this proportion rises to 75%. Over a million older people are unable to go out unassisted, three quarters of a million can't climb stairs, and a quarter of a million can't get out of bed unassisted. Today 20% of those over the age of 85, 160,000 people in all, suffer from senile dementia; if this proportion prevails, by the year 2031 this number could have grown to 350,000.

1.2.2
Impairment and Disability

The various impairments which contribute to the frailty of elderly people do not in themselves necessarily constitute disabilities. Disability, a reduction in the ability to perform a particular task or function, is a product of the interaction between a given set of impairments and the environment: people are disabled not by their impairments, but by their social and physical milieu. One main aim for those who are involved in providing housing for the frail elderly should be to reduce the disabling effects of the general environment. Good design can reduce or even eliminate disability.

1.2.3
The Economic Effects of Ageing

People now retire earlier and live longer. Although this fact ought to be a cause for celebration, it is increasingly regarded as a problem, particularly for society as a whole.

Longer periods of retirement place extra strains on savings. Although a few people are able to shed commitments and enjoy the fruits of savings and pension investments, the majority experience a steady decline in disposable income and purchasing power. This in turn leads to a decline in housing standards, general social and economic deprivation, and ultimately to marginalisation.

The elderly draw income from four sources: retirement pensions and state benefits, savings and investments, occupational pensions, and employment. The value of the retirement pension has been declining for some time when compared to average incomes in the general community. Occupational pensions are usually only taken up by professional people or those in long-term

employment, and, to be effective, rely on substantial contributions over long periods. Only about 2% of people of pensionable age are actually in paid employment.

Recent research indicates that 40% of older people have neither assets nor income and are almost wholly dependent on state benefits: these are people who live in rented accommodation and who can exercise almost no choice over how they are housed or receive care. About one quarter of this group belong to the least well off section of the general community when assessed against such criteria as income, housing and amenities.

A second band of 40% of older people own their own homes and struggle to get by on limited occupational pensions and state benefits. They are unable or unwilling to unlock the equity which is tied up in their home, and though asset-rich, they are often income-poor. Their assets may disqualify them from claiming state benefits, but their income is insufficient to give them any real choice. Increasingly they feel threatened by rules which require them to liquidate their assets in order to fund care, and they feel that they are being penalised for years of prudence.

Only about 20% of older people are believed to have made sufficient provision to cushion the effects of increasing frailty and to exercise real choice over such matters as housing and care provision.

1.2.4
The Social Effects of Ageing

The combination of frailty, bereavement and low income leads to isolation, loneliness and marginalisation. Elderly people find themselves suddenly denied the company of their lifetime partners, children and friends. In 1991 a total of 3.3 million elderly people, one in three, were living alone.

Increasing frailty cuts older people off from social intercourse: it is much more difficult to adjust to impaired hearing or poor eyesight for the old than it is for the young. Low income prevents them from making choices about housing, health and domestic care or leisure activities. Loneliness and poor housing lead to depression which in turn provokes both physical and mental deterioration which in turn increase isolation: a vicious circle.

The 'Third Age' for many older people is far from being a golden one. They are plagued by feelings of insecurity: they perceive themselves to be isolated within an increasingly violent society and live in constant fear of burglary and assault. They worry about money and about the security of their home and are jealous of their privacy and self respect. They crave the reassurance of a home which is safe and secure, warm and dry.

1.2.5
Summary

People become progressively more frail and more susceptible to illness as they grow older. Physical and mental impairments can lead to marginalisation and isolation. Older people need to live in a supportive and stimulating environment; they need housing which is secure, convenient, adaptable and affordable.

1.3
Historic Background

1.3.1
Traditional Societies

In Britain today the institution of the family is under threat and traditional kinship ties have been loosened. People now in their 80s may have surviving children who are themselves already 'old', and younger descendants who span two or three generations. Their surviving relatives, although numerous, could well be scattered to the four corners of the earth. Many young people are no longer able or willing to look after their ageing relatives, and the old are often left to fend for themselves, or the responsibility for their care is ceded to society.

In the past the elderly formed a much smaller section of the community. This was because fertility rates

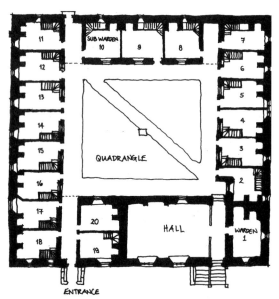

Fig. 1.3.1a: Plan of traditional almshouses

were higher and life spans were shorter. Many cultures placed great emphasis on the obligation to honour and care for elderly relatives. The family was an important social and economic unit which bound succeeding generations together. Often the ownership of property conferred a special power upon older family members.

However, it is a mistake to imagine that the elderly were always well cared for in traditional societies. In some cultures old people were literally 'cast out' when they had become too great a burden to their relatives. Even today there are nomadic tribes in the mountains of central Asia who are said to abandon their older relatives if they are unable to keep up with the family's migrating flocks.

In mediaeval Europe the Christian tradition to 'honour thy father and thy mother' was widely respected, and those old people who were not looked after by their families could seek refuge in the hospitals and almshouses which formed an annexe to most monasteries. These usually consisted of a group of small houses arranged around a courtyard with a gate and lodge. In England, after the dissolution of the monasteries, almshouses were often run by charitable foundations.

During the sixteenth century the Poor Laws established an obligation on the part of parishes to provide shelter and employment for the destitute. However, there were still many elderly people who, lacking the support of family or charitable institution, were forced to join the bands of vagrants which roamed the land.

1.3.2
Modern Britain

In the wake of the Industrial Revolution the nineteenth century witnessed an enormous surge in Britain's population and a meteoric growth in the size of its towns and cities. Old people were often casualties in this period of great change and social upheaval. Poor Law reforms led to the creation of workhouses, institutions which offered accommodation in return for work, and administered charity mixed with Christian zeal and stern discipline. Surveys conducted at the end of the nineteenth century identified old age as being one of the main causes of destitution, and there was a growing clamour from social reformers to introduce old age pensions and set up homes for the elderly.

In 1909 a Royal Commission recommended the creation of special housing for the elderly and paved the way for the development of what came to be known as 'sheltered housing'. However, during the next 40 years little serious attention was given to their design and the model for such housing remained the mediaeval almshouses.

Fig. 1.3.2a: A typical workhouse

Modern developments in the provision of special housing can all be traced back to the reforms introduced under Part III of the National Assistance Act of 1948 which delegated to local authorities the responsibility for providing both care and residential accommodation for the elderly and infirm. This led to the building of local authority residential care homes which came to be known as 'Part III Homes'.

The 1957 Housing Act encouraged local authorities to build special rented housing schemes for the more independent elderly. Following a government circular of 1969 these sheltered housing schemes were classified as Category I or Category II according to the degree of communal provision which they offered. Since the mid-1980s local authorities have been forced to withdraw from their role as housing providers, and the responsibility for developing subsidised sheltered housing has passed largely to housing associations in the 'voluntary sector' acting under the aegis of the Housing Corporation.

Private housing developers have also acted as major providers of housing for the elderly. Retirement bungalows have been a common feature of the British suburbs since the inter-war period. Recently a number of companies have been building retirement flats to standards often similar to those of Category I and Category II sheltered housing.

In 1984 the Residential Homes Act set out criteria for the registration of private residential homes. The past decade has seen a shift from public to private care provision as cuts in public spending have forced the closure of many local authority homes and social service departments have been obliged to place people in private care homes. Today fewer than 5% of pensioners live in care homes and these are viewed increasingly as an expensive and often unsatisfactory option.

Since the early 1980s the government has come to regard local authorities as enablers rather than providers in the field of housing and care for the elderly. There has been a policy shift away from institutionalised care and towards the concept of 'staying put'. The government's community care initiative supports this concept by delivering care services to individuals in their own homes.

1.3.3
Summary

In most pre-industrial societies old people were cared for 'in the community'. The institutionalisation of care is a consequence of the loosening of kinship ties which has occurred in highly urbanised modern societies. Many commentators (e.g. Valins and Salter, 1996) now predict that the wheel will turn its full circle and that the increasing cost of institutionalised care will accelerate the return to care in the community.

Fig. 1.3.2b: A voluntary sector residential care home

1.4
How the Elderly are Housed

1.4.1
Elderly Households

The present century has seen a number of major changes in patterns of housing tenure. The large-scale construction of affordable private houses between the wars saw a shift from private renting towards owner occupation. After the war massive local authority housing programmes produced a further shift away from private renting towards public renting. More recently the 'right to buy' initiative has produced a shift back from public renting towards owner occupation.

In 1991 there were 21.9 million households in Britain. Of these 66% were in owner occupation, 21% were rented from public authorities and 12% were rented privately or from housing associations. Of the households which contained a pensioner, 62% were owner occupied, 27% were public rented, 7% were private rented and 4% were rented from housing associations. Almost 50% of households in the public rented sector, and slightly more than 50% of households in the housing association sector, included at least one pensioner. The rate of owner occupation amongst pensionable households reduced in ascending age groups.

Although people of pensionable age accounted for 18.7% of the 1991 population in Britain, they were represented in 33% of all households. Out of 21.9 million households 7.3 million contained at least one person of pensionable age. In 1.8 million of these pensioners were living together with younger people. Of the remaining 5.5 million households, 3.3 million consisted of one sole pensioner while 2.2 million households consisted of two or more pensioners. Approximately 6 % of Britain's 10 million pensioners

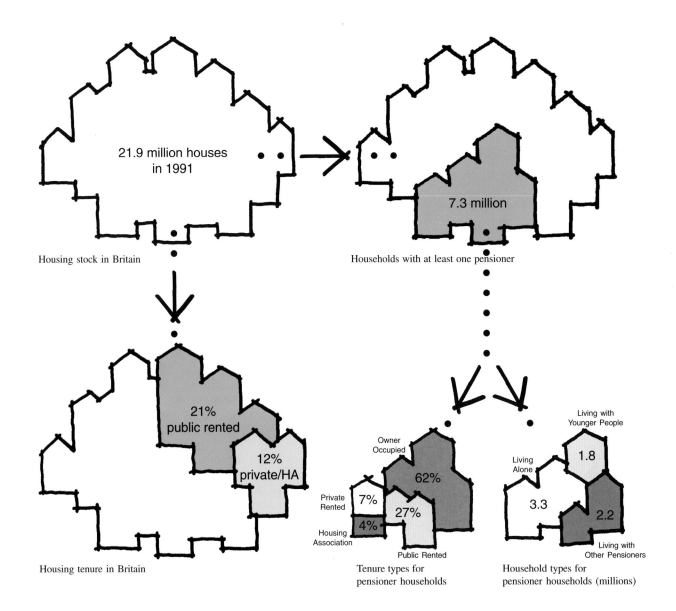

Fig. 1.4.1a: Elderly households in 1991

live in some form of sheltered housing and 5% live in residential care or nursing homes.

While the total population of Britain is growing quite slowly, social changes have produced a considerable increase in the number of households, not least amongst the elderly. Housing completions have fallen progressively during the past two decades, and although there is a theoretical surplus of dwellings over households, the unsuitability of much of the existing stock is causing shortages. It is said that 4.4 million new homes will have to be built during the next 20 years in order to eliminate existing and projected shortages and to replace redundant stock. A high proportion of these will be required to accommodate the growing number of elderly households and to address the current shortage of suitable housing.

1.4.2
Housing Condition

The 1991 House Condition Survey (OPCS, 1993) found that almost 1.5 million homes were unfit, and that a further 3 million were in need of substantial repairs. 75% of those living in the worst housing conditions were said to be pensioners and many of these were living without adequate heating or a proper bathroom. Worst off were elderly households in the private rented and owner occupied sector where about one third were in substandard accommodation.

1.4.3
Caring for the Elderly

As people become more frail they depend increasingly on care from others. This may take the form of domestic help, assistance with everyday tasks, help with personal hygiene, medical care or nursing care.

In 1985 there were 6 million carers in Britain, 75% of whom were involved with the care of elderly people (HMSO, 1985). This figure included unpaid carers such as relatives and friends, casually paid carers, fully professional peripatetic carers and institutional carers. Approximately 1.5 million older people are cared for by someone, usually a relative, in the same household.

A growing shortage of carers is predicted to develop as the numbers of older people increase in relation to the numbers of people of working age during the early decades of the next century.

The fact that many younger people continue to care for elderly relatives ought to be welcomed, in spite of the burdens and strains which this can impose. While government policies do support home carers, it is argued that much more could be done to help and encourage them.

The 3.3 million older people who live alone must resort to a variety of care systems. The active elderly may use occasional paid domestic helpers or rely on neighbours. Many frail elderly people are now supported by community care schemes.

In 1989 the government published its White Paper *Caring for People* (HMSO, 1989). This set out its commitment to provide community-based care services as an alternative to institutionalised care. The community care initiative has much to commend it, and there is no doubt that it has enabled many older people to stay at home who might otherwise have moved into special needs housing or residential care. However, peripatetic care can do little to improve the situation of frail elderly people who are isolated and lonely or who are badly housed, and becomes increasingly expensive for those who need longer periods of care.

The development of more sophisticated alarm systems has greatly extended the scope of community care services, and current developments in the field of 'smart home technology' are expected to have a huge impact in the future.

1.4.4
Exercising Choice

A number of recent studies (e.g. McCafferty, 1994) have focused on identifying older people's housing and care delivery preferences. These suggest that an overwhelming majority of people would prefer to stay in their existing homes for as long as possible, that in terms of preference and assessed need there is an over-provision of standard sheltered housing, and that the prospect of residential care accommodation fills many people with dread.

Such studies are dogged by a number of problems. One is the fact that older people often exercise very little choice over their future: indeed shrinking choice is one of the main consequences of growing old. You can't choose to move in with a relative if you don't have any, or if your relatives don't want you, or if such a move would be geographically or spatially impractical; you can't buy a retirement bungalow if you have no money; you can't move into a sheltered housing scheme if there are no vacancies, or if you don't meet the qualification criteria. Another problem, underlined by Winstanley (1996) is that older people are often confused about the options available to them, so bewildering is the range of housing alternatives, care packages and methods of payment. And finally there is the fact that older people are often unwilling to look around the corner and recognise what their future needs might be.

The situation is also complicated by the fact that as people grow older choices are made for them, directly or indirectly, by relatives, by carers, by social workers. This highlights the fact that what 'they want', what 'others want for them', what may be 'good for them', and what is 'practicably possible' are all quite different things.

1.4.5
Expectations and Aspirations

Expectations of housing are shaped very much by people's past experience, and every individual follows a unique housing pathway as they progress through life. Today's 75 year olds were born in 1922 at a time when a majority of homes in Britain were still privately rented. A high proportion of them will have spent much of their lives in some kind of rented housing. They entered adulthood during a world war and may well have moved into their first home of their own at the end of the 1940s during a period of housing shortage and rationing. Most would have grown up in houses with coal fires, and even without proper bathroom facilities. Central heating, fridges, vacuum cleaners and showers were almost unheard of until after the war.

The divisions and stratifications of class, wealth and housing tenure, which so characterise British society, endure into old age. Most people who have owned their own homes aspire to remain owner occupiers, and a majority of those who live in rented sheltered housing were renters in the past.

Some commentators, in describing the various categories of housing which are available, seem to hold out the expectation that people will actually pass from one category to another as they age. The implied sequence runs as follows: having at some point *taken the decision* to quit their life time home people *choose* to move into something smaller, perhaps a retirement bungalow; later when fully independent living is no longer practicable they *choose* to move into sheltered housing; when even assisted independent living has become impossible they *are persuaded* to move into a residential care home; finally when they are totally dependent on medical care *it is decided* that they should move into a nursing home. Such a sequence does not, of course, correspond with reality: each of these moves brings with it disruption and trauma, and for a single individual to pass through all of them would be terrible.

People often resist making moves which would be beneficial to them, or make inappropriate moves or make the right move at the wrong time. It is now widely agreed that steps should be taken to reduce the number of categories of housing and to clarify the differences between them while increasing the flexibility and cost effectiveness of care delivery systems. People would then be able stay in one place for much longer and would experience fewer disruptive moves.

1.4.6
Summary

The housing stock has not been able to respond sufficiently quickly to the demographic changes which have occurred during the past two decades and many older people are inadequately or inappropriately housed. Older people often face very little real choice in what concerns their housing or care.

1.5
Housing Options for the Elderly

1.5.1
The Range of Options

It is generally agreed that the terminology currently employed to classify housing for the elderly is no longer adequate. A number of attempts have been made to define the different categories of housing in a systematic way. Salmon (1993) uses 7 categories on a scale A to G, with a number of sub-categories. Valins (1988) uses a 1-7 numerical scale based on a system developed by Help the Aged (HtA) in 1986. This section adopts a slightly amended version of the HtA scale as follows:

Level 1: non-specialised and non-adapted dwellings ('staying put' or living with relatives)

Level 2: independent dwellings which have been purpose-built or adapted for fit and active elderly who may need some support but can generally look after themselves

Level 3: purpose-built, self-contained dwellings (to mobility standards) in groups with warden attendance and minimal communal facilities, for active elderly (corresponds to 'Category I')

Level 4: purpose-built, self-contained dwellings (to full mobility and wheelchair standards) in groups with warden attendance and access to communal facilities, for physically frail elderly (corresponds to 'Category II')

Level 5: similar to Level 4 but with extra care support available and the option to take communal meals, sometimes referred to as Category 2.5

Level 6: residential care homes for elderly who may be mentally and physically frail and in need of constant personal care

Level 7: nursing homes for elderly who are sick or very frail and need qualified nursing care

The following is a brief description of some of the options which may be open to older people today.

1.5.2
Level 1: Staying Put

Most older people would prefer to remain in their own homes. For many the family home represents their biggest single investment and symbolises their hopes and achievements. Moving can take people out of their neighbourhood and away from their friends: it implies a break with the past.

The 1981 White Paper *Growing Older* set out policies 'to enable elderly people to live independent lives in their own homes wherever possible - which reflects what the majority themselves want'. These policies have underscored government thinking for over two decades and have dovetailed with community care initiatives.

The vast majority of older people already do stay put, some of them through choice but many because they have no alternative. Specialised housing options at present only cater for one older person in eight and there are many who either cannot afford or do not qualify for them. Many older people live in homes which are badly suited to the requirements of old age: they may be too big, inconveniently sited, inadequately serviced. Behind the desire to stay put lies a fear of the future and the suspicion that the alternatives may be inadequate and costly. For many 'staying put' means 'hanging on'.

A number of agencies now exist to help people adapt and upgrade their homes. The Anchor Housing Association initiated pilot projects in the early 1980s and has established a network of 44 schemes in various parts of the country. So far it has helped 16,000 households to adapt, repair or improve their homes (Randall, 1995). Although over a hundred such schemes are now underway, these can only scratch at the surface of the problem. 'Smart home technology' is expected to play an increasingly important role in the lives of older people and its wider application could make 'staying put' a more feasible prospect.

One alternative to 'staying put' is to move in with relatives, a course of action which is still followed today by about 10% of older people. Today more and more families are dispersed. Living with relatives often necessitates a move to another part of the country, and can result in a severance of social ties. Space standards in new housing have fallen during recent decades, and many families find it difficult to accommodate an ageing relative. Family houses are often ill-suited to the needs of frail elderly people, and extensive adaptations may be necessary.

1.5.3
Level 2: Retirement Housing

Many people respond to their changing circumstances by moving into a home which is smaller and 'more convenient'. Those in rented housing often have limited choice when contemplating such a move, and may have to spend some considerable time on a waiting list, though local authorities and housing associations are usually keen to free-up family sized accommodation. Owner occupiers face a wider range of choice because retirement often coincides with the end of mortgage repayments, and they can buy a cheaper house and liquidate part of their equity.

Few of those who buy retirement homes are aware of the full consequences of ageing or can anticipate the range of impairments which will later affect them. Although they imagine that they are planning for their old age, they choose homes which are unsuited to the needs of frail elderly people.

In suburban housing estates 'Retirement bungalows' are a common feature. Bungalows typically offer two bedrooms, a dining-kitchen and a sitting-dining room and have an area of 60-70 sq.m. Although considered cheap to run and maintain, detached bungalows have a large ratio of external envelope to floor area, and therefore incur high maintenance and heating bills.

Bungalows can only be developed at low densities and are therefore usually found in suburban locations. Thus they are often badly located in relation to amenities and services. Many fail to meet mobility or wheelchair standards.

Fig. 1.5.3a: A typical suburban bungalow

Compact 'retirement flats' offer an alternative to conventional houses. Space standards are similar but prices and running costs are potentially lower. Flats tend to be found in more central locations and are therefore situated closer to amenities and services. A typical flat will have lower heating bills than a house of the same floor area, and many flats offer maintenance packages dependent on regular service charges. Older flats often fail to conform to mobility standards, and a high proportion of those located off the ground are not served by lifts. Walls and floors in cheaply built flats achieve poor standards of sound attenuation. Only 17% of British households presently live in purpose-built flats, and they are generally unpopular with older people.

1.5.4
Sheltered Housing

The first sheltered housing schemes appeared in the 1950s, but local authorities only started to build them on a large scale after 1965. An estimated 300,000 units had been completed by 1980. During the 1980s local authorities built fewer and fewer schemes, while housing associations built correspondingly more. Today there are an estimated 550,000 units of sheltered housing in Britain. Of these, about two thirds are run by local authorities and one quarter by housing associations.

A variety of categories of sheltered housing exist, and dwelling units range from compact bed-sitters through to self-contained two-bedroom apartments.

Private developers have recently started to build their own versions of sheltered housing for leasehold sale, and an estimated 40,000 units now exist, mostly in the South.

Level 3: Category I Sheltered Housing

Category I sheltered housing schemes consist of groups of self-contained dwellings. Although they lack communal facilities, they are usually overseen by a resident warden and are linked to an alarm call system. There are now about 150,000 such dwellings, most of them in the public and voluntary sectors.

Category I Sheltered Housing can take many different forms. Older local authority schemes consist of clusters of detached or terraced bungalows. Open balcony access flats were seen as a practical solution on more restricted sites and are still common in continental Europe. These are often cheaper to build and maintain than conventional flats and increase the possibilities for providing windows to kitchens and bathrooms. More recently, however, internally accessed flats have tended to predominate.

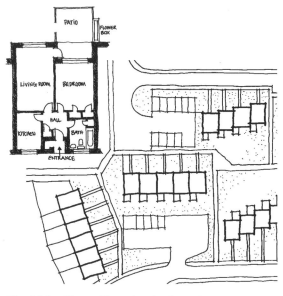

Fig. 1.5.4a: Clustered bungalow development

Fig. 1.5.3b: Retirement flats

Fig. 1.5.4b: Balcony access flats

In the past Category I Housing was often not built to mobility or wheelchair standards. Clustered bungalows pose a number of problems for frail elderly people, particularly where car access is restricted and where the site is stepped. Open balcony access flats were often built without lifts and can be treacherous in cold weather.

Level 4: Category II Sheltered Housing

Category II sheltered housing schemes consist of groups of self-contained dwellings built with a limited provision of communal facilities. Dwelling sizes vary: bed-sitter units are between 25-30 sq.m, single bedroom flats are 40-45 sq.m and two-bedroom flats are 55-65 sq.m. Schemes are overseen by a resident warden and are linked to an alarm call system. Communal facilities may include assisted bathrooms,

at least one sitting room, a room for use by a hairdresser, guest rooms, a residents' laundry and an office for the warden manager.

Schemes usually contain between 20 and 40 units. A typical 30 unit scheme might have a total area of 2,000 sq.m, equivalent to 65 sq.m gross per unit. The weekly rent for a Category II flat is about £75 including service and heating charges.

A number of private developers are now building schemes to Level 4. These are sold on long leases and are administered by management companies which, for an annual service charge, take care of running and maintenance. Residents are responsible for organising and paying for their own care. Such schemes are usually bigger than their rented counterparts. Bed-sitters are almost unknown, and fewer communal facilities are provided. A typical 50 unit scheme might have a total area of about 3,000 sq.m, equivalent to 60 sq.m gross per unit. A one-bedroom flat in a new-build scheme might cost between £50,000 and £75,000, while service charges range between £1,000 and £2,000 per annum.

There are about 300,000 Category II dwellings in existence, most of them in the public and voluntary sectors. A number of commentators (e.g. McCafferty, 1994) suggest that supply now exceeds demand, partly because so many are unsuitable for frail elderly people. Bed-sitter units are now particularly difficult to let.

Although many Category II schemes have been developed to mobility and wheelchair standards, or with the built-in potential for adaptation, a surprising number are sub-standard and would be difficult to upgrade, see Fig.1.5.4e.

Fig. 1.5.4c: A typical Category II scheme

Fig. 1.5.4d: Retirement flats, private development

- unsuitable location and siting

- steps & raised thresholds in public spaces

- narrow doorways and restricted entrance spaces

- long and confusing access corridors

- restricted bedroom dimensions, general inflexibility of space layout

- restricted bathrooms with baths rather than showers

- unsuitable kitchen planning & furniture

- unprotected hot water radiators & pipes

- unsuitable window & door ironmongery

Fig. 1.5.4e: Problems in Category II schemes

Level 5:
Category 2.5 Sheltered Housing (Extra Care)

This category has come into existence almost by default. New types of sheltered housing have evolved to bridge the gap between Category II (Level 4) and Part III (Level 6) accommodation. Many Category II schemes fail to meet full mobility and wheelchair standards. Part III accommodation, on the other hand is expensive. It can rob people of their independence and self respect and can bring about an acceleration in the process of mental and physical deterioration. Somewhere between these two, it is argued, there is a need for a type of housing which can maintain independence, can adapt to accommodate most physical impairments, can easily tap into a variety of care delivery systems and is cost-effective.

The term 'Extra Care' Sheltered Housing has been applied to a number of different types of accommodation which are aimed at filling the gap. Some, notably those operated by Methodist Homes and the Abbeyfield Societies, have evolved down the scale from Level 6 and provide bed-sitter accommodation with a strong emphasis on care provision. Others, such as those now being built by the Hanover Housing Association, have evolved up the scale from Level 4, and provide self-contained flats where the accent is on maintaining independence and adding in care when it is needed. This type of housing forms the main subject of this report and is described in much greater detail in section 1.6.

There are currently about 15,000 units in this category.

1.5.5
Level 6: Residential Care Homes (Part III Homes)

There are about 350,000 people in Britain living in residential care homes. In effect these are hostels for the very frail elderly in which residents occupy small bedrooms, enjoy the use of communal facilities and receive comprehensive domestic support and care.

Local authorities were given the responsibility for establishing subsidised residential care homes under Part III of the National Assistance Act of 1948. The 1984 Residential Homes Act recognised the need both to encourage and control the growing private residential care sector. Although private homes are not required to employ qualified nursing staff they must be registered with the local authority and are subject to regular inspections. They also have to conform to minimum standards of space and amenity.

Fig. 1.5.5a: Local authority residential care home

During the past ten years local authorities, under pressure to cut spending, have been forced to recognise the high cost of maintaining residential care homes and many have been closed. Some additional homes have been closed because they failed to meet the requirements of the 1984 Act. Social service departments have thus come to rely more and more on the voluntary and private sectors.

Many of the early homes built by local authorities set high residential and care standards. Residents would usually be accommodated in single rooms of 12-15 sq.m. A typical home for 30 residents might have a total gross area of about 750 sq.m, equivalent to 25 sq.m gross per resident. Similar standards are provided by housing associations and specialist organisations such as the Abbeyfield Societies.

Privately run residential care homes offer a very wide range of types and standards of accommodation. Small homes accommodating fewer than four residents are subject to separate controls and these sometimes offer few special features and very low standards of space, amenity or care. Many middle-range homes cater either for public-funded residents or for privately funded residents or for a mixture of the two. Top-of-the range homes cater exclusively for wealthy privately funded residents. A substantial number of residential care homes are run as charities and cater for members of particular professions, trade unions, or ethnic and confessional groups.

Few private homes have been purpose-built, and most exist in one or more older residential properties which have been adapted. The quality of accommodation and standards of space and amenity vary enormously. Many homes 'sail close to the wind' and social services departments are involved in a constant struggle to ensure that minimum standards are maintained. A typical private home might well cater for 20-25 residents in a mixture of single and shared rooms. Registration standards stipulate a minimum room size of 9 sq.m for single rooms and 15 sq.m for double or shared rooms. Most rooms have washbasins, and en suite bathrooms are a rarity. Communal facilities include a kitchen, a communal dining room, at least one separate sitting room and shared bathrooms. Staff accommodation consists of a manager's office, a staff room with toilet facilities and a sleep-over room. A lift or stair lift is required in homes on more than one floor and at least one assisted bathroom is usually provided. The total gross area for such a home might be about 500 sq.m or 20 sq.m per resident.

Staff are employed in one night and two daytime shifts to give constant support and are usually led by a non-resident manager and deputy managers.
The cost for publicly funded residents is currently

pegged at about £250 per week and they are left with only £13 per week of residual income from pension. Private residents are often required to pay in excess of £300 per week. Although capital building costs and running costs are relatively low the cost of providing continuous care is high. Staff costs constitute the biggest single budget item, in spite of the fact that care assistants are notoriously badly paid. A typical weekly wage bill would be about £2,500 or £100 per resident.

Standards vary enormously, and while excellent residential care homes exist, there are also many which offer poor accommodation and inadequate care.

Because residential care homes provide a complete support package they take away people's independence and create an environment which can erode privacy and self respect. On the other hand they offer an essential service to those who are very frail and no longer able to look after themselves. Homes often cater for a very broad range of residents, from the relatively fit to the seriously infirm. Tinker (1984) has suggested that one third of residents in care homes could have remained in a more independent situation if the right care support had been available at the right time.

1.5.6
Level 7: Nursing Homes and Geriatric Care Units

Nursing Homes and specialised Geriatric Care Units offer medical care and accommodation to the very frail elderly, and are subject to inspection by local health authorities. They exist in both the public and private sectors and are strictly controlled. Their design lies beyond the scope of this report.

Fig. 1.5.5b: A private residential care home

Fig. 1.5.6a: A modern NHS nursing home

1.5.7
Comparing the Costs

At the risk of over simplification, it might be said that frail elderly people face four choices: they can continue to live where they are, relying increasingly on care services delivered to their door; they can move in with younger relatives; they can move into some form of sheltered housing, be it in the statutory, voluntary or private sectors; or they can move into residential care accommodation. Which of these four would prove to be the most suitable depends on circumstances; which would prove to be the cheapest depends on many variables, including the amount of care provided. And the second question begs another. Cheapest for whom: residents, their relatives, the housing provider, the local authority or central government?

A number of commentators have attempted to compare costs. Tinker (1989) warns: 'Caution must be exercised in any costing exercise, and with "very sheltered housing" special care must be taken in interpreting any comparisons with other forms of housing and care because the extent of meals and care provided was so variable', and concludes that when capital, revenue and statutory costs are taken into account, 'very sheltered housing' is cheaper than residential care accommodation and only marginally more expensive than sheltered housing. Shearer (1996) carried out an exhaustive comparison of costs for an 'average resident in Extra Care Housing' and concluded that where there is a high care provision 'residential care accommodation provides the cheapest option for the public purse' while Extra Care Housing, though marginally more expensive, is a better solution for the resident, who is left with a disposable income of £128.13 compared with the care home resident's £13.75 per week.

1.5.8
Summary

Older people now face a bewildering choice of housing options produced by a plethora of competing housing providers within a complex system of rules and subsidies. 'Staying put' is a popular alternative, and while it is a practical solution for many, it holds few attractions for those who are badly housed. Sheltered housing ought, in theory, to meet the needs of a large constituency, but its current unpopularity is partly due to the unsuitability of earlier schemes. Residential care homes offer an essential service to very frail people, but they are an expensive and inappropriate solution for the housing needs of the active elderly. There is now a recognised need for sheltered housing which is flexible and which can support independent living for a broad range of older people.

1.6
Extra Care Sheltered Housing

1.6.1
What is Extra Care Sheltered Housing?

Extra Care Sheltered Housing is best described in three ways:

- in terms of what it is not
- in terms of its aims
- in terms of what it provides.

In the range of housing categories set out in section 1.5 there is a clear gap which exists between Category II Sheltered Housing and Part III Residential Care Accommodation. The former provides self-contained flats with limited communal facilities and encourages independent living. The average gross area per unit is about 60 sq.m. Capital costs are high and revenue costs are relatively low. The latter offers dependent bedrooms with a full back up of domiciliary and medical care. Here the gross area per resident might be as little as 20 sq.m. Capital costs are relatively low and revenue costs are high.

Extra Care Sheltered Housing offers more comprehensive support than standard sheltered housing, and offers greater flexibility and independence than Part III Residential Care. It provides self-contained flats to mobility or wheelchair standards with an extensive range of communal facilities. A typical scheme with 40 units would have a gross area of about 3,000 sq.m, equivalent to an average of 75 sq.m per unit.

The purpose of Extra Care Sheltered Housing is to provide housing which:

- can be adapted to suit the needs of a broad range of frail elderly residents
- minimises the effects of physical and mental impairments
- enables people to lead as full, as active and as independent a life as possible
- offers security and dignity, comfort and convenience
- offers both privacy and the opportunity to take part in a full social life
- offers good value for money
- helps people to exploit fully their entitlements to benefits while extracting maximum value from their personal savings and investments
- ensures that no money is expended unnecessarily on services or facilities which are not needed or not used
- facilitates the delivery of domiciliary and medical care either by public or private providers as and when it is required

The salient features of Extra Care Sheltered Housing:

- self-contained flats with bathroom, kitchen and separate sleeping and living rooms, designed to mobility standards with the built-in possibility to upgrade them to wheelchair standards
- daily provision of at least one cooked meal in a communal or shared dining room
- use of a communal or shared sitting room, a tenants' laundry room, a fully equipped assisted bathroom, guest rooms, and a maintained garden or open area
- access to specialised care services such as hair-dressing, chiropody etc.
- provision of at least one lift in multi-floor schemes
- provision for the storage and charging of external wheelchairs
- a non-resident manager who is responsible for managing the housing, organising social activities and co-ordinating care services
- facilities for carers, e.g. a staff room, a changing room and sleep-over rooms

1.6.2
A Home for all Seasons

One main aim of Extra Care housing is to provide elderly people with a pleasant and convenient self-contained home which can serve as the setting for independent and secure living. An individual flat ought, therefore, to be attractively designed and have no obvious features which are blatantly institutional or medical. The planning of a single person flat should allow for separate living and sleeping rooms as well as providing a bathroom and compact kitchen. A two person flat should contain an extra room which could be used as a second bedroom or a study. In both cases the spaces must be planned to allow people to introduce their own furniture and to personalise their surroundings.

As well as catering to the needs of active elderly people each flat in its basic form must be able to accommodate the most common impairments. This means that it should be designed to accepted mobility and wheelchair standards following the principles of 'barrier free design': taps should be easy to operate, sockets should be at the right height, windows should be easy to open, doors should be wide enough, kitchens should be fitted with removable units and adjustable work tops, bathrooms should be fitted with level entry showers and assisted toilets. These are all features which can be achieved with careful design at little extra cost.

In addition it must be possible to adapt each flat to accommodate a range of specific impairments which might arise in the future. This could involve removing doors, opening up walls, fitting a hoist or accommodating a carer. Increasingly it could also involve the installation of 'smart home technology'. If a resident suffers a period of illness or becomes more frail, their flat can be fine-tuned to support their condition, and the care services can be laid on.

If applied successfully this approach could enable people to remain in their homes for a much longer period than would be the case in more conventional forms of sheltered housing. The flat becomes effectively a 'home for all seasons'. As the enthusiastic manager of a new Extra Care scheme in Switzerland exclaimed without irony: 'We hope that our residents will all die here!'

Chapter 2.0
Design Criteria

This chapter discusses some of the main criteria which can be applied to the design of sheltered housing. It asks: in which ways are older people different from the rest of the population? What special problems result from the impairments which affect people as they age? What are their social needs? What particular anthropometric and ergonomic characteristics do they display? What are their environmental requirements?

2.1
Impairment and Disability

As people age they are affected by a whole range of impairments. These do not affect all people in the same way, or on the same time scale. Physical and mental impairments can be 'disabling', in that they diminish a person's ability to live the life to which they have been previously accustomed. Indeed it could be argued that impairments will have a more profound impact on the life of older people because they are less resilient, less adaptable than younger people. However, it could also be argued that, within limits, disability results not from the impairment itself, but from the interaction between the impairment and the social and physical environment. If an old person is placed in a supportive environment there is every chance that the disabling effects of an impairment can be minimised.

2.1.1
The Impairments of Old Age

The following is a list of some of the principal physical and mental effects of ageing. These can all have a profound influence on the way in which older people perceive, understand and use their environment and they must be addressed in the formulation of any design strategy.

Loss of mobility:

Difficulty in standing, walking, moving about, using steps and stairs; the need to use a stick, a frame or a wheelchair; problems with bending and stretching; difficulty in reaching into cupboards, opening windows or getting into and out of a bath; the need to spend long periods confined to a chair or a bed; increased risk of falling...

Plan all circulation spaces to accommodate wheel chairs; provide handrails in corridors, lifts, bathrooms etc.; install seats at convenient points in circulation spaces; handles, switches, sockets, knobs to be clearly visible and conveniently located; flats to be planned for flexibility and convenience, offering good visual contact with the outside world.

Loss of manual dexterity:

Difficulty with manual tasks such as opening jars, operating door or window handles, turning taps, dressing and undressing and operating controls on equipment...

Specify all handles, switches, knobs etc. with ease of operation and maximum leverage in mind; avoid stiff or fiddly controls.

Loss of physical strength and general fitness:

Difficulty in walking for any distance; difficulty in lifting, stretching, reaching; tiredness after exertion...

Keep horizontal travel distances to a minimum; lifts to be centrally located; locate vehicle drop-off as close as possible to entry / lift; design and locate stairs to encourage their use; avoid the use of heavy door closers.

Breathing difficulties:

Shortness of breath, asthma, increased sensitivity to smoke: the inability of the lungs to take in sufficient air reduces the amount of oxygenated blood and makes physical activities more difficult and resting periods longer...

Horizontal travel distances to be kept to a minimum; the environment to be dust free; heating system designed to discourage dust and micro-organisms.

Incontinence:

Inability to control bladder or bowels brought on by illness or anxiety; sudden and urgent need to use a bathroom...

Provide all flats with their own bathroom and toilet designed to full mobility standards; provide communal toilets in convenient locations and in close proximity to all facilities; specify hygienic and easily cleaned surfaces in all bathrooms (avoid carpets).

Digestive problems:

Loss of appetite, weight loss, diabetes and a restricted diet can leave a person weaker and lacking in essential vitamins and minerals; a dry mouth leads to loss of taste sensation and discomfort when talking, more difficulty in chewing, loss of appetite and less protection of teeth and gums from saliva...

Provide for a range of eating possibilities: conveniently planned individual kitchens, small group dining rooms for 'meals on wheels', communal dining rooms served by fully equipped kitchens.

Mental frailty:

Although some older people experience only gradual loss of memory many experience confusion, anxiety or depression. At least 20% of those over the age of 85 suffer from some form of dementia such as Alzheimer's disease. Dementia can affect short-term and long-term memory, and lead to disorientation, frustration, confusion, inability to make judgements, depression and even aggression; these conditions can be aggravated by the effects of insomnia...

Establish a secure, reassuring and stimulating environment; avoid unfamiliar forms or installations; create clear patterns of circulation with memorable visual events (visual contact to the outside); respect the need for privacy, security, dignity and individual expression, design to minimise frustration; encourage independence, encourage the use of personal possessions and memorabilia.

Impaired vision:

Older people may suffer from partial sightedness, short sightedness, long sightedness, blurred vision, or possibly total blindness; they experience a diminishing visual field, a reduced ability to see detail and adjust focus, and reduced lens transmission. All of these can increase the risk of falls and can seriously affect people's confidence to move around, as well as limiting the possibilities to read or watch television...

Use strong and clear colours in circulation areas with contrasts on doors, stair nosings etc.; provide adequate and even background lighting levels with highlights on important events or specific activities; avoid glare (naked light sources, windows at ends of corridors etc.); incorporate dimmer switches to allow for individual control.

Impaired hearing:

Total or partial deafness can result in isolation and loneliness. Older people may lose the ability to hear particular frequency ranges or may become highly sensitive to extraneous noise...

Incorporate good sound insulation between flats (walls, floors and ceilings!); design for low reverberation times in reception areas and in communal rooms; install hearing aid systems in communal rooms.

Impaired sense of smell:

An impaired sense of smell can reduce the ability to detect a fire. It also affects the enjoyment of food...

Install aural and visual fire alarm systems in all high risk areas.

Impaired sense of touch:

Reduced sensitivity to high temperatures increases the risk of scalding...

Specify low surface temperature heat emitters; enclose hot water supply pipes; install temperature limiting thermostatic controls on hot water taps, showers etc.

Increased sensitivity to extremes of temperature:

Metabolic changes result in old people 'feeling the cold'; inability to maintain body temperature and adjust to colder temperatures can result in hypothermia; conversely ageing of the skin and the sweat glands reduces the body's ability to lose heat in warm conditions.

Aim for high insulation standards with draught proof doors and windows, but with adequate ventilation; specify a heating system which is adequate, economical, responsive, and which can maximise comfort and offer a degree of individual control.

2.1.2
Levels of Dependency

One direct consequence of the physical and mental impairments which slowly overtake elderly people is a loss of independence, or an increased dependency on the support of others. The degree of an individual's dependency will vary according to their general state of health and state of mind and according to their surroundings. The process is reversible: after a period during which their dependency levels have increased it is quite possible for someone to stabilise, or even to regain degrees of independence.

A number of methods have been developed to measure dependency. At a general theoretical level one aim of such methods is to provide public authorities with the means to evaluate an elderly population in order to develop policy (e.g. McCafferty, 1994). At a more particular level their aim is to enable authorities and institutions to assess the needs or entitlements of individuals. Individual assessment plays an important role in admissions to local authority sheltered housing or residential care schemes, and in the determination of eligibility for subsidy in the private and voluntary sectors. Dependency levels are determined by recording how people carry out normal day-to-day tasks and how they react to particular situations. These might include: getting in and out of bed, bathing or taking a shower, getting around the house, preparing and cooking meals, using stairs, using public transport, doing the shopping and domestic chores such as housework and washing clothes.

In 1993 Anchor Housing Association carried out surveys of tenants in their sheltered housing schemes (Riseborough & Niner, 1994b). One questionnaire evaluated the degree of difficulty which respondents experienced with a range of ten day-to-day tasks. The following list ranks the tasks according to the percentage of respondents which experienced difficulty with them.

Get up and down stairs	49%
Have a bath	44%
Use public transport	43%
Do shopping	42%
Do housework	40%
Wash clothes	22%
Prepare and cook meals	18%
Get in and out of bed	17%
Get around the house	15%
Have a shower	15%

Source: Riseborough & Niner, 1994

This research led to the development of a method by which each task was scored '0' for no difficulty through to '3' for extreme difficulty, and the scores were summed to give an overall 'dependency score'.

The Clackmannan Dependency Scale, developed and used by Bond and Carstairs (1982) is more complex, involving an evaluation of five sets of criteria: three sets of functional criteria - mobility, self-care and home-

care - and two sets of clinical criteria - incontinence and mental status. These are evaluated by interview and observation and are expressed as a single value on a scale of 'A' to 'G' where 'A' indicates zero dependence, and 'G' indicates the highest level of mental and physical frailty.

Although these methods are partly intended for use in the assessment of admissions to sheltered housing, residential care homes and nursing homes, there is no evidence of their having been applied to the design of actual schemes. Research would indicate that the anticipated dependency level of residents is rarely discussed during the development stages of projects, and architects are seldom if ever briefed in such terms.

2.1.3
Disabled by Design

'So accustomed are people to tolerating poor design, that it is only when relevant faculties are diminished that some design shortcomings stand fully revealed.'

Barker, Barrick and Wilson (1995)

The designer must start from the premise that good design can have a profoundly positive effect on the way that older people live out their lives, that it can reduce the effects of physical and mental impairment, that it can combat disability. Conversely bad design can have a totally negative effect on people's quality of life: older people suffer unnecessary frustration and a growing sense of their own worthlessness as the effects of their ageing are magnified by the inappropriateness of their social and physical environments.

Anyone who is suffering from arthritis and who is wheelchair-bound ought still to be able to perform a seemingly simple task like making a cup of tea.

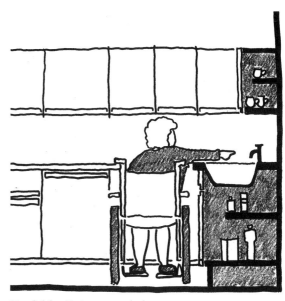

Fig. 2.1.3a: Trying to reach the tap

Fig. 2.1.3b: Trying to make a cup of tea

Unfortunately, it appears that there are many newly built and specially designed housing schemes intended for older people where making a cup of tea takes on the dimensions of a fearsome and dangerous obstacle course. To begin with, the fridge door handle is a recessed slot which makes it difficult for anyone with arthritic fingers to grasp and the milk is difficult to reach. The fridge position and the swing of the door pose problems for wheelchairs. The tea caddie is tucked away at the back of a cupboard under the worktop; its door is on powerful self-closing springs and is opened by a natty but unfunctional metal strip. The kettle is difficult to fill because the sink unit is too high and has not been designed to allow a wheelchair to slide under it and the tap handles are stiff and offer no leverage. The electric sockets are mounted on the wall above the worktop and are difficult to reach, the crockery is stored in a wall-mounted cupboard which is inaccessible, the lighting casts shadows over the worktop... Even if such a person does succeed in brewing some tea the chances are that they will scald themselves in pouring it out because the worktop is too high for them to do this safely!

What choices are there for someone facing this scenario? Go without? Call someone to help? Apply to move into a residential care home? The inability to perform a simple everyday task can breed feelings of frustration, of uselessness, of being a burden. These can lead to explosions of rage and even to bouts of depression. What is sad is that, although the problems are triggered by the person's impairments, they are magnified by insensitive design. All of these design faults could have been avoided at almost no extra cost if a correct approach had been adopted by the development team.

Over zealous design can be as disastrous as insensitive design, particularly when a designer seeks to meet the needs of one type of impairment and ignores all others. In one scheme an architect had specified raised WC pedestals for every bathroom. In attempting to cater for one group of people he made life very difficult for almost everyone else.

Another risk is that a design which is developed to combat disability can inadvertently produce an overly clinical or institutional ambience. Past methods of caring for the elderly have been more focused at the convenience of the carer than the social and emotional needs of the resident. Although the emphasis has moved away from Nightingale wards towards community care and sheltered homes, steps must be taken to keep the sometimes conflicting needs of the 'carers' and the 'cared for' in balance. Good design can help to empower individual residents by providing them with greater control over their environment, so that their convenience is accorded at least the same priority as that of the staff.

Specially designed fixtures can also create clinical environments. Valins (1996) observes 'There is an abundance of assisted devices for helping the bather or lavatory user, but most of these devices have an institutional or prosthetic appearance and are added on to the existing or ordinary fixture... While many of these products are easier to use than a traditional fixture, they are marketed as devices for the handicapped, have an institutional appearance, and have a price tag only affordable by a few'.

Many problems could be avoided if designers were to brief themselves more thoroughly and to develop their designs from a base of empirical knowledge and insight rather than from intuitive guesswork. There is a very real need for those who are involved with building sheltered housing to consult the users: the residents, their relatives and their carers.

These issues are likely to receive more attention in the future not only because of the success of campaigns which have been mounted by disability groups, but also because of the effects of the 1996 Disability Discrimination Act. This Act defines disability as 'A physical or mental impairment which has a substantial and long-term adverse effect on a person's ability to carry out normal day-to-day activities' and requires all institutions to provide safe and accessible environments.

2.1.4
Barrier Free Design

In reality it is not possible to isolate the different categories of impairment. Individuals experience their own unique combination of frailties and different impairments interact together in different ways. One impairment can be the direct result of another impairment: loss of mobility might, for instance, result from poor vision.

Fig 2.1.4a: A wide and daunting corridor

Older people are more likely to fall ill and tend to be more seriously affected by illness than younger people; they are more prone to have accidents and, because their bones are more brittle, are more likely to suffer serious injuries as a result. This does not mean that old age should be viewed as an illness, or that the impairments of ageing should be viewed either as irreversible or insurmountable. The aim of the designer should be to minimise the direct effects of impairments, to maximise safety and convenience, and to minimise the possible consequences of mishaps. This approach to design has been referred to as 'barrier free design' (Holmes-Siedle, 1996) or 'inclusive design' (Barker et al., 1995).

The designer of sheltered housing faces the problem that in any one scheme each resident will have different needs and that the spectrum of needs will vary over time. There is a very real risk that design solutions for different impairments may end up being in direct conflict with each other: a wide corridor helps the wheelchair-user but may cause problems for an unsteady walker; an environment which is 'visually stimulating' is unlikely to be 'cosy' or 'reassuring'. The aim must be, therefore, to design to the 'lowest common denominator', and to produce an environment which is acceptable to the fit and active, which is supportive to a general level of frailty and which can be 'tuned' to suit the special needs of a particular individual.

2.2
Social Wellbeing

Architects often argue about the extent to which people's behaviour is affected by their built environment. Some believe that buildings exert a controlling influence over human behaviour and that architects should see their role as one of social engineer; others believe that people are so flexible and so much influenced by other considerations that they operate independently of the buildings which encompass them. The truth lies somewhere between the two. Buildings do have enormous prescriptive and proscriptive effects on the way in which we live, but within limits. A building can't make you feel more or less lonely, but it can create the circumstances which encourage or discourage social contact .

Buildings should be viewed, not as 'machines for living in', to use le Corbusier's determinist maxim, but rather as 'enabling mechanisms'. Unfortunately we still don't understand enough about the way in which people behave in relation to buildings, and when architects set out deliberately to operate as 'social engineers' or 'social enablers' they often achieve almost the opposite effect from the one which was intended.

Because they are vulnerable and because their lives are so much more circumscribed, older people form one group whose behaviour is very much affected by buildings. It is, therefore, important that more time should be spent in studying precedents and listening to older people's comments about their surroundings in order to develop a better understanding of what constitutes an 'enabling environment'.

2.2.1
Basic Needs

Older people have the same basic needs as everybody else. They aspire to be healthy, well fed, financially secure, they want a home which is adequate to their needs, warm, comfortable, affordable and secure, and they crave privacy, independence, friendship, love and dignity. As their dependency level increases so they come to rely more and more on other people - relatives, friends, neighbours and professional carers - to assist them with daily tasks and to meet their basic needs.

Each individual's expectations of life in sheltered housing will vary according to their previous situation and the extent of their frailty. Many new residents will have recently lived through a period of hardship, discomfort, ill-health and unhappiness. Retirement, loss of a partner, or illness may have conspired to cut them off from society. After leading busy and interactive lives they may suddenly, for the first time have experienced long periods of solitude. At the same time they may have been affected by physical problems, by loss of memory or confusion, by difficulties with seeing and hearing. During a time of illness they may have had to rely on complete strangers to help them with intimate bodily functions. All of these things can isolate or desocialise people, and lead to loneliness and depression.

However, the fact that people have experienced loneliness in the past does not mean that as new residents of a sheltered housing scheme they are immediately willing or able to enter into the life of what is a fairly large community. Often the reverse is true: there are residents who find life in a sheltered housing scheme just as isolating as life in a lonely bed-sitter, partly because the circumstances of their immediate past have to some extent traumatised them, and partly because almost nothing which they have experienced in their previous lives has prepared them for life in a 'co-operative'. It is also true that older people are sometimes impatient with their fellows and find it almost impossible to tolerate the company of those who are more frail or mentally less alert than themselves.

2.2.2
Community and Privacy

One of the architect's main tasks is to plan the spatial organisation of a number of discrete elements. These elements are defined by the client's brief in terms of number and size. The main spatial constituents of a sheltered housing scheme can be categorised as follows:

- individual private dwellings
- shared communal facilities such as sitting rooms
- ancillary facilities such as assisted bathrooms
- staff areas such as offices, sleep-over rooms etc.
- service areas
- circulation areas

How these elements are organised in relation to each other will influence how they are used and how they are perceived. In particular it is important to distinguish between those which belong to the private domain and those which belong to the communal or public domains. It is possible to rank each constituent element on a scale of ascending privacy: thus the main entrance to a scheme would be ranked as very public, while the bathroom of an individual flat would be ranked as extremely private. Between these two extremes there is a range of intermediate conditions which might be described variously as semi-public or semi-private. A shared sitting room should be recognisable as the semi-private territory of a group of individuals, and yet it should be accessible to all who have the need and the right to use it. A communal sitting room is required to function as a meeting space for the whole community, and yet its design should incorporate intimate spaces which are inviting to small groups or individuals: it should be capable of being used in public, semi-public and semi-private ways.

Spatial Hierarchies

Moving from one end of the privacy spectrum to the other involves passing through a whole series of intermediate spaces and crossing various thresholds. One organisational strategy might result in abrupt transitions with few thresholds, another might create a complex hierarchy of transitions with many thresholds.

A scheme in which flats are arranged with blank flush doors opening directly on to a long dark corridor will take on an institutional atmosphere. This is in part because of the inherent nature of long dark corridors, but is also because the spatial system does not encourage any hierarchy. There are no ambiguities, no intermediate zones, no entrance recesses to give a sense of threshold, no viewing panels, no inviting benches. Only two conditions exist: the interior condition behind the door, which is wholly private, and the exterior condition within the corridor, which is wholly public.

In contrast a scheme in which flats are grouped around a well-lit core of circulation space, in which each flat entrance is recessed with a bench, in which the doors have viewing panels, in which small windows open out from the kitchens, will create quite a different ambience. The entrance operates as a threshold: the personality of the occupant is projected out from the flat to create a semi-private zone while the circulation core is shared by a group of flats and is therefore semi-public. The system is now full of ambiguities and can be modified by the residents in a number of ways: they can personalise their entrances with name boards, plants etc. and they can modify the kitchen window by adding blinds or curtains which control the degree to which they can look out or to which others can look in.

A Private Place

One aim must be to design each individual flat in such a way as to promote privacy and individual dignity without enforcing isolation. There needs to be enough space for residents to arrange their treasured pieces of furniture and to display their mementos and the symbols of their lifetime's achievements: they should be able to stamp their own personality on their flats. It is also important that each flat should connect to the

Fig. 2.2.2a: A long dark corridor

Fig. 2.2.2b: A flat full of personal furniture

outside world via at least one generously proportioned window or bay, and should have a link with the community via a kitchen window or a viewing panel in the door. Communal spaces such as corridors and sitting rooms need to be welcoming without being intrusive and every effort should be made to avoid a feeling of institution. Every resident should feel free to contract into or out of the life of the community without constraint.

Public Spaces

The communal elements within a scheme need to be designed carefully to make them inviting and undaunting.

The main sitting room should be located close to the main lift lobby and entrance with a direct connection to a garden terrace and conservatory. It should be large enough to accommodate communal events with

a single focus such as parties, entertainments, bingo sessions and residents' meetings but it must also be possible to break it down into a number of discrete areas which could be used by smaller groups for such things as tea parties and card games or by individuals. One area might relate to a fireplace, another to a window which connects to the garden or conservatory.

The dining room should also be well lit and should enjoy views out towards the garden. Older people are often jealous guardians of territory and may insist on always sitting at the same table with the same group of friends. Ideally tables will be of different sizes to accommodate different groups and each will be given a sense of individuality.

In addition to the main communal sitting room, it is becoming standard practice to provide a number of smaller sitting rooms each serving a group of flats. As well as forming the focal point for a group of flats

these can also become associated with particular activities such as needlework, bridge, or music. They may also be used by carers for serving meals to particular categories of residents.

Circulation spaces should also be designed as places for meeting and chatting. The main entrance hall is a favourite place for people to sit and gossip as they watch arrivals and departures or wait for a taxi or a visitor; it should therefore be provided with a group of seats away from the main flow and out of the draught. Corridors can incorporate small alcoves with a couple of seats, a window to the garden and a ledge for a vase of flowers. A bench on the landing of a staircase offers a place to pause for a moment and exchange pleasantries. Activity based rooms such as laundries and hairdressing salons also offer a good opportunity for contact and should be planned with adequate seating and plenty of daylight.

Non-Resident Day Care

It is becoming increasingly common for the communal areas within sheltered housing schemes to double up as day centres for non-residents. This practice brings many benefits: a scarce and expensive resource is enjoyed by a greater number of people; the unit cost of running facilities is reduced; a greater range of activities can be organised and sustained; residents have the chance to meet a wider range of people and can maintain contact with the wider community while prospective residents are able to forge a link with the residents. However, this practice does encounter opposition from residents in some schemes who see it as an invasion of territory. For this reason the main sitting room and dining room need to be carefully located so that they can be used directly from the main entrance without necessarily impinging too much on the privacy of the residents.

Fig. 2.2.2c: Mobile shop in a communal lounge

Fig. 2.2.2d: A busy entrance

Death

Death is of course a fairly common occurrence in any community of older people. While in traditional sheltered schemes sick residents might be side-tracked into nursing homes or geriatric wards when their death was imminent, it is much more likely that they will die 'at home' in Extra Care housing. The question of death is often fudged: residents are said to have 'moved on' and their coffins are discretely taken out down the backstairs. And yet many older people have a much more realistic and matter of fact view of death than they are often credited with. Death is a private occurrence which affects the whole community. There is no reason why the death of a resident should not be treated as an event: a room can be set aside for laying out the body, the coffin can be carried ceremoniously out through the main entrance foyer and those residents who wish to can pay their final respects.

2.2.3
A Balanced Community

In the 1960s providers of sheltered housing were encouraged to plan balanced communities comprising people of different ages and different degrees of frailty. It was argued that such communities would to some extent encourage mutual support, that the younger and more active residents would animate the social life of the scheme and that the warden's workload would be eased. NFHA (1991) reported that in order to sustain such balanced communities new tenancies were generally offered to younger and more active applicants, often ahead of more frail applicants whose need was greater. Observations showed that in groups of mixed dependency very little mutual support was encountered. Local authorities have recently tended to offer tenancies on the basis of need, with the result that sheltered schemes have come to cater more and

more for the frail and very frail elderly. However, in private leasehold schemes where tenants are self-selected there is a tendency for balanced communities to evolve quite naturally.

The dilemma of whether to aim for balance or to allocate to those in greatest need is re-activated by the Extra Care concept and has yet to be resolved. Should Extra Care schemes cater for a broad cross-section of residents, ranging from the active to the very frail, or should they be regarded primarily as quasi-residential homes in which almost all of the residents are highly dependent? For central government and for many local social service departments the question is academic: financial constraints dictate that because Extra Care housing is relatively expensive to provide, priority should always be given to those who have been assessed as highly dependent and for whom no other alternative housing exists. And yet, paradoxically, one of the driving ideas behind Extra Care housing is that it enables residents to 'age in place': it has been developed partly to provide frail elderly people with an alternative to residential care and partly to create a flexible option for active elderly people who want to live in greater security. If schemes are tenanted entirely by frail elderly people then half of the raison d'etre is lost, and, instead of offering a clear alternative to Part III residential care homes, they will be seen simply as a costly hybrid. Fully self-contained flats with individual kitchens and extensive communal facilities are expensive to build and are not ideal vehicles for delivering full 24 hour care. Bed-sitters with private bathrooms offer a potential saving on capital and running costs and may be better configured to deliver care to some categories of residents.

The dilemma of whether or not to plan for balanced communities is complicated by the fact that people with different levels of dependency are often seen, or

see themselves, to be incompatible with each other. Experience would suggest that people who start off at the same dependency level will offer mutual support to one of their number who develops a physical impairment, though they might be less willing or able to cope with someone suffering from dementia. On the other hand people who are at different levels of dependency from the outset are much less likely to form mutually supportive relationships.

Any group of forty to fifty individuals is bound to encompass a broad range of characteristics: residents may come from different social, educational and cultural backgrounds, they may belong to different ethnic or religious communities, and they may exhibit widely different degrees of frailty. Should we encourage people who suffer different impairments, or who have different faiths, or who belong to different ethnic groups, or who come from different social backgrounds to live in the same mutually supportive community or should they all be housed in their own special categories of housing? Is it too much to hope that someone in a wheelchair and someone who is partially sighted might be able help each other in a symbiotic way?

2.2.4
Clusters

A scheme of forty flats could theoretically be arranged as a single aggregation of units, each one served by a common circulation system. Such a layout, it might be argued, would be non-hierarchical and would place every individual in the same neutral relationship to every other. Residents could mix freely with one another and develop relationships in a random manner. Conversely a scheme can be broken down into smaller groups or clusters. This can happen quite accidentally, as a result for instance of the way that a scheme is divided vertically into separate floors, or it can be deliberately engineered.

Arranging flats into clusters can help to minimise any sense of institution. Instead of living in one unit of a large organisation, residents would find themselves living in a cul-de-sac containing between six and ten flats, and sharing between them a small sitting room. Such a cul-de-sac provides an immediate sense of community, a semi-private world which intercedes between the intimacy of the individual dwelling and the scale of the collective. It sets up a group of neighbours who may keep an eye on each other and even offer mutual support. Clusters can be planned in a range of sizes in order to provide greater flexibility and to encourage diversity.

The clustering principle offers a possible solution to the problem of how to cater for people with special needs. A cluster can be set aside for people who are especially frail, or who are mentally infirm. This allows them to remain a part of the larger community while separating them to some extent from those more active residents with whom they are becoming increasingly incompatible. It also produces considerable advantages for the care team who can focus their attentions on one group. Similar clusters could be established for people who are partially sighted or for people from a particular ethnic or religious group.

Critics of clustering would argue that it represents a form of social engineering and that the creation of arbitrary groups discourages the development of richer and more appropriate relationships outside of the cluster. However, there is evidence to suggest that many residents do establish relationships outside of their cluster and distinguish clearly between 'friends' and 'neighbours'. On balance the potential advantages of clustering seem to outweigh the risks.

2.2.5
Caring for the Carers

Any discussion about social issues would be incomplete without some mention of the needs of staff. The well being of the residents will be affected by the well being and morale of the staff, be they managers, carers, domestics or kitchen staff.

The role of the scheme manager is changing (NFHA, 1996). In the past, managers of sheltered housing schemes were often referred to as 'wardens'. They lived on the job, and acted as guardians, carers and general factotums. Today many managers in Extra Care schemes live off-site and operate more specifically as organisers and facilitators. In such cases the manager is responsible for ensuring that the heating is working, that the building is properly maintained, that the post is delivered, that social activities take place on a regular basis, and that care delivery is

properly co-ordinated. The responsibility for managing care delivery is sometimes devolved to a separate care manager and the care team itself might be supplied by a separate agency or be employed directly or indirectly by the local authority social services department. Care services may also be arranged by the individual who is in receipt of the care.

The manager needs an office next to the entrance with a clear view of the approach, of the entrance lobby and of the lift and main stair. This office is the main hub of all communications, it acts as the eyes and the ears of the scheme and guards its first threshold. It should be easy to approach, while still providing the manager with a degree of privacy.

The care team needs to have a general office and staff room as well sleep-over rooms, washrooms and changing facilities. The office should be situated near to the manager's office, but tucked well away from view. Carers tend to be poorly paid and there is often a high rate of staff turnover, particularly when agency staff are used. This can be highly unsettling for residents. Carers need facilities which are pleasant and relaxing and which offer them a high level of privacy. Their case meetings should be held behind closed doors and should never take place in communal rooms which are in the full view of residents.

2.3
Designing for Minorities

The majority of sheltered housing schemes are built to meet the needs of older people from the general community, and it is assumed that the special needs of each individual can be accommodated by tinkering with or particularising the common denominator solution. However, sizeable minority groups exist in sufficient numbers to warrant the existence of specialised facilities, either in the form of entire schemes or in the form of dedicated clusters within schemes. These groups may share a common impairment such as blindness, deafness or dementia, or they may belong to a particular ethnic or religious group.

A full treatment of this complex subject lies beyond the scope of this book, though a few observations on the needs of ethnic minorities are presented below.

2.3.1
Ethnic Minorities

Britain's different ethnic minority groups have grown as the result of particular patterns of immigration. These groups vary in size, concentration and degree of assimilation and each displays its own demographic characteristics. First generation immigrants who were born into an entirely different culture, may never have adjusted to the British way of life and some of them may never have learnt English. They remain true to their traditions and continue to practice their own religion. Although the extended family system often remains strong among such groups and older people are often cared for within the community, there is now a growing need for specialised sheltered housing for particular ethnic minorities.

Older people of the first immigrant generation are often difficult to accommodate within a stereotypical sheltered scheme and they may encounter racial or cultural discrimination from fellow residents who have had little contact with minority communities during their earlier lives. Subsequent generations of older people will tend to have much more in common with the general population, but may still be differentiated by religion, by dress and by dietary preferences. They are likely to have experienced various forms of racial discrimination during their lives and may well feel

reluctant to live in a mixed community. As minority groups slowly assimilate into the main population so the special needs of their older members will tend to disappear, though problems of racial and cultural discrimination may sadly persist.

In the past there was a tendency to treat the different minority groups simply as sub-sets of the same general problem. In reality each ethnic group is unique, and members of one group are as different from the members of another as they are from the general population: the one thing which they might have in common is a sense of alienation. Certain ethnic groups are further divided into mutually exclusive sub-groups by religion, by language or by caste. It is not sufficient, therefore, simply to operate sheltered housing schemes for a mix of ethnic minorities.

The needs of first and second generation minority groups are often best catered for in special schemes

Fig. 2.3.1a: Group reading space at an Asian day centre

and a number of housing associations do exist to serve particular communities. However, such schemes are only feasible in areas where there is a substantial catchment population. In areas where a minority community is too small to sustain a whole scheme it may be difficult to find appropriate accommodation. Here the concept of clustering comes into its own: a single group of flats can be converted to meet the special needs of a particular group of residents who would then exist as a sub-group within the main scheme. Such a solution can appear to be overtly segregationist, but it does offer a workable compromise.

2.3.2
Special Design Needs

In a recent survey commissioned by Odu Dua Housing Association (Bright, 1996) ethnic minority groups and sheltered housing providers were asked to identify the main barriers which older people from minority groups faced when entering sheltered housing. Of the nine major barriers which were identified, inappropriate design and poor location were ranked fourth and fifth respectively.

The general housing needs of ethnic groups have been described in the North Housing Trust's excellent design guide (Penoyre & Prasad, 1993). The special needs of older people will vary from community to community and the following notes simply touch on a few of the issues which might arise.

Communal Areas

Several cultures require that men and women remain segregated on social occasions, a fact which necessitates the provision of at least two communal sitting rooms. In a recent scheme for the Indian community the male residents, who were in a minority, insisted on taking over the only lounge, leaving the women to make do with a small area of the entrance hall. In this case the need for two separate lounges could have been met by providing a single large room which was capable of sub-division into two unequal parts.

Some groups require special rooms for religious observance. For Moslems two simple rooms, one for women and one for men, would suffice, while Hindu residents would welcome the provision of a small shrine room dedicated to a favoured deity.

The Need for Special Cooking Facilities

Many groups are bound by strict dietary rules whose observation may necessitate the provision of specially designed and equipped kitchens. These strictures will apply equally to individual kitchens and to central communal kitchens. Jewish customs require food to be prepared according to Kosher rules, and strictly orthodox Jews will not allow utensils to come into contact with non-Kosher food. Hindus may be strictly vegetarian, or, if they eat meat, may require that two separate sets of utensils be used for meat and vegetables.

Many older people, and not only those from minority groups, are reluctant to cook on electric hobs because of their slow response. Furthermore there are cooking techniques which cannot easily be adapted to electric cookers: Chinese wok cooking requires a highly responsive heat source, while Indian chappatis need to be cooked on a naked flame. Electricity is by far the safest cooking fuel and many agencies are understandably reluctant to introduce gas supplies or to condone the use of paraffin stoves in sheltered housing schemes.

Bathing and Toilet Facilities

The rituals of personal hygiene vary enormously from culture to culture and are often subject to arcane taboos:

- Hindus abhor baths and require water to flow down over them towards the earth: while a shower might suffice, they prefer to dowse themselves with a bucket. This requirement can be met by providing a standard flush floor shower and seat with an additional tap for filling a bucket.
- In some cultures squat pans are preferred to pedestal WCs. Indeed there are many health experts who maintain that squatting offers a more hygienic and more natural method of bowel evacuation.
- Many cultures use water for anal cleansing and view the western use of 'toilet paper' with distaste. In such cases it is quite sufficient to provide a tap or a shower hose next to the WC. Attempts to persuade people to use bidets or air-dried 'superloos' have been greeted with understandable derision.

Location

People from ethnic minorities are understandably reluctant to move away from their family and friends. Many have had very little exposure to the way of life which exists outside of their own community and rely heavily on the network of special shops, cinemas, cultural centres and places of worship which has grown up in their area. As minority ethnic groups are usually concentrated within inner city districts this suggests that an urban location with good public transport connections would usually be ideal.

Gardens

Gardening is a popular pastime with many older people and offers an excellent form of exercise. Many first generation immigrants came originally from farming backgrounds and welcome the chance to work again with the soil and to grow their own preferred herbs and vegetables.

Language and Culture

Many first generation immigrants have never learned to speak or read English. This can pose difficulties for carers and can affect such things as the safe operation of alarm call systems. Substantial numbers are illiterate in their own language, which means that they can't read signs which have been translated for their benefit. In such communities it is important to provide rooms for language and literacy classes, and to set aside a space where regular group readings from books and newspapers can take place.

Wherever possible some staff members in special schemes should belong to the appropriate ethnic group. Not only can they then communicate with the residents who have language difficulties but they can also assist in the preparation of appropriate food and can help with personal care and hygiene.

2.4
Spatial Criteria

2.4.1
Anthropometric Data

'The formulation of design criteria for buildings depends to a considerable extent on the dimensional characteristics of people at rest and moving, and on their range of physical capabilities in terms of strength and flexibility.'

(Goldsmith, 1976).

Anthropometry is the comparative study of sizes and proportions of the human body. Any design of buildings or their interiors must proceed from a knowledge of human dimensions. Anthropometric data provide information about the human body and its spatial characteristics: these include the heights of key parts of the body such as the head, the shoulders, the knuckles and the knees, as well as the length of limbs and the extent of reach.

Anthropometric measurements vary considerably from individual to individual, and they alter with age. People actually shrink as they get older and they lose the ability to stretch and reach. The anthropometric characteristics of someone who is wheelchair-bound will be quite different from someone who walks with a zimmer frame and different again from someone who walks unaided.

The fact that anthropometric data are based on statistical averages presents the designer with a problem: if a design is based on average data, then its dimensions will be too large for half of the population and too small for the other half. Such an approach could exclude large numbers of the tallest or the smallest. It is necessary for any element to be either

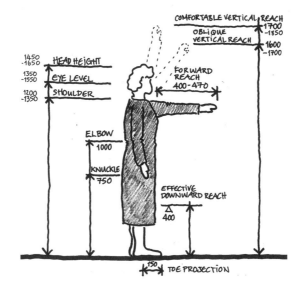

1. Comfortable vertical reach
2. Oblique vertical reach
3. Head height
4. Eye level
5. Shoulder level
6. Elbow level
7. Knuckle height (comfortable downward reach)
8. Effective downward reach
9. Comfortable forward reach
10. Toe projection

Fig. 2.4.1a: Approximate reach dimensions of an ambulant woman aged 60+ standing (Source: Goldsmith, 1976)

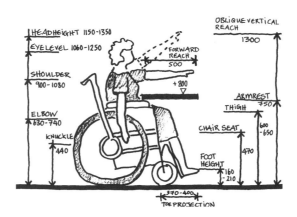

1. Comfortable forward vertical reach
2. Head height
3. Eye level
4. Shoulder level
5. Chair armrest level
6. Elbow level
7. Thigh level
8. Chair seat level, centre front edge (with cushion if used)
9. Knuckle height
10. Foot height
11. Effective forward reach
12. Toe projection beyond face of chair arm

Fig. 2.4.1b: Approximate reach dimensions of a woman in a wheelchair (Source: Goldsmith, 1976)

small or large enough to suit most people. Thus, the side of a bath must be low enough for the vast majority of people to negotiate with ease, while a doorway must be wide enough for all but the most exceptionally wide to pass through. Designers must analyse all the critical variables and base their decisions on the characteristics of the potential users. If a design

decision is likely to exclude part of a population then provision must be made to enable those who are excluded to make adjustments or adaptations.

Goldsmith (1976) states: 'Housing criteria are generally based on the physical characteristics of women rather than men' and argues that: 'The physical performance of women, particularly in respect of reaching ability, is more constraining than that of men...Among elderly people, where disability is most prevalent, there is a preponderance of women'.

Figs 2.4.1a & b illustrate the critical anthropometric measurements for a woman aged 60+ who is ambulant or able bodied and a similar woman who is wheelchair-bound. These measurements should be taken into account when designing a spatial environment for older people.

2.4.2
Ergonomic Data

Ergonomics is the study of people in relation to their living and working environment. The ergonomist sets out to ensure that equipment is designed to minimise physical effort and to maximise efficiency.

As people grow older they become progressively less mobile and less able to adjust to their reduced mobility. Housing for older people must be designed to take into account the physical limitations of its occupants. Normal standards based on averages derived from the active population need to be called into question and, if necessary, more suitable standards should be developed.

For example, the standard kitchen worktop is 600mm deep from front to back. This is a dimension which balances a desire to maximise the depth and area of a work surface against people's need to be able to reach things like shelves and electric sockets. Older people will be less concerned about the area of the worktop and more concerned about the ability to reach. For them a 500mm deep worktop could offer a better compromise. Again the standard height for a worktop is fixed at 900mm to suit normally erect adults. However, many older people prefer to sit whilst

working and others are obliged to operate from a wheelchair. For them 900mm is too high and they need space under the worktop in which to fit their knees. Thus, in a kitchen which is designed ergonomically to suit older people, kitchen fittings are replaced by a worktop which is supported on adjustable brackets, while the fixed drawers and cupboards are replaced by mobile consoles.

It is important to distinguish clearly between those dimensions which should be fixed and those which should be variable. The heights of key pieces of equipment are often critical and need to be made adjustable. It is difficult to adjust the height of standard fittings which are already in-situ, but it can be relatively simple and inexpensive at the outset to incorporate a simple system which enables the heights of key items like worktops and washbasins to be adjusted. What is important is that the designer should be prepared to 'question' and 'rethink' a

design which has become fixed in people's minds as an absolute standard. It is also crucial that any new design should be acceptable to the user.

The question of whether or not to install wall cupboards and shelves poses an interesting dilemma. Although wall cupboards provide valuable storage volume for items which are seldom used, they are likely to be beyond the reach of many older people. Such items can always be brought down or put away by friends.

Fig. 2.4.2a: Ergonomic data

2.4.3
Wheelchairs

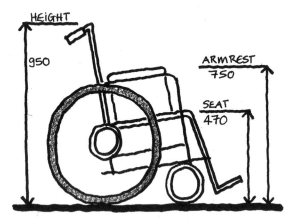

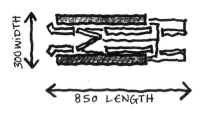

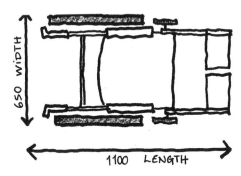

Fig. 2.4.3a: A self propelled wheelchair

A significant proportion of residents in Extra Care housing can be expected to use wheelchairs either permanently, occasionally or for short periods, and so schemes must be designed to cater for wheelchair access.

Because older people find it difficult to learn to operate manual wheelchairs, and often lack the necessary physical strength, there is a growing preference for powered wheelchairs. Powered wheelchairs are slightly bigger and heavier than those which are manually powered because they incorporate motors and batteries but they offer a greater degree of independence. As battery design improves so powered chairs will become smaller, lighter and more manoeuvrable and their controls will become more user friendly.

Many people use their wheelchairs only when they leave their flats. For this reason it is important to provide a space in the entrance hall to park and recharge a chair when not in use. Unlike manual chairs, powered chairs can't usually be folded.

Electric scooters or 'buggies' which are designed for outdoor use are much bigger than indoor electric wheelchairs. These need to be stored in a recharging room near to the scheme's main entrance. This room needs to be big enough to allow residents to transfer from their indoor chair to their outdoor chair.

Wheelchair sizes vary from model to model: standard self propelled wheelchairs for indoor use are approximately 1100mm long by 650mm, and fold down to approximately 850mm long by 300mm. Electric indoor wheelchairs can be up to 1200mm long and 700mm wide.

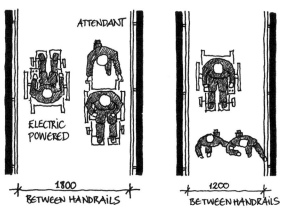

Fig. 2.4.3b: Recommended widths of corridors for two-way and one-way traffic

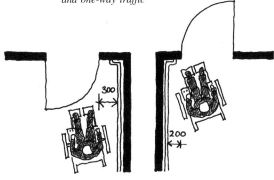

Fig. 2.4.3c : Negotiating door openings in a wheelchair

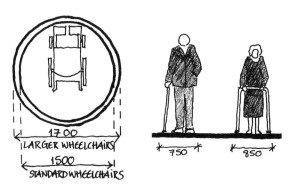

Fig.2.4.3d :
Wheelchair turning circles

Fig. 2.4.3e:
Ambulant disabled people

The wheelchair is not a static object: it is a moving vehicle. Sufficient space must be allowed for wheelchairs to turn corners and, within activity areas, to turn on themselves. It is also important to allow space for people to transfer between their wheelchair and their shower, their toilet or their bed. Doorways require special attention: there needs to be space to approach the door, to reach for the handle and to open the door.

2.4.4
Mobility Standards

Much of the literature on designing for the disabled draws a clear distinction between 'mobility standards' and 'wheelchair standards'. This distinction was created in a joint circular published in 1974 by the DoE and Welsh Office and amplified by two Housing Development Directorate (HDD) occasional papers (Goldsmith 1980a, 1980b). Whilst the normative basis for the distinction has now been overtaken by more recent legislation the two terms continue to be used.

The joint circular recommended that housing for general purposes should be provided 'with certain features so designed that it is suitable for many handicapped people as well as for those who are not handicapped'. This type of housing was never intended specifically to meet the needs of people who were wheelchair-bound and was referred to as 'mobility housing'. A later HDD occasional paper (Goldsmith, 1980a) discussed the concept of 'mobility housing' and its design implications in some detail. It stated that mobility housing is 'ordinary housing modified to be more convenient for handicapped people to move about and live in'.

The main recommendations of the occasional paper on 'mobility housing' were as follows:

- Access should be via a ramped or level approach with a flush threshold
- Internal planning should allow for easy movement by ambulant handicapped people, as well as by those in wheelchairs
- 900mm doorsets (giving 750mm clear openings) should become standard and the minimum dimension for corridors should be 900mm
- At least one bedroom and a bathroom should be located at entrance level

These standards fell well short of the standards needed for full wheelchair accessibility and were intended to make a proportion of general purpose housing more accessible to the 'general disabled'. They were based on an implicit assumption that wheelchair-users would be unlikely to use their wheelchairs within their homes. Goldsmith (1980a) argued that: '... mobility housing is potentially suitable for: 1. all ambulant disabled; 2. those who use wheelchairs but are able to transfer and move a few steps... with something to hang on to. It is not convenient for the chair bound... or for those with very large wheelchairs. It is estimated that mobility housing could cater for between 50 per cent and 75 per cent of people with wheelchairs'.

2.4.5
Wheelchair Standards

'Mobility standards' were drawn up to encourage local authorities to build a proportion of their general purpose housing to standards which would render them more accessible for disabled people.

A second HDD occasional paper was written as a follow-up to 'Mobility Housing' and was entitled 'Wheelchair Housing' (Goldsmith 1980b). The purpose of this paper was to provide design guidance on the housing needs of wheelchair-bound people. This paper defined what today is referred to as 'design to

wheelchair standards'. Wheelchair housing was needed by 'people who, on account of disability, cannot conveniently be placed in mobility housing... People with disabilities tend to deteriorate physically and, while in the short term mobility housing may be adequate, in the long term they may be satisfactorily catered for only in wheelchair housing'.

Selwyn Goldsmith was involved in an uphill struggle to improve standards of accessibility and to raise general levels of awareness amongst designers. If today some of his recommendations seem to err on the cautious side this is in part a tribute to his achievement and in part the result of recent developments in the design of wheelchairs. The use of powered wheelchairs is now much more commonplace than it was in 1980 and, although they have become smaller, they are still bigger than manual wheelchairs. The 'mobility standard' recommendation for 900mm doorsets to achieve 750mm clear openings is too tight for powered wheelchairs: clear openings of 800mm or ideally 850mm are now recommended. Again a 900mm corridor is too narrow to allow a wheelchair to make a tight turn and 1200mm is now recommended.

It is dangerous for the designer to proceed from the premise that residents of sheltered housing are generally healthy and active people, a few of whom may occasionally experience problems with mobility. Today it is necessary to turn this premise on its head: most residents of sheltered housing will at some time experience difficulties with mobility, and only a few will remain fully active and mobile. This is not to suggest that elderly people should be regarded per se as being disabled. However, although designers of sheltered housing in the past could get away with designing to 'mobility standards' the Extra Care concept demands that all flats be designed with the built-in capability to be upgraded to full 'wheelchair standards'.

Design Recommendations

The following summary recommendations are an updated version of the 'wheelchair standards' as defined in the original HDD paper (Goldsmith 1980b).

Location:
- The scheme should be sited near to shopping facilities, in an area free from steep inclines
- Residents should be able to look out onto scenes of activity

Access:
- The approach to any entrance should be ramped

Entrance doors:
- Minimum 950m doorsets, to give 800mm clear openings
- Viewing panels should be fitted to doors
- A letter cage should be fitted
- Thresholds should be flush

Internal circulation:
- Corridors to be minimum 1200mm wide with 950mm doorsets to facilitate 90° turns
- Wheelchairs need a 1500mm diameter circle in which to turn completely through 180°
- All doors to have minimum 950mm doorsets to achieve 800mm minimum openings
  - Doors must be correctly positioned to allow for door swing, position of handles etc.
  - Sliding doors are a suitable substitute for rooms such as bathrooms, but they should achieve a clear opening of 800mm

Door and window ironmongery:
- Handles to internal doors should be at standard height of 1040mm above floor level
- Kick plates should be fitted to minimise damage from wheelchair footrests

- Window openers should be accessible and easy to manipulate

Taps:
- Lever tap fittings preferred
- Taps must be accessible

Floor finishes:
- Should be slip resistant
- The needs of ambulant disabled people should be given priority over wheelchair users in the specification of finishes

Walls and floors:
- Partition walls to bathroom and WCs must be sufficiently strong to allow for the fitting of support rails
- Corners need to be protected against damage (plaster specification)
- Ceilings should support the weight of a hoist

Heating:
- Should be individually controllable and have controls which are easily manipulated

Electrical:
- Switches and sockets to be at 1040mm above floor level

Alarm systems:
- Emergency alarm system required

Kitchens:
- Should be planned as a recess off the sitting room: drive in and reverse out
- Allow space for wheelchair turning circle of 1500mm
- Fit adjustable height worktops
- Specify a split level cooking unit with built in hob and waist height oven

- Shallow sinks (140mm deep internally)
- Swivel taps to be fitted - so that kettles can be filled without lifting them off the worktop
- Preparation area:
  - 500mm deep is sufficient
  - Provide knee access and leg room
  - Pull-out boards can provide alternative (or additional) working levels

Storage:
- Leg-room is needed below worktops
- Wall units can be useful for long-term storage
- Specify movable storage consoles

Living rooms:
- Window sill height of 600mm recommended
- Avoid transoms in the zone 1000-1200mm above floor level
- Bay windows are recommended

Bedrooms:
- Space to facilitate transfers from wheelchair to bed
- Space to approach wardrobes, dressing tables etc.
- Clothes cupboards should have an unobstructed access and adjustable height rail

Bathrooms:
- Showers are preferable
- Allow space for wheelchair turning circle of 1500mm diameter
- Washbasins should project to allow wheelchairs to slip under
- WC position should permit frontal, oblique or lateral transfer from wheelchair with or without assistance
- Allowance should be made for the fixing of support rails to the side wall adjoining the WC, while a hinged horizontal rail should be fixed on the open side

2.5
The Visual Environment

2.5.1
Visual Impairment

It has been estimated by the Royal National Institute for the Blind (RNIB) that while only about one person in sixty in the general population is registered as suffering from a visual impairment, the proportion of people over the age of 75 is one in six (Barker, Barrick & Wilson, 1995). People over the age of 75 are estimated to account for two thirds of the total number of those who are visually impaired. On average there could be as many as half a dozen people suffering from serious visual impairments in a typical sheltered housing scheme and special care must be taken to design a suitable visual environment.

Older people who become partially sighted or blind are much less able to adjust to their affliction than those who are younger. It is estimated that when older people lose their sight it can take as long as two years for them to familiarise themselves with the layout of a typical sheltered housing scheme. Older blind or partially sighted people can experience difficulty in managing a large flat. Those who are less mobile prefer to live in a small flat or bed-sitter where the layout is simpler to visualise, with fewer doors to negotiate and less furniture to bump into.

At the design stage, everything possible should be done to ensure that a scheme will be legible and memorable for blind people and that it will be safe and easy to negotiate for those who are partially sighted. People who are partially sighted rely on extra visual stimuli such as contrasting colours and highlights, while blind people rely on other sensory stimuli. Fortunately many of the strategies which are designed to help the visually impaired will also

bring benefits to people suffering from confusion or memory loss.

Whilst it is important to consider the needs of those who suffer from some form of serious visual impairment, it is also important to bear in mind that almost all older people experience at least a degree of restricted vision. Older people need on average at least twice the illumination than younger people in order to perform a given task.

Apart from total blindness the main types of visual impairment associated with old age are:

- Hypermetropia
  Long-sightedness or hypermetropia results from the failure of the cilliary muscles. Old people may suffer from a combination of short and long-sightedness.
- Age-related macular degeneration
  This affects central vision and makes the eye more sensitive to light.
- Cataracts
  These are caused by a clouding of the lens which decreases the amount of light able to pass into the eye. It causes blurred and dimmed vision. Glare presents a special problem: light is scattered across the lens obscuring vision, like bright sunlight hitting a dirty windscreen. Cataracts also yellow the lens and affect the perception of colour.
- Diabetic retinopathy
  This causes patchy vision.
- Glaucoma
  This can result from damage to the optic nerve or an increase in pressure on the eye. It causes tunnel vision and reduces peripheral vision, making it difficult to see obstructions or moving cars.

2.5.2
Design Strategies for the Visual Environment

The following is a list of design strategies which aim to improve the quality of the visual environment to benefit both the partially sighted and those with normal sight.

Lighting

Although older people need high levels of overall lighting in order to see and to perform normal everyday tasks, concentrations of excessive light can be troublesome for people with impaired vision.

- Glare and bright reflected light cause particular problems. Shiny reflective surfaces should be avoided, particularly in communal and circulation areas. Large windows placed at the ends of corridors can cause discomfort and confusion.
- Elderly people have problems to 'accommodate' quickly when the level of lighting changes. Care should be taken to ensure only gradual or phased transitions from room to room by creating zones of 'intermediate lighting'. This is particularly important at the main entrance where, at night, people are moving from a dark exterior to a brightly lit interior.
- Problems of retinal accommodation and disability glare can be minimised by using either indirect lighting, where the actual source of the light is hidden from the eye, or diffused lighting, where the light source is camouflaged.
- Background lighting should be adequate and evenly distributed. The use of dimmer switches enables people to adjust the level of lighting to the task in hand.
- Directional task lighting is needed for such activities as reading, sewing or food preparation.
- Windows are important both for the visual link which they provide and as a source of daylight. However, the strength and quality of daylight may need to be modified by curtains, blinds and external sunshades.
- Wall and ceiling surfaces should have a light hue in order to reflect as much light as possible. This is particularly important in schemes with deep plans.
- Notice boards and signs need to be well lit, though individual spotlights can cause streaks or cones of light which make notice boards difficult to read.
- Shadows can create confusing information and even camouflage potential hazards. They can create the illusion of steps which don't exist or obscure actual steps. Care must be taken to prevent low sunlight from casting strong shadow patterns.

 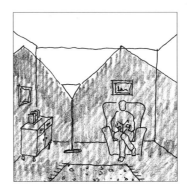 

Fig. 2.5.2a: Two examples of inadequate and uneven lighting   *Fig. 2.5.2b: Ideal lighting*

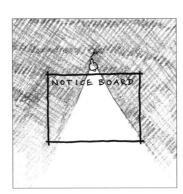  

Fig. 2.5.2c: Glare at end of corridor   *Fig. 2.5.2d: Bad corridor lighting*   *Fig. 2.5.2e: Lines of strong shadow*

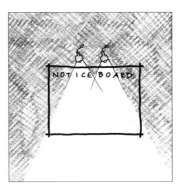 

Fig. 2.5.2f: Two examples of inappropriate lighting   *Fig. 2.5.2g: Improved lighting*

Contrast

Partially sighted people rely on contrasting tones and colours to help them identify important objects or to differentiate between surfaces. Although colour contrasts can be effective many partially sighted people rely more on tonal contrast: it should be borne in mind that a pair of contrasting colours like red and green provide almost no tonal contrast.

- Colour and tonal contrasts can be used to pick out a door from its surrounding architrave, or a stair nosing from the tread. They can be used to locate light switches and handrails in corridors, and to accentuate the junction between a wall surface and a floor.
- Features such as clocks and notice boards need to employ strongly contrasting graphics.

There is a danger that colour schemes which are designed only with contrast in mind will appear garish or unpleasing to the normally sighted. The University of Reading is currently carrying out research on the use of colour and contrast in environments for the partially sighted. The intention is to produce a design guide which will include colour wheels and charts for use in the design of contrasting colour schemes.

Pattern

Surfaces of walls, floors, tables and worktops which carry strong decorative patterns give out ambiguous information and can be confusing for the partially sighted. A swirling carpet pattern makes it more difficult to distinguish items of furniture and almost impossible to find small objects which have fallen to the floor. Strongly patterned wallpapers make it difficult to distinguish doors and can cause wall and floor planes to merge. On the other hand a regular and strongly contrasting geometric floor pattern can be

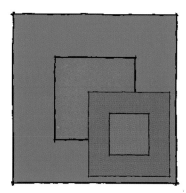

Fig. 2.5.2h: Contrasting colours with poor tonal contrast

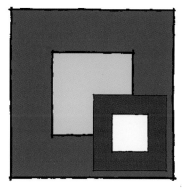

Fig. 2.5.2j: Contrasting colours with strong tonal contrast

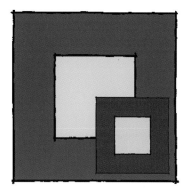

Fig. 2.5.2k: Tonal contrast

Fig.2.5.2m: A yellow hand rail

Fig. 2.5.2n: Use of colour

helpful in certain situations.

Unfortunately there is a lack of precise information which can help the designer in this area. Large swirling decorative patterns are thought generally to be more confusing, while small regular patterns tend to merge and look more solid. It is advisable to treat walls as plain undecorated surfaces with strong colours of light hue. It is also important to design rooms as a single entity in which wall, ceiling and floor surfaces are considered together with lighting, furniture and soft-furnishing.

Texture

Tactile stimuli can be sensed via the hands or feet and can play an important role in helping blind and partially sighted people to function independently.

- Changes in floor surface and texture can act as location indicators or can give warning of hazards. Carpets, tiles, boards, vinyl sheets and bricks all exhibit different degrees of bounce and produce distinct tactile and aural information.
- Tactile warning mats should be placed at the top and bottom of stairs.
- Handrails can be made from a variety of materials, or can be marked with grooves or bumps to identify the different parts of the scheme. The ends of handrails can be marked by projecting dowels.
- Controls on such things as cookers, showers and heating units should carry clear tactile signals.
- Rectangular pieces of furniture can help people to orientate themselves, though sharp corners may cause injury.
- Signs should carry tactile information and strong graphics.
- Textured wall surfaces can help with orientation but rough textures could cause injury and should be avoided.

Fig. 2.5.2p: Tactile handrail

Fig. 2.5.2q: Absence of tactile information on controls

Fig. 2.5.2r: Changes in floor surface

Fig. 2.5.2s: Tactile signage

Design Criteria

Other Sensory Information

People who are blind or partially sighted develop enhanced sensitivity to other forms of stimuli. Sound, smell, touch and air movement all play a part in helping people to map their surroundings.

- The acoustic quality of a space can be quite distinctive.
- Auditory signs can be triggered by smart cards and can provide information about location or warn of hazards - "mind the gap!"
- Aromas can identify particular rooms, such as a kitchen or a laundry. Materials and finishes carry aromas: polished timber, new carpet, heavy curtains.

Layout Logic

Clear and logical layouts help older people to form strong mental images of a building and avoid problems of disorientation and confusion.

- Complex multiple choice situations should be avoided.
- Meandering corridors can be confusing; arbitrary changes of direction are disorienting.
- Important facilities should be located in a clear and consistent way: toilets for instance should be placed near to lifts.
- In large rooms the layout of furniture should be logical and, within limits, unvarying.
- Fire escape routes should be simple and clear, and escape stairs should communicate clearly the level of each landing.

Obstructions

People who are blind or partially sighted navigate on the assumption that everything is in 'its proper place'.

When things crop up in strange places they can cause problems. Care must be taken to avoid creating unexpected obstructions such as overgrown vegetation in a garden or a protruding fire extinguisher in a corridor or a low table in a sitting room. These can impede progress or precipitate a fall. On the other hand anonymous 'clutter free' spaces can also fail to provide visually impaired people with 'signs'. A radiator on the wall of a corridor may be a potential hazard, but it could also serve as a 'marker'. If things like radiators aren't recessed then they should be specified with rounded edges so as not to cause injury.

Partially sighted people may collide with hinged doors and some commentators recommend that sliding doors should be fitted to all cupboards. However, sliding doors do not offer the best solution for elderly people with diminished strength, and have a reputation for jamming. One solution would be to dispense with cupboard doors altogether.

Fig. 2.5.2t: Recessed radiator and fire extinguisher in corridor

Signs

Signs are a necessary feature of communal buildings. However, the use of too many signs will cause confusion and visual 'noise', and convey an institutional feeling. It is important to ask the question: 'Is this sign really necessary?'. The use of abstract graphic signs can be effective, but unfamiliar symbols can cause confusion. Not all of the symbols used to indicate male and female toilets are as clear as their designers intended.

- Signs should be designed using large clear lettering, contrasting tones and non-reflective surfaces.
- Letters should be embossed and not engraved.
- Signs should be located at between 1.2m and 1.5m above floor level to allow them to be both seen and touched.
- Braille signs should be included wherever appropriate.
- Notice boards should be large and well lit and should be located in a prominent place with plenty of space. They should have dark, non-reflective backgrounds and should employ a system which dispenses with the use of pins.
- Lettering should be in lower case
- Clear layout plans can be installed at the main entrance to a scheme to help people develop a clear mental picture of where they live. These can use raised surfaces and strong colours.

2.6
The Acoustic Environment

2.6.1
Hearing Impairments

It is estimated that 17% of the general population suffer from problems with their hearing. However, people are more likely to experience problems as they grow older: they may become partially or wholly deaf; they may find difficulty in hearing particular frequencies; they may become hypersensitive to sounds of particular frequencies; they may lose the facility to separate one sound source from another.

People who are affected by hearing difficulties late in life find it much harder than younger people to adapt to their new situation or to learn to cope with it. They often experience problems in learning to use a hearing aid, in learning to lip-read or in a learning sign language.

Partial or total deafness can lead to frustration, isolation and depression. Hearing problems can also affect balance and induce feelings of dizziness, thus increasing the risk of falling.

2.6.2
Modifying the Acoustic Environment

The acoustic character of a space is determined by its size, its proportions, by the absorptive properties of its main boundary surfaces and by the nature of its contents. Highly reflective surfaces produce long reverberations and can lead to a confusion of sound stimuli, as for instance in a swimming pool. Highly absorptive surfaces will tend to muffle and swallow sound, as for instance in the lounge of a hotel.

A high level of background noise is particularly troublesome for people with hearing problems, especially those who use hearing aids. For this reason the communal spaces within a sheltered housing scheme need to be designed with absorptive surfaces so as to achieve fairly low reverberation times and cut down on echo. This is particularly important in dining rooms where there is a lot of background clatter, and in sitting rooms where a number of different conversations can be taking place at the same time. Hard surfaces on the floors and walls of corridors will produce long echoes and generate an institutional ambience.

Sound transmission from room to room is a common source of discomfort and irritation in any apartment building. Air-borne sound is transmitted across walls, floors and ceilings; structure-borne sound is transmitted through the building fabric. Lifts and staircases are a source of both air-borne and structure-borne sound. Unwanted sound may also emanate from the outside: from busy streets, from neighbouring buildings and from passing aeroplanes. The problem is exacerbated in sheltered housing by the fact that some residents are hard of hearing and turn up the volume of their audio equipment, while others are highly sensitive to sound.

2.6.3
Aids and Appliances

In addition to the now familiar hearing aid, many new appliances are now available to help those with hearing difficulties.

- Alarm systems in sheltered housing should include flashing lights as well as sound. Vibrating alarms can be fitted under pillows or worn under clothing.
- New developments include portable amplifiers for listening to the television and personal pagers which respond to the telephone, the doorbell or the general alarm system.
- Glass panels in doors will give a person with hearing problems more confidence to enter a room.
- Communal rooms which are used for talks and entertainment can be fitted with an induction loop which transmits amplified sound to hearing aids.
- Deaf people who rely on lip-reading and sign language need adequate lighting to be able to see clearly.

2.7
The Thermal Environment

The thermal environment exerts a considerable influence on the physical and psychological wellbeing of the elderly. Older people are particularly sensitive to the cold and show a much stronger preference for warmer temperatures than younger and more active people (Collins et al., 1981; Collins 1986). It is vital, therefore, to provide them with a high standard of thermal comfort, especially during winter months.

Thermal comfort is determined physiologically by the body's production of metabolic heat, its ability to transfer that heat into the surrounding environment and its ability to maintain its own working temperature. However, the perception of thermal comfort is subjective and varies from person to person according to their individual characteristics and to their environmental circumstances. Individual characteristics include such variables as clothing or level of activity while environmental circumstances include air temperature, surface temperature and relative humidity.

2.7.1

Individual Characteristics which affect Thermal Comfort

An environmental design strategy for sheltered housing must take into account the special needs of older people. In particular it is important to identify those individual characteristics which are likely to modify or compromise the design. Designers need to understand exactly how the thermal comfort of older people is affected by their physiology, their general state of health, their level of activity, their clothing, their patterns of behaviour and their state of mind. Other characteristics such as ethnicity, gender or build may also have an influence but are usually less significant.

Physiology

In order to survive, human beings need to maintain a constant deep body temperature. When the temperatures of the air and the surrounding surfaces fluctuate, the body undergoes a series of physiological changes to regulate its heat gain or loss. These include blushing and sweating to dissipate heat, blanching to conserve heat and shivering to generate heat. In a cold environment, human blood is diverted towards vital organs in order to maintain internal body temperatures, leaving the extremities such fingers and toes feeling cold and uncomfortable. Under extreme conditions, the human nervous system slows down and the core body temperature drops (McIntyre, 1983).

Older people suffer from a decline in their cold defence mechanisms. They tend to feel much colder than younger people and are more vulnerable to infection and illness (Collins et al., 1981). They also show low resistance to respiratory related infections and in cold conditions may experience high blood pressure, cold strokes or heart attacks. Prolonged exposure to cold temperatures is a major cause of clinical hypothermia

which can lead to other secondary disorders (Collins, 1986).

As people age their skin loses its ability to retain or dissipate heat, they suffer from poor blood circulation and they become less sensitive to surface temperature. This loss of skin sensitivity makes older people vulnerable to burns and scalds. When they feel cold they are naturally drawn towards a fire or a radiator but their skin is unable to cope with the influx of heat and they may be unaware of any injury which they are suffering. This is a particular problem for those suffering from dementia who are unable to associate the sensation of pain with its cause. For this reason it is important to limit the temperature of all exposed surfaces and all water supplies to a maximum of 43°C.

Levels of Activity

The human body gains heat mainly through metabolism - the conversion of body fuel or food into energy or activity. When the level of activity increases metabolic heat generation rises and excess heat must be dissipated in order to maintain a constant body temperature. Older people become progressively less active and may eventually become totally sedentary. They may suffer from loss of appetite and under-nutrition or they may experience a lowering of their metabolic rate. For these reasons they are no longer able to generate sufficient body heat and consequently they feel cold.

Clothing

Clothing insulates the human body against heat loss. As the thickness of clothing is increased, so the importance of the surrounding thermal environment is reduced. Extra clothes can increase overall body comfort in cold conditions, but clothing must be distributed evenly to avoid localised discomfort. Cold

hands and feet can produce an overall sensation of discomfort even when the general level of body insulation is adequate.

It has been shown that the effect of clothing insulation is greater at higher metabolic rates (McIntyre, 1983). This means that although younger and more active people with higher metabolic rates can successfully compensate for a cold environment by increasing their level of clothing, older people, who have a lower metabolic rate and who are less active, are much more dependent on a warm environment.

Behaviour

Younger people are more successful in adapting to a wider range of environmental conditions in order to minimise thermal discomfort. They can increase activity, change clothing, adjust heating levels and promote air movement. However, old age reduces peripheral temperature perception and older people respond less effectively and less quickly to changes in the ambient temperature (Collins et al., 1981). In a cold environment older people are less able to perceive accurately any reduction in peripheral temperature and are thus slower in taking compensatory action. Delays in putting on extra clothes or adjusting the heating level can lead to discomfort or distress.

State of Mind

The perception of thermal comfort is subjective and varies from individual to individual. In winter many younger people are able to adjust psychologically to a cooler environment and as a result can happily tolerate a lower level of ambient temperature (Cena et al., 1986). Older people who make similar mental adjustments run the risk of suffering from thermo-regulatory distress because they are physically less adaptable.

A person's state of mind can have a marked effect on subjective thermal sensations (McIntyre, 1983). Perceptions of thermal comfort can be influenced by a number of external factors such as room colour and lighting. The installation of a dummy fireplace, for instance, can induce sensations of warmth. These psychological effects can be exploited in the design of internal environments, though with older people there is a real risk that falsely induced sensations of comfort can mask physical distress.

2.7.2
Environmental Circumstances which affect Thermal Comfort

Individual characteristics are to some extent subjective and may be modified by behaviour. Environmental circumstances, on the other hand, are more operational, more measurable and therefore more susceptible to design. The four primary environmental circumstances which affect the thermal comfort of the elderly are air temperature, surface temperature, air movement and relative humidity. These may be regulated by the thermal performance of the building envelope and by the provision of space heating and ventilation.

Relative Humidity

Humidity affects the body's ability to lose heat by evaporation, although at normal temperatures it has little bearing on perceived warmth. Most older people would hardly notice changes in humidity levels in the range between 30% and 70%.

High levels of humidity can be harmful for people who are susceptible to chest infection. They bring increased risks of condensation which supports mould growth and can cause asthma and cold-related symptoms such as sneezing and runny nose. However, humidity levels should not fall below 30% as this may cause dryness to skin, eyes and nose. The mucous in the nose normally traps bacteria and viruses, and a dry nose can make people more susceptible to winter illnesses.

Air Movement

The velocity of the air relative to the body influences heat loss through convection and evaporation. Sedentary old people are especially sensitive to air movement or draughts. When air movement exceeds a velocity of 0.1m/s, higher room temperatures are needed to maintain the same feeling of thermal comfort. Air velocities above 0.3m/s would lead to complaints of draught and are therefore unacceptable except in summer. Unless mechanical ventilation is used, air velocity within most modern buildings is usually less than 0.1m/s, and air movement does not have a significant effect on thermal comfort. Mechanical air extracts in kitchens and bathrooms only disturb the air close to inlets and pose little threat to thermal comfort.

Air and Surface Temperature

The balance between air temperature and the combined net effect of the temperatures of surrounding surfaces - known as the mean radiant temperature - has a considerable influence on thermal comfort. High radiant temperatures can compensate for low air temperatures: it is possible to sit quite comfortably in a swim suit surrounded by snow if there is strong sunshine. Conversely high air temperatures can compensate for low radiant temperatures: the build up of warm air within an igloo reduces the effect of radiant losses to its icy walls. However, maximum comfort will only be achieved when the two are in balance, particularly for sedentary older people. Discomfort can result from an imbalance of radiant heat sources: someone sitting by a fire in a cold room on a cold day with their back to a large single glazed window will experience excessive radiant heat loss on one side of the body and excessive gain on the other. Any such imbalance of radiant temperatures should be kept within a 10°C range.

As a general rule people feel more comfortable when the air temperature around their feet is slightly higher than that around their head, and when the temperature of the floor is slightly higher than that of the ceiling. This may be particularly true for old people with circulatory problems who suffer from cold feet. If ceiling heating is used, temperature asymmetry should be less than 5°C. If underfloor heating is used the surface temperature of the floor should not exceed 29°C.

Fig. 2.7.2a: Big variations in radiant temperature cause discomfort

Thermal Comfort Indices

One thermal index used in the UK for specifying the level of thermal comfort is the 'dry resultant temperature' (CIBSE, 1986b). This takes into account the combined effect of air temperature, mean radiant temperature and air movement and provides a more effective way of specifying comfort than does air temperature alone.

British Standards now used 'operative temperature' as an index of thermal comfort. Under normal conditions of air movement this is almost the same as 'dry resultant temperature'.

2.7.3
Thermal Comfort

The thermal comfort of older people is influenced by six principal factors: clothing, type of activity, room air temperature, mean radiant temperature of the surrounding surfaces, relative humidity and the velocity of air passing over the skin. The thermal requirements for older people can be specified in relation to three main types of activity: rest or sleep, sedentary activities and bathing/showering. A summary of recommended dry resultant temperatures for different parts of a sheltered housing scheme is given in Fig. 2.7.3a.

Although the metabolic rate is much lower during sleep, bedclothes reduce heat loss, and temperature levels can be lower than the daytime average. Air velocity should be kept below 0.2m/s and persistent flow of air in one direction should be avoided. Relative humidity can normally be kept within the acceptable range of 30% - 70% through background ventilation. When a bedroom is not in use its temperature level can be kept lower than that of a living room.

Older people may spend much of their time in sedentary activity and are likely to be clad in several layers of clothing. The air velocity experienced by the elderly should be maintained below the threshold of 0.2m/s and there should be no persistent air flow in any one direction. Any large cold surface which can cause excessive radiant heat loss from one side of the body should be avoided. The balance between radiant temperature and air temperature should be kept within recommended limits.

When taking a bath or shower, the whole body is in direct contact with the surrounding environment and is subject to high rates of heat loss. A higher temperature level is therefore required. Air movement should be reduced to the minimum to reduce convective heat loss and large cold surfaces should be avoided to reduce radiant heat loss. The relative humidity level may rise above the recommended upper limit of 70% and this should be restored by operating an air extract in a position close to the moisture source and over-running it after bathing is complete.

	Dry Resultant Temperatures	C
1	Living rooms	23
2	Bedrooms	21
3	Bed-sitting rooms	23
4	Bathrooms	24
5	Residents' toilets	21
6	Staircases and corridors	20
7	Staff rooms	20
8	Entrance hall and foyer	22

Fig. 2.7.3a: Recommended 'dry resultant temperatures'

2.7.4
Air Quality

Human comfort is very much influenced by air quality. Older people who spend a high proportion of their time indoors are particularly affected by internal atmosphere and need to breathe in air which is fresh and free from pollution. Good air can be defined as 'air which is free of pollutants that cause irritation, discomfort or ill health to occupants' (Liddament, 1996).

Indoor air quality is affected by three main factors: pollution generated within the building, pollution which enters the building from outside and ventilation.

Pollution

The main pollutants which are generated within buildings are water vapour, odour and particulates. Water vapour is a by-product of metabolism and is also produced from activities such as cooking and washing. When the humidity level of the air increases, dampness and condensation will occur on cold surfaces. If such conditions persist they encourage the growth of mould and parasites and thus increase the risk of respiratory-related infections. Odours are generated by metabolism and by such activities as cooking and smoking. Although odours are rarely harmful, they can be upsetting and may induce depression or stress. Particulates include dust, pollens, fungal spores, fibres, bacteria and smoke particles. Large particulates may cause stains on wall surfaces or furnishings. Small and microscopic particles have properties similar to gaseous compounds and can cause respiratory problems.

The most effective method for controlling indoor pollutants is to remove their source: pollution from tobacco smoke, for example, can be eliminated by banning smoking. A second method is to ventilate at source: air extracts in bathrooms and kitchens remove odours and excessive moisture before they can diffuse. A third method is to employ general ventilation. Pollutants such as carbon dioxide, odour and water vapour can be removed by dilution.

Ventilation

Adequate background ventilation is necessary both for health and for comfort. Health depends on air which contains sufficient oxygen for respiration, which is free of excessive concentrations of harmful bacteria, noxious gases, dust or odours. Comfort depends on the control of heat and humidity and on the movement of air to promote body cooling.

Older people are particularly vulnerable to infection and it is important to ensure that ventilation provides sufficient fresh air to dilute and remove harmful bacteria. All habitable rooms should be provided with some form of permanent trickle ventilation. Bathrooms and kitchens should be mechanically ventilated in a manner which avoids the direct recycling of vitiated air.

Chapter 3.0
Planning

This chapter looks at the various stages in the overall planning of an Extra Care housing scheme: how does a project begin? What determines its feasibility? What are the roles of the different players? What are the main elements of a scheme? What are the criteria for selecting a site? How should the site be organised, planned, landscaped? What will determine the overall form of a scheme?

3.1
Project Planning

Although Extra Care housing may be provided in the voluntary, private or public sectors, this section focuses mainly on the way in which projects are planned by housing associations, with occasional references to private developers.

3.1.1
Project Inception

The ways in which projects are conceived and born can vary from sector to sector and from organisation to organisation. The aims and priorities of a private housing developer are quite different from those of a housing association or a local authority.

The Public Sector

Although local authorities were once the main providers of sheltered housing, during the past ten years they have almost ceased to build new schemes and, as existing schemes have been transferred into the voluntary sector, their role as estate managers has

contracted. Some local authorities have gone so far as to transfer their entire housing stock to what are called local housing companies. If present trends continue local authorities may eventually cease to be providers of sheltered housing. In the future, however, they will take on a much bigger role as purchasers, inspectors and licensing authorities and will continue to influence the development of new projects. As purchasers they can exercise a controlling influence over the number of subsidised places within their area, they can support new schemes with grants and they can make land available to housing associations, while as planning authorities they can influence the scale and location of developments.

The Voluntary Sector

The voluntary sector is now the biggest provider of sheltered housing and Extra Care housing. There are a total of 1,400 housing associations affiliated to the National Housing Federation (NHF), half of which build and manage sheltered housing. These include small community-based associations, housing associations which cater to the needs of a very specific constituency and large associations which serve a variety of constituencies. In the past new projects were often born out of opportunity - the fact that a suitable site had been found or that funding was available - or out of an association's need to develop its estate. Today projects are much more likely to develop in response to an identified need and there are a number of safeguards in place to ensure that this is so. Associations work in partnership with local authorities in assessing demand and developing strategies to address needs. There is also a growing number of associations which no longer develop or build but which see their role simply as that of estate managers.

The Private Sector

Private sheltered housing for sale did not exist in Britain prior to 1977. However, during the past twenty years a new market has grown up and today it is estimated that there are over a hundred developers and construction companies in the field. Private schemes offer elderly home owners the opportunity to carry their equity with them into old age. For this reason they are likely to become an increasingly popular alternative in the future as greater numbers of owner occupiers reach retirement age.

Private developers have to operate within a highly competitive and fluctuating market. When they launch a project they have to gamble on how the market will develop over a period of up to two years. Their first problem is land: in order to start a project they need a site with outline planning permission which is at the right price and in the right locality; their second problem is finance: in order to progress a project they must first find an affordable source of funding.

3.1.2
Feasibility

The ultimate test of the feasibility of a scheme is to be able to demonstrate that it will meet a real demand and that the total costs of the development will not exceed the total anticipated dividends.

The Voluntary Sector

The parameters which determine the feasibility of a scheme in the voluntary sector are relatively complex. Most housing associations originally came into existence as alternative providers of subsidised housing and still operate as registered charities or 'not for profit' organisations. They are financed from a number of different sources, which include government grant and private borrowing. In theory a housing association assesses feasibility in the same way as a private developer: the total development costs must relate to anticipated revenues. However, revenues will depend on a number of variables including projected rents, estimates for voids and anticipated subsidies.

The following is a simplified list of steps in the assessment of feasibility:

- local needs for sheltered housing are assessed
- 'market' rents are estimated
- assumptions are made for the level of 'voids' which can be expected
- a site is identified
- building and consultants, costs are identified
- 'in-house' development costs are identified; bigger associations can cross-subsidise from past projects, to mask high 'in-house' development costs.
- possible subsidies are estimated and subtracted from the land and development costs in order to calculate mortgage requirement
- net income is estimated from projected revenues, taking into account management and maintenance costs as well as losses due to voids
- net income is compared to the cost of servicing the mortgage
- if the scheme doesn't 'stack up' it is abandoned

The Private Sector

The parameters which determine the feasibility of a private development are relatively easy to identify. The total cost of the development must not exceed the gross development value. The total development cost includes land costs, consultants' fees, construction costs, financing costs and profits. The gross development value must reflect the total receipts and income which can be expected to accrue from sales, ground rents and annual charges.

One difficulty facing the developer stems from the fact that two years can elapse between inception and completion and during this time the market can change completely. In assessing the feasibility of a scheme the developer must evaluate the demand for sheltered housing in a particular area and make accurate projections for future sales. The main variables in the developer's equation are the cost and the potential of the site, the cost of financing the development and the ultimate selling price of a flat. Bigger developers purchase options on sites in suitable locations so that they can start building when the prospects are judged to be good.

The past ten years have seen a considerable swing in the demand for private sheltered housing and prices tumbled when the market collapsed at the end of the 1980s. Although the theoretical demand for sheltered housing has exceeded supply, actual demand has been limited by the fact that when the housing market was depressed prospective purchasers were unable to sell their existing houses with sufficient margin of equity to set against their future recurrent costs.

3.1.3
Project Funding

The Voluntary Sector

Before 1988 sheltered housing in the voluntary sector was funded almost entirely by central government through the Housing Corporation. However, during the past decade the funding regime has altered dramatically and the proportion of Housing Corporation grant has diminished. Housing associations have been obliged to augment grant funding with funding from private financial institutions. Today the average Social Housing Grant (SHG) is about 55% though it can drop to as low as 25%.

The Treasury determines the total size of SHG in any year and channels it through the Housing Corporation. The Housing Corporation enters into a dialogue with local authorities in order to assess local housing needs. Local authorities each submit a 'housing strategy statement' to the Housing Corporation and from this a 'housing needs index' is established. This defines needs and priorities in terms of categories of housing and numbers of units. A housing association must then bid competitively for grant funding through a local authority within the limits of its housing needs index. In this way the government acts through the Housing Corporation to exert a controlling influence on the volume of new construction, its location, its standard and its quality.

The Housing Corporation sets cost norms for each unit in each category of accommodation for any given locality. These can be used to calculate the Total Cost Indicator (TCI) for a scheme. In applying for a grant a housing association must submit a 'total scheme qualifying cost' (TSQC) which is the sum of the estimated 'capital cost' and 'on-cost'. The TSQC would not normally exceed the TCI. Housing associations must make their bids for SHG each November, a fact which produces a 'tidal effect' in voluntary sector activity. The shortfall between TCI and SHG is sometimes made up from private loans using the property as equity. This practice can result in higher rents.

The Private Sector

Private developers generally finance new developments by borrowing from private financial institutions such as banks, building societies and pensions funds. The profitability of a project will depend very much on the cost of borrowing, and the length of time between inception and sales.

3.1.4
Management

The Voluntary Sector

The organisational structure of housing associations varies according to the size of their estate and the main thrust of their activities. The large and medium sized associations typically operate with a departmental structure which differentiates between the following functional groupings:

- Housing Management (HM) Department
  Manages the Association's estate. It is generally responsible for the day-to-day running of schemes. Its role in the development of a new project is to determine local need, advise on lettability, organise feedback from existing tenants and help in drawing up the brief.
- Finance Department
  Secures funding, monitors feasibility and sets financial guidelines for new developments.
- Development and Technical Services
  Identifies land opportunities, bids for grants, employs consultants, selects contractors, develops briefs in conjunction with HM, manages contracts and puts completed schemes into commission. Subsequently it takes on the responsibility for scheme maintenance.
- Care Management
  Some associations are directly involved in the provision of care, particularly in the context of Extra Care housing, and run a separate department which has specific responsibility for care management. Others prefer to adopt a role of 'care enabler' and treat care management as a sub-function of housing management. In either case there is a need for close co-operation with local social service departments in order to develop long-term care provision strategies.

Once a project is underway a project team is set up with representatives of each of the main departments and with representatives of the local authority's social services department. During the early stages it is important that Development and Technical Services and Housing Management work closely together, though once the project is on site the former assumes the role of project manager, while the latter takes charge of lettings.

The Private Sector

Developers exist first and foremost to develop and build new schemes. Some developers act as developer/contractors or are closely linked to contracting organisations, while others employ contractors to build on their behalf. Few developers of sheltered housing are interested in the management, maintenance or care provision for a scheme once it has been sold, and it is common for them to entrust this to a separate management company. The management company levies an annual service charge from individual leaseholders which includes ground rent and a contribution towards the costs of maintenance, scheme management and services. Management companies may be linked to the developer or they may be quite separate organisations. In some cases the management company purchases the freehold of the scheme from the developer.

3.1.5
Consultants

The design of a complex building such as an Extra Care housing scheme requires the involvement of a range of specialist consultants which might include an architect, a quantity surveyor, an engineer and a landscape designer. Although a few housing associations and development companies employ their own in-house specialists, the majority rely on outside consultants. The Housing Corporation's 'Scheme Development Standards' (1995) require housing associations which undertake development on a regular basis to maintain lists of approved consultants.

Wherever possible the key consultants should be appointed during the very early stages of a project so that they can be involved in assessing the feasibility of alternative sites and strategies. However, the cost of initial feasibility studies is not regarded as being part of the actual cost of a project. The Housing Corporation in its Good Practice Guide (1989) states: 'The [Housing] Association may need the services of consultants at an early stage in order to undertake initial assessments of scheme proposals...Unless consultants agree otherwise, the [Housing] Association will be responsible for any fees arising out of inception and feasibility work'. As a result consultants are often expected to carry out work during initial stages without any guarantee of remuneration.

Unfortunately it is quite common for schemes to be cancelled or set aside, particularly if they are unsuccessful in the annual round of SHG bidding. Consultants working 'at risk' can find that a project is abandoned after they have 'nursed' it for several years and may work up two or three aborted schemes for every one which goes ahead. This system has two consequences: some of the more reputable practices are now reluctant to work in the voluntary sector while those which do are only able to invest minimum effort during the key early stages of a project.

During recent years development has come increasingly to be 'finance led' rather than 'design led' and quantity surveyors have taken over from architects as lead consultants. The adoption of new procurement routes such as 'design and build' has led to earlier involvement of contractors and a reduced role for consultants.

The Architect

The overall planning and detailed design of a scheme is usually entrusted to a firm of architects. The architect's full service as defined by the Royal Institute of British Architects extends from initial feasibility studies through to the approval of final accounts. This includes the development of the brief, the preparation of sketch designs, the submission of planning and building control applications, the preparation of detailed designs and specifications, the preparation of tender documents and site supervision. Ideally architects should be appointed during the early stages of the project so that they can contribute to the development of the brief. The architect is responsible for developing the overall concept of the scheme, and under the terms of a traditional appointment, acts as a guardian of the interests of both the client and the contractor.

The fact that the architect's role has shrunk in recent years may be due partly to the increased complexity of building operations and the consequent need to involve other specialised consultants. Today many institutional clients are driven by very narrow concepts of 'value' and sometimes ignore the benefits which good design will bring. The recent vogue for fee tendering is based on a false premise that design expertise can be measured in an objective way, and fails to balance 'time, effort and experience' against 'quality' and real cost. A quickly designed building is likely to be an unsatisfactory one.

The system of procuring buildings in the voluntary sector is increasingly 'finance led' and may be less sensitive to design quality. Architects are expected to give away their 'big idea' in order to win the right to earn a fee by producing working drawings. The most crucial stage in the development of a project is often rushed through without a proper investment of time and resources and without proper consultation and evaluation. Some clients now dispense with their architect's services during the construction stage, and lose the benefits of impartial quality control in an often misguided attempt to save money.

It is sometimes assumed that all architects are equally capable of designing any type of building, though, like other professionals, in reality they often specialise in particular building types. The time scale on most projects makes it impossible for architects to learn their way into a new building type, and for this reason a shortlist of architects for a sheltered housing project should only include firms which have a proven track record in the specific field of design for the elderly or in the general field of housing. The Housing Corporation's 'Scheme Development Standards' (1995) require that consultants be 'vetted in respect of relevant skills' and that 'the range of their skills and capacities should fairly represent the range and scale of expertise required'. Observation would suggest that this is a requirement which is often ignored.

The Quantity Surveyor

Quantity surveyors have an important role to play in voluntary sector housing because of the complex nature of funding procedures. A firm of quantity surveyors will steer a project through the financial approval stages, establish cost targets, prepare bills of quantities, assist in the preparation of specifications, evaluate tenders, manage the financial side of the contract, carry out valuations and prepare final accounts. Quantity surveyors ought to be appointed during the early stages of a project so that they can advise on financial viability. Although quantity surveyors are usually appointed directly by the client they need to work in close collaboration with the architects.

Engineering Consultants

The complexity of modern building construction makes it advisable to use the services of specialist engineering consultants. In traditional procurement systems these were employed by the client and might have included structural engineers who would be responsible for structural design and calculation, heating and ventilating engineers who would be responsible for the design of the heating system and mechanical and electrical engineers. Increasingly these services are offered directly or indirectly by contractors and their specialist sub-contractors. In order to ensure that the particular heating and hot water needs of sheltered housing are addressed, clear performance specifications and employers, requirements should be issued to consultants and contractors.

Landscape and Interior Design Consultants

The scale of most sheltered housing schemes does not usually warrant the use of specialist consultants for interior design and landscape design. Where they are used it is important that they should be appointed in consultation with the architects and that they should work under the architects, overall direction. This will ensure that unity of the scheme's concept is maintained.

3.1.6
Developing the Brief

It is essential that client organisations provide consultants with a clear and comprehensive set of project aims and requirements in the form of a written and illustrated brief. The brief should define the main parameters of the project in terms of accommodation, range of activities, performance specification and environmental standards. In the absence of a good brief it is unlikely that the consultants will be able to develop a design which will meet the specific needs of the project.

Basics

The Housing Corporation's Good Practice Guide (1989) recommends that a brief should contain the following information:

1. the timetable for the scheme
2. physical site details, including information from structural, site or geotechnical surveys
3. proposed accommodation, including dwelling mix and sizes, layout and landscaping, car parking etc.
4. any known special planning requirements such as the use of local materials
5. any conditions of purchase or legal restrictions affecting rights of light and access, preserved buildings, trees or services crossing the site
6. any conclusions resulting from feasibility studies carried out by the client organisation
7. building and service performance standards, standards of construction, finishes and fittings and maintenance requirements etc.
9. contract procedures and completion arrangements;
10. how the project is to be managed and maintained
11. the budget for the scheme

To these one might add:

- a clear statement which defines the aims of the project, and sets out its main priorities in relation to general policies of the client organisation
- a description of the quality of the environment which is to be created
- a description of the lifestyle which is to be sustained

Formulation

A brief should be drawn up as a collaborative undertaking involving representatives from every part of the client organisation, including wardens, scheme managers and carers. Wherever possible the views and opinions of residents in existing schemes should be taken into account.

Larger associations often employ standard briefs and specifications which are carried over from one project to the next. Where this happens it is important that the performance of key features be properly evaluated before they are replicated.

Smaller housing associations may have limited experience of developing new projects and sometimes enlist larger associations to operate on their behalf. When they do act as developers it is essential that they use experienced consultants who are involved directly during the brief-making stage.

The initial brief should not be treated as a tablet of stone but as a dynamic overture to the project. It is important that clients invite their consultants to comment on the implications of the brief and contribute to its refinement and development. It is helpful, for example, if key members of the development team accompany the architects on joint visits to existing schemes: these might include in-house schemes, schemes built by other associations and examples of the architects' own previous work. Such visits can help both the architect and the client to develop initial ideas and to define a set of clear aims for the project.

Evaluation

Once a project is underway every effort should be made to avoid unnecessary changes, because these can result in costly abortive work and cause delays. However, it is also necessary to subject a scheme to rigorous testing during the design stage. For this to take place the architects need to present their design proposals in ways which are fully comprehensible to all the members of the team. Architects forget that many people have difficulty in reading drawings. A musician can look at a page of notes and hear the music coming off the page; an architect can look at a plan and envisage the building. All too often clients are disappointed by a final building because it fails to match the impression which they had formed of it during its early stages. Sketch models and CAD simulations which show the scheme in its setting or which focus on the design of an individual flat or a communal space can be helpful both to client and architect, and can be used in meetings which are held to introduce the emerging scheme to members of the local community - such meetings can play an important part in the early development of a scheme.

3.1.7
Approvals

Any building project must be built in accordance with existing legislation and should conform to relevant British Standards relating to construction.

Projects built with Housing Corporation funding must obtain final approval before a contract is let and must demonstrate that the project costs fall within the TSQC and that the design conforms to the Corporation's Scheme Development Standards.

In addition the following approvals must also be obtained:

- Planning Consent
  The enactments of current planning law are mainly contained in the Town and Country Planning Act of 1971. A new building should conform to the general requirements of any

existing Structure Plan or Local Plan. It is advisable to obtain Outline Planning Permission for a project at the inception stage. Full Planning Permission should be sought when firm proposals have been developed.

- Building Control Approval
  Local authorities exercise control of building through powers invested in them under the Building Regulations and Building Acts of 1984 and 1991. It is an offence to commence building works without first making a proper written application, to fail to issue the proper notices or to build contrary to the Building Regulations.

3.1.8
The Building Contract

In the past the traditional procurement route for housing associations involved raising finances, acquiring a site, commissioning a design and appointing a builder to construct a new purpose-designed building. Finances came mainly from government, the contractor was selected by competitive tender and a traditional form of building contract was employed.

Today housing associations may adopt one of a variety of procurement routes: they can obtain finance from banks, local authorities or financial institutions as well as from government; they may elect to convert an existing building, to purchase a ready made building from a contractor or to lease a building which has been purpose-built for them by a developer.

Types of Contract

The following are a few of the alternative types of building contract which are currently in use:

- Traditional Contracts
  Under a traditional contract a shortlist of approved contractors is invited to submit sealed tenders on the basis of a set of drawings and a bill of quantities and the contract is awarded to the lowest tender against a fixed sum on one or other of the standard forms. The main advantages of this method are that the client keeps control of the contract through appointed consultants, the relationship between the client and the contractor is clearly defined, there is full price competition, high standards of construction are achieved, and there are no conflicts of interest. The main disadvantages are that the stages are sequential and are therefore wasteful of time, and the cost is determined at a fairly late stage in the process.

- Design and Build
  Under the 'design and build' system the contractor's offer is based on an outline description of the project. The contractor takes responsibility for detailed design as well as the construction. The advantages are that the various stages of the traditional contract are telescoped together, the contractor can offer advice at an early stage and the client is given an early indication of the final cost. The disadvantages are that the client may lose control over quality, there may be only limited price competition, and variations are subject to cost penalties. However, collaborative forms of design and build contract have been developed during recent years to counter these disadvantages.

- Management Contracts
  The project is run from an early stage by a project manager who controls an array of separate sub-contractors, each one of which is responsible for a package of work which is defined by a performance specification. The advantages are that the duration of the project is reduced, without necessarily affecting the standard of construction. The disadvantage is that cost control and cost certainty can be reduced.

- Turnkey Contracts and Private Finance Initiatives
  Under a turnkey contract the developer takes over the full responsibility for financing and developing the entire project, and the potential client either guarantees to purchase the complete building, or agrees to lease it for a fixed number of years. This offers advantages to client organisations which lack project management expertise and have difficulty in raising capital. The disadvantages are that it removes much of the client's control over detailed design and specification, and can be expensive in the long term.

3.2
The Brief

An Extra Care scheme will usually consist of a group of flats with a variety of supporting facilities. The number and mix of flats is determined on the basis of projected demand while the nature and extent of the supporting facilities depend on the operational concept which is adopted.

3.2.1
Mix

Today most schemes contain a majority of one-bedroom flats with smaller numbers of two-bedroom flats and bed-sitters. This corresponds to current perceptions of demand.

Single people are currently in a majority among those who live in Extra Care housing, and there is no reason for supposing that this will change in the near future. Bed-sitters have become increasingly unpopular with older people and most would prefer to occupy a flat with a bedroom which is separate from their living room.

Couples and people who choose to live together form a significant group and they will normally require a flat with two bedrooms.

Increasing numbers of single people would like to have the use of a second bedroom and are prepared to pay for the privilege. On the other hand there are those for whom a bed-sitter may be the most suitable alternative.

3.2.2
Size

Sheltered housing schemes are generally smaller in Britain than in other European countries. In northern Europe schemes of more than a hundred units are not uncommon, and there is a tendency to locate different categories of housing on the same site. A typical scheme in Switzerland might consist of a group of about sixty Category 1 sheltered flats, a further group of about forty bed-sitters for the frail elderly and a separate care home for thirty residents.

The fact that in Britain different categories of housing are financed and licensed in different ways discourages this sort of mixed development. Although dual registered residential care/nursing homes are quite common, the combination of sheltered housing with residential care accommodation is almost unknown.

In Britain sheltered schemes in the public and voluntary sectors contain an average of between thirty and forty units and rarely exceed fifty. This is in part due to a belief that larger schemes risk becoming institutional and in part the result of local authority allocation policies. In the past the use of live-in warden-managers may also have been a limiting factor.

Private developer schemes often contain between forty and seventy units. These higher totals result from the need to maximise the number of dwellings in relation to basic infrastructural and communal provisions.

In Extra Care housing the use of non-residential scheme managers in association with flexible care teams seems to remove one of the limits on scale, but worries about possible links between size and ambience remain. Larger schemes do bring some real advantages: they can support more communal facilities, they encourage a greater choice and range of activities, and they tend to contain a wider cross-section of residents.

3.2.3
Operation

As well as varying in size, number of units and mix, Extra Care schemes also vary considerably in the way in which they are run. Three areas are important in this respect: the management system, the care delivery system and the system of food provision.

- Management
  In many Extra Care schemes live-in wardens have been replaced by non-residential scheme managers. This has occurred in response to a need to separate the day-to-day running of a housing scheme from the provision of care. The manager ceases to be an overworked factotum who is responsible for everything from light bulbs to resuscitation and who is unable ever to escape fully from the job, and becomes a professional with a clearly circumscribed job description. The manager is an enabler, an advocate for the residents and a mobiliser of resources.

- Care Delivery
  Some housing associations take on a direct responsibility for the provision of care, whilst the others prefer to act simply as enablers. Care may be provided by outside agencies on an individual basis or it may be provided in a comprehensive manner by the local social services department. In either case there is a need for a care office, a staff room, toilets, changing facilities and sleep-over accommodation. These might be located beside the scheme manager's office, but should be separated to some extent from the main communal areas.

- The Provision of Food

    The policy on the provision of cooked meals varies considerably from scheme to scheme. At one extreme there are schemes in which no communal dining facilities are provided: tenants are expected to prepare their own food in their own kitchens, possibly assisted by a carer, or they have cooked food delivered to them in their flats. At the other extreme there are schemes which provide cooked meals in a central dining room. In this case participation may be voluntary, or it may be mandatory in so far that meals are paid for as part of the service charge. Supporters of the latter arrangement argue that older people benefit from a regular cooked meal and from regular social contact, and that the operation of a pay-as-you-eat system is difficult to fund or manage. Supporters of the former argue that any mandatory system is a threat to independence. Between these two extremes there are schemes in which some tenants cook for themselves while others eat meals which have been prepared by carers in small communal dining-kitchens. Finally there are schemes which operate a hybrid of all of these alternatives.

3.2.4
The Schedule of Accommodation

The schedule of accommodation can be broken down into three main categories:

- residential
  accommodation

- essential communal
  and support facilities

- optional communal
  and support facilities

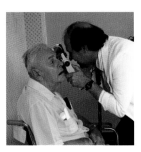

The residential accommodation will consist of a mix of independent flats of three principal types:

One-Bedroom Flats:

These have an area of between 40 sq.m and 50 sq.m and consist of an entry space, a sitting room, a bedroom which is large enough to take two single beds, a bathroom and a kitchen. Although intended for one tenant they may be used for a couple or for two people sharing, or they may need to accommodate occasional visitors or carers.

Two-Bedroom Flats:

These have an area of between 60 sq.m and 70 sq.m and contain an extra bedroom. Some would argue that two-bedroom flats offer much greater amenity to single people, making it easier to accommodate visitors and carers. However, this raises a question of cost: will purchasers in the private sector pay an extra 30% on the purchase price, will providers in the voluntary sector agree to fund the extra cost?

Bed-sitters:

These have an area of between 25 sq.m and 35 sq.m and consist of an entry space, a single living/sleeping space with a bathroom and minimal cooking facilities. Although bed-sitters may be suitable for very frail people or those with poor eyesight they have gained a bad reputation because, in the past, they were often built to mean space standards and without en-suite bathrooms.

The communal and support facilities will vary from scheme to scheme according to the operating concept which is adopted. A basic scheme will contain the following elements:

Communal Rooms:

- A main sitting room: this should accommodate all of the residents, and may be used for full-scale meetings or entertainments, as well as for casual social encounters.
- Smaller sitting rooms: these are needed for group activities such as classes, board games, religious observance, handicrafts etc., and may be located in other parts of the scheme.
- The entrance hall: this should be conceived, not simply as a left over space, but as an important social gathering space.

Staff Accommodation:

- The manager's office: this should be in a central position.
- Care office, staff room, staff toilets and sleep-over accommodation.

Support Spaces:

- Communal toilets in strategic locations.
- Assisted bathrooms: two fully equipped bathrooms would normally be needed in a medium sized scheme.
- Guest rooms: at least one suite of overnight accommodation for visitors is needed; this should contain a double bedroom and a bathroom.
- A consultancy room: this may used by a doctor, a chiropodist, a hairdresser etc.

Ancillary Spaces:

- Sluice rooms and staff workrooms.
- Laundry room: operated by staff but accessible to residents.
- A wheelchair room: used for storing and recharging electric wheelchairs.
- Facilities for storing refuse.
- Plant and maintenance rooms.

Site Amenities:

- Sheltered outside terraces
- Gardens
- Parking spaces: for staff, visitors and possibly a few residents
- Delivery court: a screened court with delivery bay and pick up facilities for refuse.

Dining Facilities:

Some schemes offer extra support services such as meals.

- Main dining room: this needs to be big enough to accommodate all residents in one or two sittings
- Kitchens and stores
- Small dining rooms: these may be provided as an alternative to or in addition to the main dining room and are used for serving meals to small groups of residents.

Day Centre Facilities:

Some schemes will function as day centres for non-residents. This suggests that the dining room and kitchen will need to be enlarged and that extra spaces will be needed for any additional activities.

- Additional consultants rooms
- Additional activity rooms
- Day centre team office.

The above list contains most of the individual elements which could form the constituent parts of a scheme. Their size and number will vary according to the scheme's overall size and operational model. Each separate element is treated in some detail in Chapter 4.

3.3
The Site

The southern half of Britain is one of the most densely settled areas in the world. Land-use is subject to strict planning control and vacant land scheduled for housing development is in short supply. Today's developers are being forced to turn more and more towards 'brown land' and inner city areas rather than green field sites. They are rarely in the position of being able to go out and 'choose a site': more typically they are presented with a proposal for a site from some third party and must decide whether or not it 'stacks up'. For this reason it is important to establish a clear set of criteria for site appraisal. One aim of site appraisal must be to test the basic feasibility of a site: many sites are simply not suitable for sheltered housing, be it for reasons of location, cost, topography or surroundings. Once the basic feasibility of a site is established the next aim must be to identify the type of scheme for which it is best suited.

3.3.1
Location

Almost all studies of 'difficult to let' sheltered housing identify poor location as one of the main factors which contribute to a scheme's unpopularity. Although many residents have fairly clear ideas about what constitutes a poor location, and inaccessibility seems to figure strongly among these, it is more difficult to give a precise definition of what constitutes a good location. Many people elect to move into a scheme for positive reasons which seem to be important to them at the time, only to discover the drawbacks after they have moved in or when they have become more frail.

A particular location might be ideal for one category of resident and not for another. A scheme in a rural area with a large garden and fine views over rolling countryside could appeal to people who have access to some form of personal transport, but may not suit someone who was dependent on public bus services. A scheme on a compact inner city site would not suit a keen gardener but could be ideal for anyone wanting to remain close to amenities or to their original community.

The following is a list of criteria which relate to choice of location:

- Demand for Sheltered Housing

    It is important to locate a scheme in an area where there is an identifiable demand for sheltered housing. Different housing providers serve different categories of demand and operate within different sets of parameters. A private developer will want to be reassured that flats within existing schemes are selling well, that there are no other new schemes in the pipeline and that the area is not already saturated. A housing association will seek to assess the demand within the voluntary sector and will also need to take into account the local social service department's projections for assessments and subsidies.

- Proximity to Public Transport

    Easy access to a frequent bus service offers residents the potential of independent mobility and is a boon to staff and visitors. A scheme would ideally be sited within 500m of a bus stop and connected to it by a safe, level and well-lit route. The bus stop itself should have a shelter and a seat.

- Proximity to Family or Friends

    Many people want to remain close to their previous home with its network of neighbours and community ties, or they want to move closer to their family.

- Proximity to Catchment Population

    A scheme should be strategically located in relation to as large a catchment population as possible. Fig 3.3.1a shows a schematic plan for a town of 3km radius with a population of 100,000 and gives estimated 1km radius catchment populations for 3 alternative locations. A scheme at the edge of a town serves a relatively small catchment population compared with one located within an inner residential area.

The catchment population within a kilometre radius of each of three sites is as follows:

site 1 . . . 10,000
(boundary of central area and inner residential area)
site 2 . . . 14,000
(boundary of inner and outer residential area)
site 3 . . . 3,000
(edge of town)

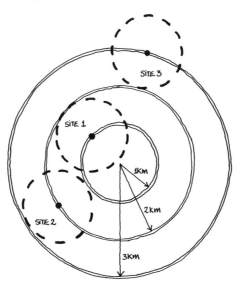

Fig. 3.3.1a: Alternative locations within a typical town of 100,000 population

- Proximity to Amenities

    Ideally a scheme will be located within walking distance of a local corner shop, and be a short bus ride or taxi trip away from a health centre, a supermarket, a post office, a library, a bank, a pharmacy, a pub, a place of worship, a day care centre, a cinema, a park etc.

- Characteristics of the Immediate Area

    Sheltered housing is probably best located within an existing residential neighbourhood which is well endowed with trees and greenery. Adjoining roads should be safe and quiet and the surrounding area should be reasonably flat. A site should be located well away from busy roads, airports and factories, and from any other obvious sources of noise or pollution.

- Characteristics of the Site Itself

    The site should be large enough to accommodate the appropriate type of accommodation and to meet projected needs for car-parking, gardens etc. It should be reasonably flat but without risk of subsidence or flooding. The ground conditions should be conducive to supporting buildings of the appropriate number of floors and there should be an absence of toxic waste material.

- Services and Infrastructure

  It is important to select a site which is already fully serviced with mains electricity, water and gas supply, and telephone and IT connections. If these are not present, the cost of providing for them must be taken into account.

- Legal Restrictions

  The full implications of any covenants, rights of light or access, preserved buildings, tree preservation orders or underground services must be taken fully into account.

- Site Cost

  The cost of the site should relate to the projected gross development value of the scheme and should offset the cost of any improvements which might be necessary.

The relative importance of the above criteria will vary from scheme to scheme. It is possible that some characteristics of a site will be in direct contradiction to each other: for instance a site which is directly on a bus route is likely to suffer from traffic noise and pollution.

3.3.2
Size

The gross area of a scheme will include communal and circulation spaces as well as net residential space. The net area of a typical one-bedroom flat is about 47 sq.m, but the total area of a scheme can be 'guesstimated' using the approximate unit value of 80 sq.m gross per flat, with the proviso that this value will vary according to the mix of dwellings and the extent of the communal facilities. Thus a scheme with forty flats can be assumed to have a gross area of approximately 3,200 sq.m.

The footprint of a building is the area of a site which it actually covers: as a rough approximation it can be thought of as its total area divided by the number of floors. A building of 3,200 sq.m built on two storeys has a footprint of 1,600 sq.m; a four-storey building would have a footprint of 800 sq.m. The total site requirement will be the sum of the building footprint area and the areas required for other activities and needs. These include car-parking, access and garden areas, as well as set-backs and building lines.

A forty unit scheme built on two storeys will require a minimum site area of about 3,500 sq.m to accommodate its footprint of 1,600 sq.m and the other basic site activities. In contrast a six-storey scheme in which car parking and servicing are accommodated in a basement will have footprint of only 530 sq.m and can fit onto a site of less than 1,000 sq.m.

It is becoming increasingly difficult to find affordable sites within existing residential areas of towns. Providers of sheltered housing thus face a dilemma: 'brown' sites within a town's central area may be available at the right price and offer reasonable proximity to amenities but are rarely located within attractive or secure neighbourhoods; spacious sites in suburban areas may also be available but these are often remote from amenities and badly served by public transport; infill sites in inner residential areas are likely to be small and costly.

In conducting site appraisals the conflict between size and location will be a recurring dilemma. Large sites tend to be found in less convenient locations, remote from large catchment populations; well located sites tend to be expensive and therefore smaller. On balance most commentators seem to agree that, where a clear choice exists, location is more important than size.

3.4
Alternative Building Forms

3.4.1
The Number of Floors

Early local authority sheltered housing schemes were usually built to one or two storeys. In some inner city housing developments sheltered housing would be located alongside the primary school and the health centre as the only low buildings within a cluster of residential tower blocks. Today, paradoxically, tower blocks are no longer considered appropriate for families with children and many have been converted for the use of older tenants while the original sheltered housing has been cleared to make way for low-rise family housing.

It is now generally accepted that single-storey schemes, while achieving the seemingly important benefit that all flats are on the ground, require unrealistically large sites and set up excessive horizontal travel distances. Older people have also become much more concerned about security and for this reason many would actually prefer to live on an upper floor. Interestingly a study of early single-storey schemes reveals that relatively few actually allow direct access from flat to garden.

In a two-storey scheme about a third of all residents might live at ground level with two thirds living one flight of stairs away from the ground. Psychologically there is still a strong sense of contact with the ground, and the scale is still 'domestic'. A lift is required though many residents still feel encouraged to use the stairs. In larger schemes the horizontal travel distances can still be considerable.

Once a lift has been installed it eliminates the main restraint on increasing height. A lift can just as easily serve six floors as two, and increasing the number of floors will result in progressively shorter horizontal distances from flat to lift. Within certain limits, it will also reduce unit construction costs. However, schemes of three storeys or more lose any sense of domestic scale and are more likely to be viewed as institutions. Residents on or above the third floor are unlikely ever to use a staircase and the consequences of a lift breakdown, even for a short period, become more and more serious. Increasing height also gives rise to worries about fire safety and the evacuation of non-ambulant residents.

3.4.2
Height and Site

The size of a site will influence the building footprint, and the footprint will determine the number of storeys. This chain of relationships can be represented by a couple of simple equations:

$$80 \times n = \text{total area of scheme in sq.m}$$
(80 sq.m is assumed to be the gross area per unit, and 'n' is the number of floors)

$$80 \times n = f \times s \text{ sq.m}$$
(where 'f' is the footprint area and 's' is the number of storeys)

Fig. 3.4.2a illustrates three alternative configurations for a scheme of 40 units. The two-storey example has a footprint of 1,600 sq.m and a residual area of 1,900 sq.m The four-storey scheme has a footprint of 800 sq.m and a residual area of 1,500 sq.m. Above this height savings can only be achieved by creating basement parking and rooftop terraces.

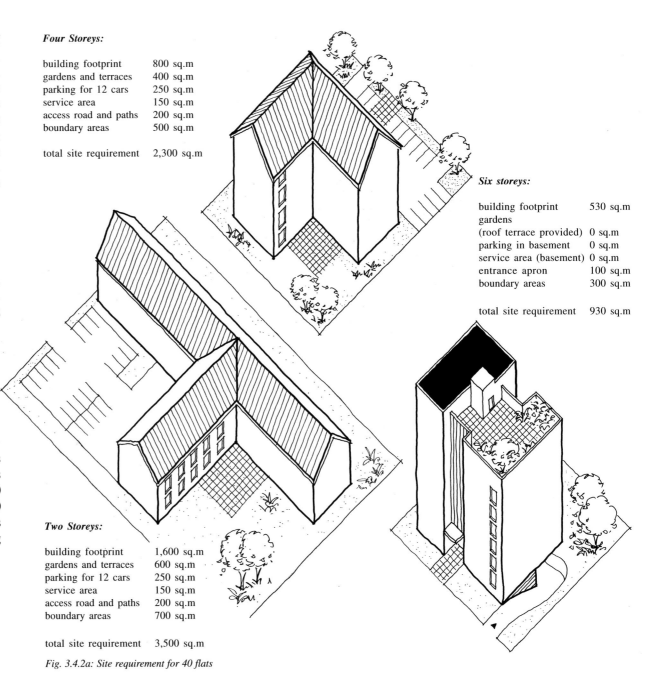

Four Storeys:

building footprint	800 sq.m
gardens and terraces	400 sq.m
parking for 12 cars	250 sq.m
service area	150 sq.m
access road and paths	200 sq.m
boundary areas	500 sq.m
total site requirement	2,300 sq.m

Six storeys:

building footprint	530 sq.m
gardens	
(roof terrace provided)	0 sq.m
parking in basement	0 sq.m
service area (basement)	0 sq.m
entrance apron	100 sq.m
boundary areas	300 sq.m
total site requirement	930 sq.m

Two Storeys:

building footprint	1,600 sq.m
gardens and terraces	600 sq.m
parking for 12 cars	250 sq.m
service area	150 sq.m
access road and paths	200 sq.m
boundary areas	700 sq.m
total site requirement	3,500 sq.m

Fig. 3.4.2a: Site requirement for 40 flats

One limiting factor on the height of a scheme will be the attitude of the local planning authority. Planners are often guilty of using purely subjective criteria to curtail the height and scale of buildings and operate with a sometimes misplaced desire to limit 'over development', often flying in the face of logic and reason. However, there is a growing acceptance of the need to encourage more sustainable forms of urban development, to protect green belts, to exploit existing urban infrastructure and to develop intensive uses for 'brown sites'.

3.5
Site Planning

In developing a building form for a given site the designer must take into account emerging ideas about site layout and the general disposition of the constituent elements. These in turn must respond to the nature of the various boundaries, the preferred point of access, any possible sources of noise and pollution, problems of privacy and overlooking, view, sunpath and prevailing winds and the need for car-parking and servicing.

3.5.1
Boundaries

It is dangerous to assume that all sites are simple rectangles, with three sides relating to neighbouring properties and one side fronting onto a street. In reality sites come in all shapes and sizes. There are sites with two or even three sides fronting onto streets, and sites without a street frontage where access roads must pass between neighbouring properties.

When carrying out a site appraisal it is useful to make a simple scale model in order to study the influences of surrounding buildings. Such a model can be of cheap card, ideally to a scale of 1:200, amplified with

photographs which illustrate the scale and character of surrounding buildings.

Any buildings which are situated close to boundaries must respect the rights to light and ventilation of neighbouring properties. Building regulations proscribe the location of openings within 2.7m of common boundaries and limit the use of materials which pose a fire hazard. The heights of buildings and their distance from boundaries will also be subjected to planning control and possible appeals by neighbours.

Where one or more boundaries face onto busy roads it may be considered prudent to push the building back from the road and to use parking and service areas as a buffer zone. However, a busy road can also serve as a point of interest: many older people would prefer to have a window which looked out into the busy world than one which looked into a peaceful garden. Judicious tree planting can be used to cut down on the visual intrusion of traffic and can also have some small effect on both noise and pollution. It may also be possible to develop a building form which minimises the number of flats which face the road and which acts as a protective wall to the interior part of the site. Those flats which do face the road will need windows which provide good sound insulation and special systems of ventilation. Pushing the building back into the site can have a negative effect on the amenity value of the rear part of the site.

The exact point of access to a site must be determined in discussion with both the highway and planning authorities. Access points should not interfere with busy junctions and need to be located in such a way as to give maximum visibility both to emerging vehicles and to on-coming traffic. It may be advantageous to provide separate points for entrance and exit.

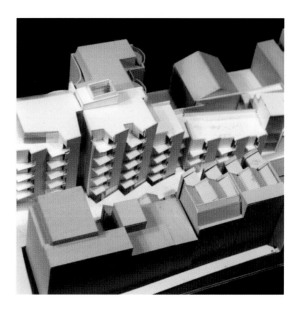

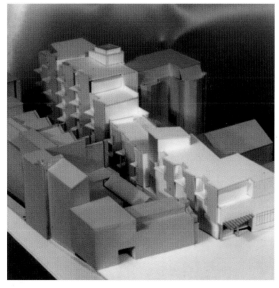

Fig. 3.5.1a: A simple site model

3.5.2
Activities

A site can be thought of as a large enclosure divided into separate 'rooms' which are consecrated to particular activities. These rooms include, of course, the internal elements of the scheme which are located at ground floor level. The position of the building footprint on the site will define areas which are 'front', 'back' and 'side'.

Areas which belong to the 'front' may be adversely affected by traffic noise and lack of privacy. On the other hand the 'front' can provide an interesting visual link with life in the street and provide a grandstand view of all the comings and goings. 'Side' areas are likely to be relatively narrow and may suffer from overlooking. The 'back' area can be developed as a series of secluded garden spaces, though it might be subject to overlooking from neighbouring properties.

Fig 3.5.2a shows the site plan for a four-storey block on a site of 3,320 sq.m. The building footprint is 830 sq.m and covers 25% of the site. The building straddles the site in such a way as to divide it equally between front and back. The dark grey zones denote private internal spaces while the light grey zones represent internal areas which form a part of the public realm. The rear gardens and terraces (5 & 6) have an area of 1,000 sq.m. The front parking and access courts have an area of 700 sq.m.

1. *Car Park and Service Area* (400 sq.m)
   This is located immediately adjacent to the site entry point and connects directly with the service entrance. It forms a buffer between the building and the road
2. *Front Garden* (250 sq.m)
   This offers an outdoor sitting area beside the road with a clear view of entrance and main driveway.
3. *Driveway and Entry Area* (250 sq.m)
   The main entrance is placed directly on axis with the site entry point and is fully controlled by the manager's office. It is directly accessible by car or ambulance and is protected by a glazed porte-cochère. The doorway links directly with the lift and main staircase and offers visual links through to the communal areas and the garden beyond.
4. *Communal Areas* (110 sq.m)
   The sitting room and the dining room are situated between the entry zone and the back garden. They face south and south-west and enjoy afternoon and evening sun. A conservatory/garden room acts as a buffer space between them and the garden.
5. *The Garden Terrace* (300 sq.m)
   This is a paved area which serves as an extension of the main sitting and dining rooms and can be used for meals.
6. *Garden Areas* (700 sq.m)
   The different parts of the garden can be developed as different environments defined by hedges and walls and each one devoted to a particular theme.
7. *Side Gardens* (350 sq.m)
   The side garden strips have very little amenity value, but can be used as kitchen gardens. Provision should be made to maintain an access for fire engines.

3.5.3

Key:

MO: Manager's Office
CSR: Communal Sitting Room
D: Dining Room
C: Conservatory

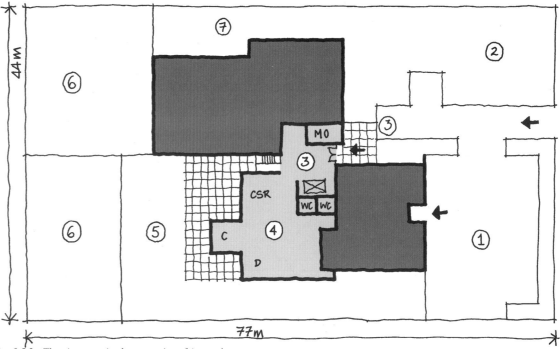

Fig. 3.5.2a The site conceived as a series of 'rooms'

Orientation and Aspect

Although older people can suffer extreme discomfort as a result of solar gain and may need to avoid direct sunlight, they can still derive great physiological and psychological benefit from the sun. A room which faces north could also face a wonderful panoply of trees which, because they are facing south, receive full sunlight and register the progress of the day. However, as a general rule, flats which are exclusively north-facing should be avoided if at all possible, and all inhabited rooms should receive some direct sunlight for a part of the day. On the other hand rooms which face south-east or south-west may suffer from excessive solar penetration and need to be provided with some form of protection.

Too many designs are developed on the simple assumption that the sun rises in the east and sets in the west. In fact, as the sun moves backwards and forwards between the winter and summer solstices it follows a sequence of over 180 unique sweeps across the sky. In summer it rises in the north-east, performs a high arc and sets in the north-west; in winter it rises in the south-east, performs a low arc and sets in the south-west. The effects of these changing sunpaths can be studied using a simple model of the scheme to a scale of 1:200 and a device to simulate shadows such as a heliodon or a sundial. These different sunpaths can be exploited to achieve maximum penetration during winter months when the sun angle is low and to limit penetration in the summer when it is high.

Outdoor sitting areas need to be protected from wind. Although the prevailing wind direction may be known, it is often difficult to anticipate what influence the buildings themselves will have on microclimate and air flow. Tall buildings can have a marked effect on wind direction and can set up areas of turbulence. Where the building height exceeds 4 storeys it may be necessary to take special steps to reduce turbulence.

As well as orienting the buildings to achieve optimum insolation it is also important to consider aspect and views. As people get older they become less mobile and their world starts to shrink. This tendency towards introspection can be encouraged by design strategies which prioritise such values as privacy, security and warmth. It is therefore important that the exploitation of view and the creation of links with the outside world should also be given due attention. The fact that a site doesn't offer great scenic views is not important. Older people need to have a window onto the world: some are happy to be able to look at a few trees and watch the changing pattern of sunlight, others prefer to look down onto a busy road and watch the traffic. Every flat ought to have at least one large window. Ideally such a window would project outwards in the form of a bay or bow in order to increase the potential field of vision and, incidentally to capture more sunlight. It should also be designed with a low sill so that people could look out and downwards from a seated or even a lying position.

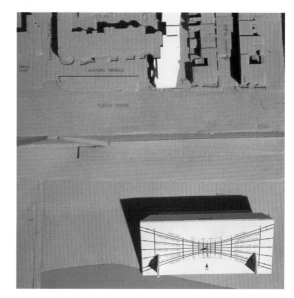

Fig. 3.5.3a: A simple site model with sundial

Fig. 3.5.3b: A bay window offering wide views

3.5.4
Car-Parking and Servicing

Attitudes towards car-parking are currently in a state of flux. Local authority planners who until recently were demanding relatively high numbers of parking spaces are now seeking to limit them. There is little point here in trying to second guess what a particular planning authority might require, though it is still important to try to identify what the needs of a scheme might be in purely functional terms.

The highest priority must be given to providing unobstructed access for taxis, minibuses and ambulances to the building's main entrance and access for services and deliveries to the service entrance. The next priority is to provide parking spaces for the scheme manager, the care manager and any visiting doctors or nurses. Parking spaces for other staff might be given a lower priority depending on the site location: it could be argued that those who do use cars might very well park them in surrounding streets.

The question of whether or not to allow parking spaces for residents raises an interesting dilemma. If the scheme is conceived essentially to serve only the very frail elderly then it is highly unlikely that any of them would be car users. However a resident might still need a parking space for a relative or a private carer. On the other hand if a scheme serves a broader cross-section of residents then there could well be those who drive cars and who need parking spaces.

In the light of the above it would seem that the minimum strategy would be to provide for twelve cars, half of them in wide bays with access strips for wheelchairs. A more realistic strategy would be to provide for eighteen cars, again half of them in wide bays. The provision of twenty-five parking spaces might be considered generous but not outrageously so. In every case it is necessary to provide an unobstructed apron at the main entrance for taxis and ambulances and a service parking bay next to the service entrance.

Powered wheelchairs and electric buggies are becoming increasingly popular with residents of sheltered homes. It is now essential to provide garaging and recharging facilities for about one resident in eight. Such a garage should be located close to the main entrance and be directly accessible from the site entry point.

On tight urban sites it might be necessary to provide for car-parking and service areas at a basement level. As a rough rule of thumb it is necessary to allow about 30 sq.m gross per car space. Basement provision for twelve cars and a service bay could cost as much as £200,000 at 1997 prices, increasing the construction cost for a 40 flat scheme by about 12.5%

3.5.5
The Entrance

The entrance to a scheme is very important and needs to be designed with great care. It should be conceived as a single space which belongs partly to the interior and partly to the exterior, one of the series of 'rooms' into which the site is divided. The main entrance door should be clearly visible from the site's main entry point and the approach should be entirely free of steps. Taxis and ambulances need to be able to approach right up to the main entrance and alighting passengers should be protected by a glass-covered porte-cochère. A comfortable bench is useful for people who are waiting for taxis and provides a good vantage point from which to watch the world go by.

The entrance and its approach should be clearly visible from the scheme manager's office. The entrance foyer

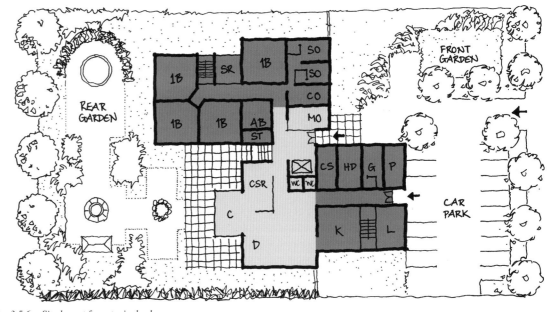

Fig. 3.5.6a: Site layout for a typical scheme

must be designed as a positive space in its own right and not simply as a circulation area. It needs to be large enough to serve as a waiting area both for those who are arriving and those who are departing, a place in which to sit for a while, to meet people and to gossip. The lift and main staircase need to be clearly visible and immediately accessible.

3.5.6
Site Layout

Fig. 3.5.6a provides more details of the hypothetical layout for a four-storey scheme which was illustrated in Fig. 3.5.2a. This scheme has been developed to illustrate some of the main issues which need to be addressed in the design of a typical site layout. The building footprint occupies 830 sq.m or 25% of the 3,320 sq.m site.

A line of trees screen the front part of the site from the busy road. The main driveway runs directly to the main entrance area which is protected by a canopy. The entrance area is surveyed by the manager's office. The foyer gives direct access to the lifts, the main communal areas and the rear. The care team are located next to the manager's office but away from the main communal areas. A cluster of higher dependency flats is located next to the care office. The main sitting and dining rooms connect directly to a garden terrace.

The parking and service areas relate to the service entrance. The parking and access surfaces occupy 650 sq.m or 20% of the site.

The rear garden covers 1,000 sq.m or 30% of the site and is divided into a series of separate environments.

3.6
Landscape Design

Many older people derive great pleasure and benefit from getting outside and walking around a garden. Those who have been keen gardeners may welcome the opportunity to 'potter'. The fact that gardens in sheltered schemes are often under-used may reflect partly on poor accessibility, partly on the attitudes of staff and partly on poor and unimaginative design.

3.6.1
Overall Planning

The overall size of a garden will be determined by the amount of land available once other site uses have been accounted for. The scope for landscaping will be limited by budgetary considerations: the amount of money available to establish it in the first place, and the amount of money available to maintain it subsequently. Even though some residents may elect to help with gardening tasks, the overall maintenance of a garden necessitates the employment of a gardener on a regular basis.

There is no need for a garden to be large in order to be successful: a pleasant garden can be created in a space of about 500 sq.m. Larger gardens can be planned as a series of separate environments or 'outdoor rooms'. These can each be devoted to creating particular moods: one might incorporate water, one might be a scented garden, another might be a 'wild garden'.

Different areas of a garden can be developed to different standards of accessibility and protection. Those closest to the point of entry to the garden should be least challenging: they need to be level and fitted with handrails. Other more remote areas might involve changes of level and use ramps or even short flights of steps. The layout can be conceived as a series of short promenades which are capable of being combined together to form a longer circuit for more active residents.

The site must be carefully planned from the outset so that the gardens relate to the buildings in such a way that they receive adequate sunlight and are protected from prevailing winds. It is important to ensure that sitting areas receive sunlight either in the morning or in the late afternoon, and that they are protected in some way from midday summer sun. Carefully placed deciduous trees will offer shade in the summer and admit sunlight in the winter.

It should be possible to go out directly into the garden from the main lift and stair lobby without having to negotiate steps or steep ramps. Doors should be easy to open and fitted with flush thresholds as well as adequate doormats and foot scrapers. An access route might also be provided from the sitting room and dining room via a main terrace. The exact relationship between buildings and garden needs to be carefully considered: parts of the garden ought to be visible from the main sitting and dining rooms and from individual flats.

In some locations there may be worries about site security: a gated perimeter could be required in order to prevent the ingress of unwanted outsiders, or, where there are residents with dementia, to limit egress.

At least one toilet should be located within the scheme at ground floor level close to the door into the garden. In a larger garden it might be advisable to install a separate external toilet.

3.6.2
Detailed Landscape Design

Older people are likely to be unsteady on their feet and may suffer from impaired vision. They are liable to fall at the slightest provocation and, because they have brittle bones which fracture easily and are slow to mend, when they do fall they may suffer serious consequences. They tire easily and need to be able to sit down regular. They will enjoy sitting in a warm and sunny spot but may prefer to keep out of the direct sun. The following are points to bear in mind during the design stage:

Planting:

- Raised planting beds make it easy for older people to appreciate both the appearance and the smell of plants. Retaining walls provide a convenient sitting surface.
- Plants should be selected to give a changing display throughout the year.
- Partially sighted people appreciate flowers with strong colours at the red and yellow end of the spectrum.
- Blind and partially sighted people appreciate plants with distinctive perfumes.
- People suffering from dementia often eat flowers and berries: all poisonous plants should be avoided.
- Some plants attract birds and wildlife.
- Residents from other lands may like to plant their own native culinary herbs.

Changes in Level:

- Sudden obstructions and level changes must be avoided at all costs.
- Ramps should be short in length and limited to a maximum gradient of 1:20.
- Steps should only be used where they are absolutely necessary and needed to be designed with great care.

Shelters:

- Covered walkways offering protection from the elements.
- A gazebo or summer house offers shade and protection from wind as well as providing the ideal setting for outdoor social activities.
- A garden shed is needed to store tools and equipment.
- A potting shed or a greenhouse might be provided in schemes where some of the residents are keen gardeners.

Seating:

- Terraces and sitting areas should be laid out as flat and even surfaces with slight falls to avoid ponding.
- Furniture should be robust and stable. Warm materials such as timber are preferable to cold materials such as cast iron.
- The sitting surfaces of benches should be well drained.
- Seats should be provided at regular intervals in sheltered and sunny spots.
- Seats should be located so that people can converse easily with each other.

Screens:

- Hedges and walls can be used to delineate the separate parts of the garden and to create wind breaks.
- A south-facing brick wall stores heat and can form the ideal containment for a group of seats.

Surfaces:

- Garden paths should have firm, semi-porous, non-slip surfaces.
- A suitable surface is provided by in-situ concrete with exposed aggregate surface which is tamped to give texture. Control joints and edges can be picked out in strongly coloured tiles or brick paviours.

- Bituminous materials are also suitable providing they are given a surface dressing to enhance the texture.
- Paving slabs and brick paviours are subject to movement and need careful maintenance.
- Loose materials such as gravel are to be avoided.
- Edges and boundaries can be picked out with strongly coloured tiles or paviours.
- Hazards and changes can be indicated with grooves or channels to help blind people with sticks
- Drainage gulleys and gratings should be carefully protected
- Care should be taken to avoid ponding.
- Regular maintenance is needed to repair cracks and to prevent the build up of lichen.

Lighting:

- Lighting should be installed on all main pathways and terraces which are likely to be used in the late afternoon or evening. Low-mounted downlighters are preferable.

Pathways:

- Paths need to be wide enough to allow people in wheelchairs or with zimmer frames to pass each other (ideally 1.8 m).
- Handrails should be installed in those parts of the garden used by the more frail residents.

Fauna:

- Older people enjoy watching birds and animals. Bird boxes and tables will attract birds and other forms of wild life.

3.6.3
A Detailed Example

The basic principles of landscape design are illustrated here in a hypothetical example. Figs 3.6.3a & 3.6.3b show sketch proposals for the main open spaces in the notional scheme which was previously described in Figs 3.5.2a & 3.5.6a. It should be stressed that these sketch proposals have not been costed: they are intended simply to hint at what is possible. It is also worth remembering that gardens are not instant creations: they can start from simple beginnings and evolve over a number of years.

The rear and front gardens each have an area of 1,000 sq.m and are planned as follows:

1. **Access to the Garden**
   A door beside the main staircase provides a direct link from the entrance foyer (33) to the garden. This has a ramped approach and flush threshold. Two toilets are close by (34).
4. **The Conservatory, or Garden Room**
   Connects the main sitting room (2) and the dining room (3) to the terraces and sitting areas.
5. **The Sitting Room Terrace** (50 sq.m)
   This offers a sheltered sitting area which receives south and south-west sun.
6. **The Dining Room Terrace** (50 sq.m)
   The dining room opens out directly onto this terrace which can be used for open air meals in summer.
7. **The Perfumed Garden**
   This is a small court immediately below the main terraces. Wooden benches nestle in between raised planting beds which contain strong smelling herbs and flowers. The central planting bed incorporates a bird bath and bird tables.
8. **The Sundial Court** (80 sq.m)
   This square court has a raised planting area with a large sundial at its centre. A summer house (9) occupies the southern side of the court and provides shade, shelter and a wind break.
10. **The Greenhouse**
    Available for the use of keen gardeners. It is separated from the summer house by a sold brick wall which acts as a heat store, warming the back of the summer house.

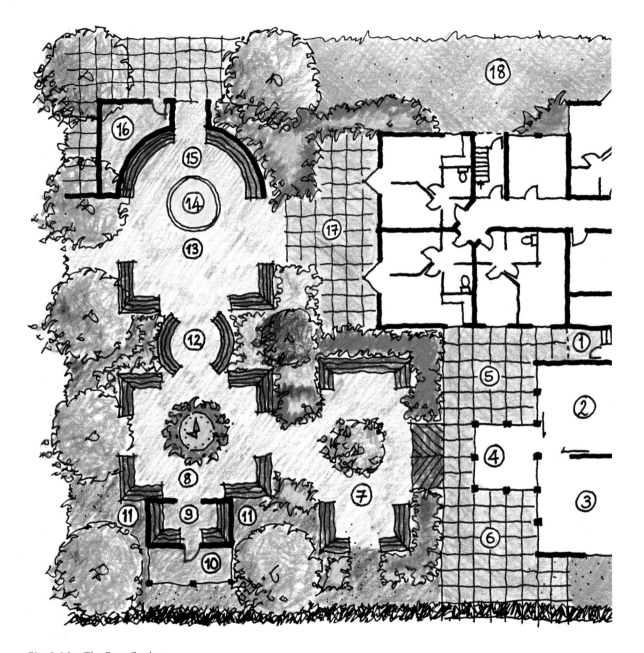

Fig. 3.6.3a: The Rear Garden

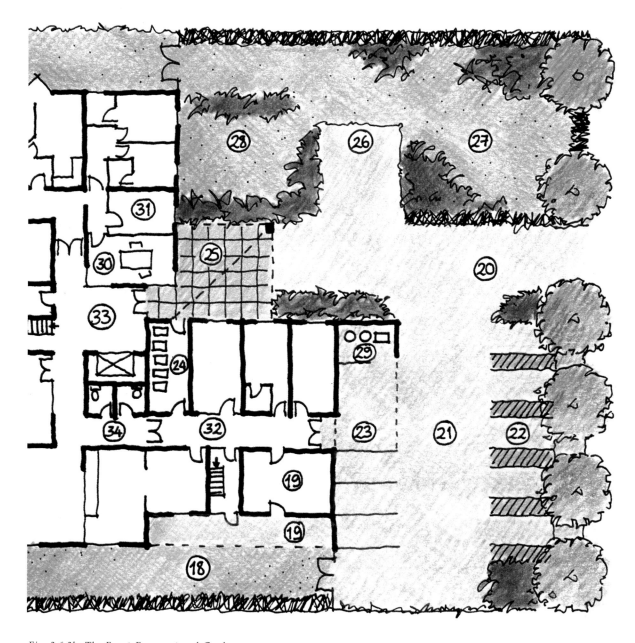

Fig. 3.6.3b: The Front Forecourt and Garden

11. **Small Vegetable Plots** are located beside the greenhouse.
12. **The Honeysuckle Arbour**

    The Honeysuckle Arbour is a small sitting area formed by a trellis and straddles the pathway which leads from the Sundial Court (8) to the Pond Court (13).
13. **The Pond Court** (110 sq.m)

    This large court is closed at its northern end by a curved brick exedra (15) which supports two arcs of south-facing benches. The pond itself (14) is contained within a raised retaining wall and is stocked with goldfish.
16. **Garden Shed** and **Work Area** located behind the exedra.
17. **Private Terraces**

    Two ground floor flats open onto private terraces, screened from the Pond Court by raised planting beds.
18. **Narrow Pathways** lead along the sides of the building through security gates into the front forecourt area. Active residents can make a 250m circular tour of the whole site.
19. **The Laundry** and **Clothes Drying Area** located side by side.
20. **The Driveway**

    The entrance drive leads directly to the main entrance and is fully visible from the manager's office (30).
21. **The Car Park** (360 sq.m)

    This contains twelve parking bays. Half of these are wide bays with extra strips for wheelchairs (22).
23. **The Service Delivery Bay**

    This connects directly with the main service corridor and incorporates a screened bin enclosure (29).
24. **The Wheelchair Store**

    Space is provided for five outdoor wheelchairs to be parked and re-charged. The store is directly accessible from the driveway and connects through to the service corridor (32).
25. **The Porte-Cochère**

    A glazed porte-cochère provides a sheltered approach to the main entrance (33). Taxis, minibuses and ambulances can draw up under the canopy and can reverse into the turning bay (26). The entrance forecourt and driveway are overseen directly from the manager's office (30) and the care office (31).
27. **The Front Lawn** provides a sitting area for the more active residents and offers a view of the road.
28. **The Staff Lawn**

    A small outside sitting area for staff is situated next to the care office (31).
32. **Clear Access Route**

    A clear access route for fire-fighting equipment must be maintained.

3.7
Cost Planning

One aim of any initial feasibility study is to achieve a balance between the estimated total development cost and the anticipated gross development value of the project, and one main outcome is an explicit set of cost targets. The total development cost includes the cost of land, site development, consultants' fees, development costs and profits as well as the cost of construction. Targets for the cost of construction may be presented as global costs, as elemental costs or as unit costs. Elemental costs are those for particular building elements such as the roof or the external windows. Unit costs can be expressed as costs per square metre, costs per flat or costs per resident. As the project progresses the cost targets are monitored by the quantity surveyor or financial adviser in a series of cost estimates.

3.7.1
Factors Which Affect Cost

There are factors affecting the cost of a development which fall outside the narrow limits of the building contract and which lie beyond the control of the designer: these include the cost of the site, the nature of the ground conditions, the extent of any landscaping, the general tendering climate and the cost of building materials. However the cost of construction can be determined within certain limits by the nature and quality of the design. Three aspects of the design are important in this respect: the size of the building, the nature of the building envelope and the general level of specification.

- The Size of the Building
  It is self evident that the area and volume of a building will have a direct bearing on costs. All too often target areas are set in terms of the net areas of principle elements rather than the gross area of the whole scheme. In Extra Care housing the accepted net area for a one-bedroom flat is about 45 sq.m.

  The total gross area includes the areas allocated for communal and service provision and circulation as well as the area of the actual dwellings. In buildings of this type the normal allowance for circulation is about 20%.

  A scheme of 40 flats where the average size per flat is 45 sq.m will have a total net area of 1,800 sq.m while its total gross area might be about 3,200 sq.m, depending on the extent of communal facilities. The gross area per unit in this case would be 80 sq.m. If the space allocated to communal spaces were to increase, the unit area would also increase; if the area of circulation were to creep up this would also affect the unit area. Such increases will have a marked effect on the total construction cost, the overall project cost and, inevitably, the cost per unit.

- The Nature of the Building Envelope
  The ratio of external envelope area to the building volume and the relationship between external wall area, ground floor area and roof area will both affect costs. Complex plan forms with shallow floor plates and a high incidence of re-entrant surfaces will increase the external wall to volume ratio and increase costs. Increasing the number of floors will reduce ground floor and roof areas. However, beyond a certain number of floors the reductions are offset by a reciprocal increase in the proportion of the external wall component.

- The General Level of Specification
  The total construction cost is the sum of the costs of the individual elements. If the cost of windows is increased this will affect the estimates for that particular element and will have a knock-on effect on the total cost of construction. A relatively small increase in the cost of a major element like, for instance, external brickwork will have a marked effect on the total cost, while a substantial increase in the cost of a single element like a lift might be less significant. The general level of specification will affect the cost of each element and will have a cumulative effect on the total cost of the project.

3.7.2
Achieving Cost Savings

From the above it can be seen that if there is a need to make savings on the cost of construction, these can be achieved in three ways: either the whole building must be made smaller, or its overall form must be simplified, or one or more elements must be subjected to reductions in specification.

Reductions in the size of the building might be achieved by reducing the number of units, but this would affect the anticipated gross development value; they might also be achieved by tightening up on circulation or shrinking the communal facilities, but such changes could affect the efficient workings of the scheme if taken to the extreme. Simplifying the shape of the building can reduce the extent and cost of the external envelope, but there might be negative side-effects on other aspects of the design. Reductions in specification can achieve substantial savings if applied to a sizeable building element but these can seriously affect the quality of the scheme.

The implication of any cost saving for the lifetime costs of a building should be assessed. The specification of an electric panel radiator heating system in place of hot water radiators will save on capital costs but will produce much higher running costs.

Cost savings made during construction can also affect long-term maintenance costs and reduce the life span of a building. The cost of the roof might account for as little as 4% of the total building costs. A reduction in specification might achieve a 20% saving in the cost of that element, but it would only achieve a 0.8% saving on the whole contract, which in turn might result in a saving of about 0.5% on the total development costs. However, the long-term performance of the roof could well be seriously compromised: leaking roofs can cause expensive damage and are costly to repair.

Unfortunately many institutions are reluctant to invest adequately in their buildings: compared with those of other European countries it can be argued that British buildings are characterised by low initial capital investment and low maintenance expenditure. We suffer from 'Cheap Building Syndrome'.

3.7.3
Unit Costs

In late 1996 it was possible to build Extra Care housing to reasonable standards for about £550 per sq.m. At this rate a development of 40 flats with a total area of 3,200 sq.m would cost a total of £1.75 million to construct. However, once the cost of land and other development costs had been taken into account, the gross development cost might come to about £2.5 million. A one-bedroom flat of 45 sq.m might be thought to cost about £25,000, though its unit construction cost taken across the whole scheme would be more like £45,000 and its unit development cost would be close to £65,000.

These figures imply that a unit in the private sector would have to sell for an average £65,000. However the developer might set part of the development costs against the anticipated annual service charge. In addition the developer could juggle prices: early sales could be subsidised by later sales, smaller flats could cross-subsidise large flats, ground floor flats could subsidise third floor flats, etc. Individual flats might sell for anything between £45,000 and £75,000.

The implications for a scheme in the voluntary sector are more complex. A part of the development cost would be covered by Social Housing Grant (SHG). The local authority might offer a grant to cover a part of the cost of the community facilities and might provide a cheap site. The balance finance would have then to be raised from private financial institutions. Once these various grants had been taken into account the average development cost per flat might be about £45,000 in which case the full cost rental would be about £380 per month, excluding service charges.

3.8
A Matter of Design

'Over the past decade, Housing Associations have become major developers on a national scale. We are now having a significant impact on the look of villages, towns and cities. However, if we are honest, our developments do not always enhance them. The processes of mass housing have led to increasingly bland and standardised solutions, frequently devoid of character and the ability to delight. Whilst technically there is little doubt that the houses we build have improved, this has often been at the expense of the aesthetic.'

Antonia, Marchioness of Douro, The Guinness Trust (Owen and O'Dwyer, 1990)

3.8.1
The Image of Sheltered Housing

Owen and O'Dwyer (1990) have pointed out that Britain is a small country with a remarkable variety of building styles which have developed from local traditions and their response to local physical and climatic conditions. But the construction processes of the late twentieth century have largely destroyed this regional variety. Development is concentrated on the mass production of 'little boxes' to which the builders add a variety of window patterns and 'stick-on porches'.

Sheltered housing schemes often appear simply as 'slightly bigger boxes' in the suburban continuum and are festooned with the same cheap stick-on porches and bays as their smaller neighbours. They are rarely singled out for the quality of their architecture and usually look as if they have been designed by a committee and subjected to the excessive zeal of planning control officers.

Fig. 3.8.1a: Welfare State Modern

Fig. 3.8.1b: Institutional Brutalism

Early sheltered housing schemes were built mainly by local authorities and adopted styles which varied between 'Welfare State Modern' and 'Institutional Brutalism'. Figs. 3.8.1a & b both show schemes designed by eminent architects but both seem to announce: 'abandon hope all ye who enter here'.

Today most sheltered schemes are built either by housing associations or by private developers. Until quite recently many housing associations did not consider themselves to be in a 'market place' and gave relatively low priority to the appearance of their schemes. Their main aim, and that of their chosen architects, was often to 'keep the planners happy'. This has resulted in the development of what might be described as a 'Neo Workhouse' aesthetic: hard red bricks, dark concrete-tiled roofs of indeterminate pitch and underscaled plastic bay windows. We half expect to find Mr. Micawber and Miss Havisham lurking behind the lace curtains.

Developers have a more hard nosed approach: they are selling a product and they need to know their market. However, like car manufacturers, they offer only limited choice, and their aim is always to form taste rather than follow it. Developers seek to achieve what they now call 'kerb appeal' and have recently opted for the sort of nostalgia which is associated with the television revivals of the novels of Jane Austen. This approach can be seen in the ersatz sitting rooms which are often located next to the front door: chintzy curtains, flock wallpaper and Constable's 'Hay Wain' above the mock Adam fireplace with its coal effect fire.

Housing developers seem sometimes to attach almost as much importance to names as to style. Early local authority schemes often employed the word 'house' and commemorated the names of local politicians. Developers prefer words like 'court', which promises

Fig. 3.8.1c: Kerb appeal: two schemes, two sitting rooms, one design

a large enclosed garden, or 'lodge', which suggests an appendage to some great mansion. They often add names which carry a hint of royalty: 'Albany Lodge', 'Alexandra Court', 'Victoria Lodge', 'Windsor Court' etc.

The question of style is not an easy one to resolve. A sheltered housing scheme will typically contain about forty flats, and therefore presents a facade which is made up of a repeat pattern of small openings. Most people would agree that every effort should be made to avoid creating the appearance of an institution, that some hint of domestic scale would be desirable and that an attempt should be made to relate to, though not necessarily to ape, the character and scale of the surrounding area.

The problem stems from a dilemma about image: sheltered housing is still a new building type and, in the search for relevant precedents, it is all too easy to

Fig. 3.8.1d: Vernacular Modernism: sheltered housing, Byker

invoke the spirit of, for example, the 'almshouse'. A sheltered housing scheme is not *'a hostel'*, nor is it *'a hospital'*. However, other possible models do exist. When a group of residents in Switzerland were asked to comment on the modern design of their scheme, they were all very positive about its image, which they likened to *'a holiday hotel'*.

3.8.2
Good Design

Design is often dismissed as a matter of taste, of fashion or of individual preference. And yet 'quality' is something which transcends taste and style.

Old people themselves are seldom consulted about design. Many of today's elderly were born at the end of the First World War and were young adults during the years after the Second World War. They belong to that generation which rejected the 'dark satanic mills' of the industrial city and espoused the clean white modernism of the 'Brave New World' which was heralded by the 1951 Festival of Britain. Although there are no grounds for claiming that they have remained champions of modernism, there is also no evidence to suggest that they are all keen to retire into the world of Charles Dickens.

It has been argued in Chapter 2 that older people need a supportive environment which can minimise the disabling effect of any impairments which they may suffer. They need clear and legible layouts, light and airy interiors, strong contrasting colours, properly designed doors and windows, furniture which is both functional and attractive. They also need a clear identity and a sense of belonging. What they clearly don't need are small windows, florid wallpaper, dark swirling carpets or heavy old-fashioned furniture.

A well designed building will meet the needs of its

clients and users and offer good value for money. It will use space and resources efficiently and exploit the potentials of its site to the full. A well designed building will also improve the social, physical and psychological wellbeing of its users and make a positive contribution to its neighbourhood. Finally, it will give pleasure to all those who enter it and who look upon it.

A number of architectural practices have offered promising alternatives to the prevailing aesthetic rut in which so much sheltered housing is now stuck.

Fig. 3.8.1e: Swiss Modernism: Chur and Davos

PRP Architects (formerly Phippen Randall and Parkes) is a firm of architects which has specialised in sheltered housing and has established a very clear attitude towards style with a series of buildings which use traditional materials in a clear and contemporary manner.

Photos by Peter Cook

Fig. 3.8.2a: John Kennedy Lodge, London (PRP Architects)

Fig. 3.8.2b: Alan Morkill House, London (PRP Architects)

Fielden Clegg are a young Bath-based practice with a growing reputation for producing social buildings of great sensitivity and quality.

Photos by Simon Doling

Fig. 3.8.2c: Bengough's House, Bristol (Fielden Clegg)

Fig. 3.8.2d: Bridge Care, Bath (Fielden Clegg)

Planning

Peter Cook

70

Planning

Chapter 4.0
Detailed Design

This chapter is presented in the form of a series of design studies which cover the main elements of a typical scheme. The studies are numbered as follows:

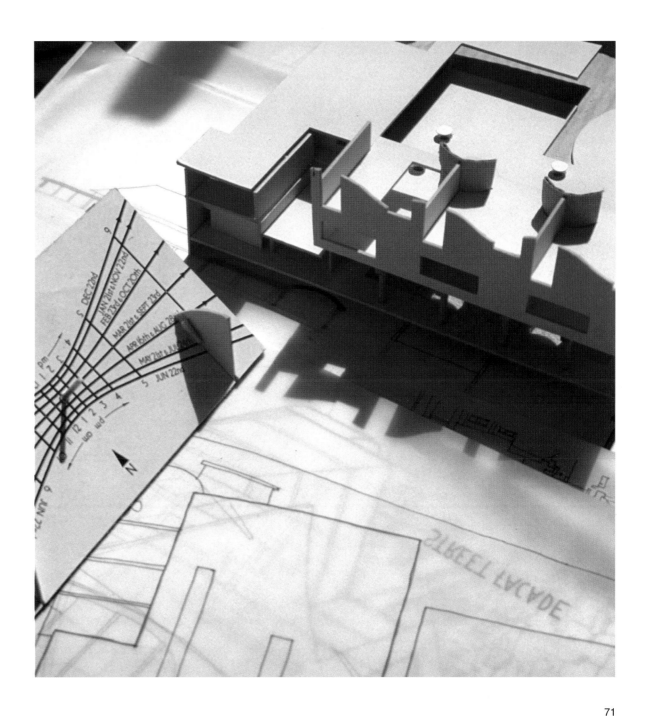

4.1 Flat Types

4.1.1
One-Bedroom Flat

One-bedroom flats have become, and are likely to remain, the most common unit of accommodation in Extra Care housing. Although they are generally intended for a single occupant, they are sometimes occupied by two people: couples, friends, siblings. Single occupants may also need to put up a relative or a 'sleep-in' carer for a short period.

A flat should be designed to support independent living and to accommodate normal day-to-day activities such as sleeping, bathing and dressing, cooking and eating, watching TV and entertaining friends. It needs to incorporate the following:

- a bedroom big enough to accommodate a single bed with full wheelchair accessibility and with space for a second bed if required
- a sitting room in which two or three people can sit together in comfort and where at least two people can eat a meal
- a kitchen in which meals for one or two people can be prepared
- a fully wheelchair-accessible bathroom
- a hall which acts as a buffer zone between the communal corridor and private living areas and is big enough to park a wheelchair
- adequate storage in each of the main activity spaces

Although a flat must be designed to be accessible to frail elderly people who may be wheelchair users, it should not take on the appearance of a hospital ward. A design must be flexible in order to meet the needs of a wide variety of occupants: there is a need for short-term flexibility to accommodate a sudden bout of illness or a visiting relative; there is a need for progressive flexibility as an individual's needs change with increasing age; there is a need for long-term flexibility to accommodate changing tenancies or changes in the way that a scheme is managed.

Flats should be designed to ensure privacy for their occupants, without positively discouraging contact with the outside world. The entry serves as a buffer zone, but it should also be welcoming; windows provide an important view of the world, but they must also guarantee privacy. Planning and construction should minimise the intrusion of noise from neighbours, from communal areas and from the outside.

Areas

The generally accepted area for a one-bedroom flat is about 45 sq.m. It will usually consist of a number of discrete cells or compartments which accommodate specific activities or sets of activities. The following is a list of the usual compartments with recommended areas:

entry space	5.0 sq.m
bathroom	5.0 sq.m
bedroom	14.0 sq.m
kitchen/cooking area	5.0 sq.m
sitting/eating area	17.0 sq.m
total	46.0 sq.m
storage (5 cu.m)	2.0 sq.m
included within the above	

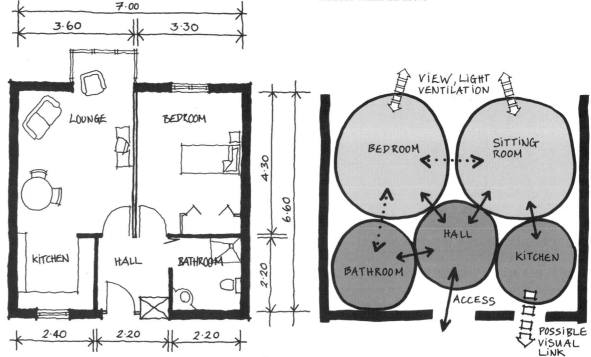

Fig. 4.1.1a : A one-bedroom flat in a 6.6 x 7.0 m shell (46.2m²)

Fig. 4.1.1b: Space relationships in a one-bedroom flat

Compartmentation

While it is important to segregate the various compartments, it can also be advantageous to allow them to combine in different ways. The compartments listed above would require a total of seven doors if they were to be completely segregated. Doors take up space and may be troublesome for the frail or those in wheelchairs. People's need for compartmentation will change over time and there should be a degree of built-in flexibility. Everyone prefers to have a totally closed-off sleeping area when they are fit and well, but those who are confined to their bed for long periods might want to open their bedroom up to their living room. Many people prefer to close off their cooking area, but those who are frail might find it easier to operate with an open kitchen.

Planning

Although it might seem that all five of the main compartments would benefit from windows to provide views and natural light, some windowless spaces are bound to occur in any aggregation of flats which share common party walls and which are served by an internal circulation system. The fact that an entry space must connect to a main internal circulation route usually precludes it from having an external wall, while bathrooms for older people actually benefit from being windowless because glass surfaces act as cold radiators and because the walls are needed for equipment.

Most people would prefer their kitchen to have a window. However if bedroom, sitting room and kitchen are to occupy the same external wall, the plan length will have to be about 9m. Such a wide fronted flat is very difficult to plan, and would be expensive in terms of external wall ratio and energy consumption. Fig. 4.1.1c shows a wider fronted flat where the widths of the lounge and the bedroom have been compromised in order to accommodate the kitchen on an external wall. McCarthy & Stone have recently built schemes which incorporate an ingenious 'bay window kitchen' in order to accommodate this preference in a more economic way, Fig. 4.1.1d.

Fig. 4.1.1b shows the main spatial elements of a flat and the system of links between them. Bedroom, sitting room and bathroom are all accessed from the hallway. Accessing the kitchen from the living room offers improved fire safety as well as increased convenience. The potential to open up the bedroom to the sitting room and to connect it directly to the bathroom would benefit people who were ill or very frail. The possible window connection from the kitchen to the corridor offers a valuable link with neighbours.

Fig 4.1.1a shows a possible layout for a 7.0 x 6.6m shell. The following points can be noted:

- the bathroom is adjacent to the bedroom and a direct connection can be made if necessary
- the partition between the bedroom and the sitting room can be removed if necessary - for this reason it should be kept free of services
- there is space in the hall to manoeuvre and store a wheelchair
- the kitchen can be open or enclosed and can be linked to the corridor by a small window
- a bay window is added to the sitting room to improve the range of view and to catch sunlight
- storage is distributed around the flat

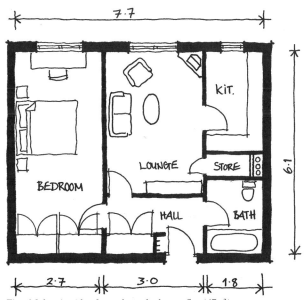

Fig. 4.1.1c: A wider fronted one-bedroom flat (47m²)

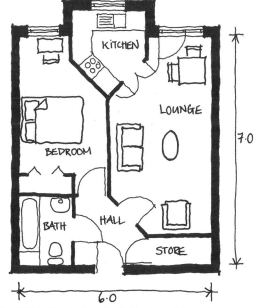

Fig. 4.1.1d: Sketch plan of a McCarthy and Stone flat

4.1.2
Two-Bedroom Flat

There is evidence in the private sector of a growing demand from single people for larger flats with an extra room which can be used for putting up a guest or a sleep-over carer. However, two-bedroom flats will usually be occupied by two people. It is dangerous to assume that two people who live together will necessarily be a 'couple' and that they will require a larger 'double bedroom' and a smaller guest room/study. A two-bedroom flat may also accommodate friends or siblings who choose to share a home but still require separate bedrooms.

A two-bedroom flat should support independent living and accommodate normal day-to-day activities in the same way as a one-bedroom flat. It needs to incorporate the following:

- two bedrooms which can be planned as either a 'double' and a 'single' or as two rooms of equal size:
  - where bedrooms of different sizes are provided, the main bedroom should accommodate two single beds and the second bedroom should accommodate one single bed; both must provide wheelchair accessibility
  - where bedrooms of the same size are provided, both should be big enough to allow for wheelchair accessibility
- a sitting room in which two or three people can sit together in comfort and where at least two people can eat a meal
- a kitchen in which meals for one or two people can be prepared
- a fully wheelchair-accessible bathroom
- a hall which acts as a buffer zone between the communal corridor and private living areas and is big enough to park a wheelchair
- adequate storage in each of the main activity spaces

A two-bedroom flat should afford the same degree of external privacy as a one-bedroom flat, while still encouraging social contact. In addition it should offer the possibility for two people to maintain a degree of privacy from each other within their home. The partitions between the three inhabited rooms should offer a degree of acoustic separation, so that, for example, one occupant can watch TV while the other is sleeping. The rooms should be planned to enable individuals to pursue their own interests or to entertain their own friends.

Areas

The generally accepted area for such a flat is 63 sq.m. The following is a list of the usual compartments with recommended areas:

entry space	6.0 sq.m
bathroom	5.0 sq.m
1st bedroom	13-15.0 sq.m*
2nd bedroom	11-13.0 sq.m*
kitchen/cooking area	6.0 sq.m
sitting/eating area	18.0 sq.m
total	63.0.sq.m
storage (7.5 cu.m)	3.0 sq.m
included within the above	

* It should be possible to alter the sizes of the bedrooms to suit the particular needs of the occupants.

Compartmentation

As there will normally be a greater need for compartmentation and internal separation than in flats intended for single occupation it should be possible to isolate the three principal rooms from each other. However, people's need for compartmentation will change over time and there should be a degree of built-in flexibility. There is some advantage in placing one of the bedrooms beside the sitting room in order to make it possible to combine the two during a period of long illness.

Planning

Because two-bedroom flats are likely to attract a range of combinations of occupants there is a very real need to plan for flexibility. The two occupants of a flat may have quite different degrees of dependency and may experience quite different sets of impairments. It may happen that one is quite fit and acts as a quasi-carer for the other. However, it not uncommon for people to come together because of a shared impairment: two deaf people or two partially sighted people might choose to share a flat. In such instances there would be a strong argument for making special adaptations throughout the flat. It is also possible that both occupants could be wheelchair users, suggesting a need to plan spaces for the simultaneous use of two wheelchairs.

Fig. 4.1.2a: A dining space

In a standard situation the bathroom, kitchen and entry are likely to be located along an 'inner wall', leaving the three principal living rooms to occupy an external wall. These three together require a length of between 9.5m and 10m which suggests a plan depth of between 6.3m and 6.5m.

With the 9.7 x 6.5m configuration shown in Fig. 4.1.2b, the following points can be noted:

- bedrooms and bathroom are 'zoned' to give privacy
- doors are arranged to allow direct access from both bedrooms to the bathroom
- the partition between the two bedrooms can be

moved as can the partition between the left hand bedroom and the sitting room, thus a variety of room configurations are possible

- there is space in the hall to manoeuvre and store a wheelchair
- the kitchen can be open or enclosed and can be linked to the corridor by a small window
- a bay window is added to the sitting room to improve the range of view and to catch sunlight
- storage is distributed around the flat

Fig. 4.1.2c demonstrates how the plan illustrated in Fig. 4.1.2b can be adapted to meet a variety of needs.

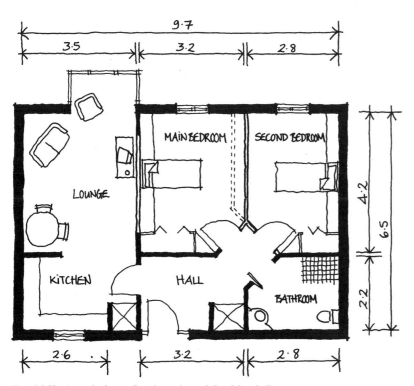

Fig. 4.1.2b: A two-bedroom flat planned in a 9.7 x 6.5m shell

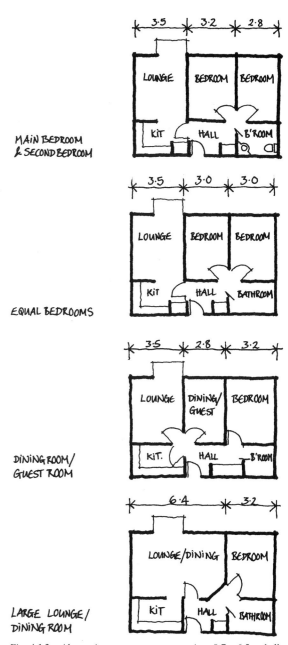

Fig. 4.1.2c: Alternative room arrangements in a 9.7 x 6.5m shell

4.1.3
Bed-sitter

Bed-sitters have gained a bad reputation and are often labelled as 'difficult to let'. However, the bed-sitters which were criticised in the past usually lacked private bathrooms and were very small. Such is the stigma which has now attached itself to bed-sitters that it may be time to re-christen them 'studio flats'. Certainly this is a name used by estate agents and corresponds to the names given to such flats in France and Germany.

In fact a single-roomed flat with its own private bathroom and a basic cooking facility offers a number of advantages to certain categories of resident. They provide a single generous space with all amenities and facilities immediately to hand, they offer a high degree of flexibility and they are easy to maintain. People who are partially sighted or who are suffering from dementia or who are confined to their beds for long periods may find it much easier to live in a flat which is more compact, which is not divided into different compartments and which is relatively easy to run.

Although conventional one-bedroom flats are the preferred option for most people, it may be beneficial to provide a small number of bed-sitters in Extra Care schemes. These might be scattered throughout the scheme or concentrated within a cluster.

Compartmentation

As its name implies, the bed-sitter consists of one primary compartment: a room which is used for both daily living and sleeping. In addition there is a need for an entry space to act as a buffer to the outside and a fully equipped bathroom.

Areas

Although bed-sitters in the past were designed with an area of about 20 sq.m, today the recommended norm in sheltered housing is about 30 sq.m. The following is a list of the main compartments with recommended areas:

entry space	5.0 sq.m
bathroom	5.0 sq.m
bedroom/sitting room	20.0 sq.m
total	30.0 sq.m
storage (5 cu.m) included within the above	2.0 sq.m

Fig: 4.1.3a: A studio flat

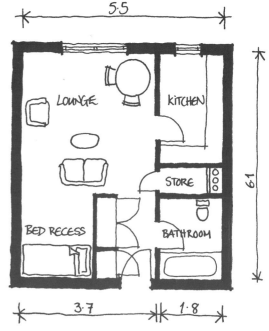

Fig: 4.1.3b: A studio flat

Fig. 4.1.3c: Plan of a 5.5 x 6.1m bed-sitter

Detailed Design

Food Preparation

Should bed-sitters be provided with fully equipped kitchens? The provision of full cooking facilities within a single cell dwelling is fraught with problems: increased fire hazards, cooking smells etc. The case for providing bed-sitters in Extra Care schemes rests on the special needs of categories of people who are unlikely to want to cook full meals for themselves. It is therefore possible to suggest that people who want full cooking facilities should be encouraged to occupy one-bedroom flats, and that the provisions for cooking in bed-sitters should be limited. A small kitchen corner should include a sink and a small fridge with power points for a kettle and a microwave.

Planning

One main disadvantage of bed-sitters is that they offer very little privacy within the flat: the sleeping area will generally be on full view to visitors, and there is often no possibility for someone to dress in private when visitors are present. It is for this reason that some attempt should be made to articulate the plan to enable the sleeping area to be screened off when not in use. The main room should be planned to allow for its sub-division into clear activity zones. The cooking corner should also be fitted into an alcove space.

Fig. 4.1.3d shows a possible layout for a 5.6 x 5.6m shell. The following points can be noted:

- the main living area is a 4.2m square with alcoves for sleeping and cooking
- the sleeping alcove can be screened by a curtain
- the cooking alcove can be contained by a sliding or folding screen
- the hall allows for wheelchair manoeuvres and storage

The main advantage of the bed-sitter is that it offers the potential of good accessibility for the very frail or the partially sighted. There are no doors within the main living zone and the bathroom is directly accessible via a twin-leaf door. Residents who are confined to their beds for long periods are not imprisoned within a small cell-like bedroom, but have the full use of the facilities within the flat. The plan is easy to visualise and memorise for those who suffer from poor vision or short-term memory loss.

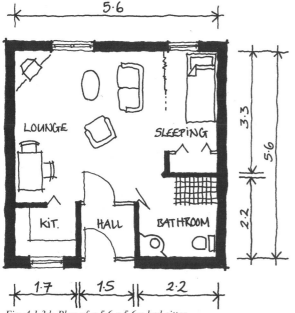

Fig. 4.1.3d: Plan of a 5.6 x 5.6m bed-sitter

Fig. 4.1.3e: A personal museum

Fig. 4.1.3f: A cooking corner in a bed-sitter.

4.2 Key Spaces

4.2.1
The Flat Entrance

The entry space acts as a buffer between the outside world and the world of the individual, in just the same way as the entrance hall to a conventional house. It includes the space immediately to the outside of the 'front door' as well as the hallway within. The doorway itself should be conceived as a threshold: it is both a barrier against intrusion, extraneous noise and prying eyes, and a place of welcome. It should guarantee privacy but encourage neighbourly contact and should offer each resident the opportunity to establish their identity.

The Outer Threshold

- the entrance should be set back from the main circulation tract within its own threshold area
- provide a small bench where two neighbours could sit
- provide a shelf for deliveries and with space for a plant or flowers
- provide a small but clearly visible name board: names and numbers should be embossed and should be set in contrasting colours
- residents should feel free to personalise the area around the doorway and to paint the door in their own chosen colours
- doorbell and letter box should be located at about 1.1m above floor level
- down-lighters should be used to highlight each entry space and to provide adequate illumination for handles, keyholes, signs etc.

Fig. 4.2.1a: An illuminated doorway

Fig. 4.2.1b: Front doors

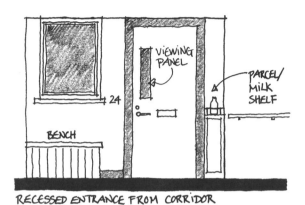

RECESSED ENTRANCE FROM CORRIDOR

The Front Door

- the door itself should be welcoming: not a blank plane with a small spy hole, but a real 'front door', brightly painted with a sizeable viewing panel at a height which suits both standing and seated people (1.2 - 1.8m above finished floor)
- all door furniture should be easy to operate: chunky lever handles, large and highly visible keyholes (or remote controlled locks), all placed at about 1m above floor level
- the threshold should be flush with the general floor level
- door closers should be adjusted to allow doors to be opened with minimum pressure; the closing action should incorporate a delay and a final damping to avoid any risk of trapping people or knocking them over
- door surrounds should be fitted with seals to prevent the sound of 'slamming' and to improve sound reduction

Fig. 4.2.1c: A letter box cage

Fig. 4.2.1d: Stretching to reach the spy hole!

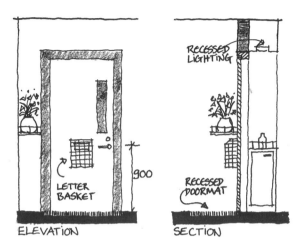

ELEVATION   SECTION

The Inner Threshold or Hallway

- the hallway should be spacious and well lit
- the doormat should be recessed to be flush with the general floor level
- the bells for the flat door and the main front door entry phone should be clearly distinguishable
- provide a letter box with a cage
- there must be enough space for someone in a wheelchair to manoeuvre and turn
- provide space for a wheelchair to be parked with an accessible socket for recharging
- automatic door openers can be fitted for wheelchair users
- provide a sizeable cupboard to store outdoor clothes etc. - hooks should be located at about 1.2m above floor level

4.2.2
Sitting Rooms

A sitting room is used for the full range of day-to-day activities and must accommodate a variety of personal belongings and furniture. There should be space for two or three people to relax with space to watch TV and space for two people to sit and eat a meal.

It is often said that a sitting room needs a focus. This could take the form of a fireplace with mantleshelf containing a protected radiant electric fire. Such a fire provides useful top-up heating, especially when the primary system is only designed to provide background heating.

It is normally accepted that the minimum dimension for the width of a sitting room should be 3.5m. A room of 3.5 x 4.5m has an area of 15.75 sq.m.

Checklist

- allow space for at least two large easy chairs, or a chair and a sofa (sofa bed?)
- allow space for a small dining table and two chairs
- allow space for a cupboard or sideboard
- allow space for a TV and hi-fi
- provide two lighting connections in the ceiling with dimmer switch (possible remote control)
- Provide an adequate number of electric sockets (at least 4 doubles, one to each wall) 900mm above floor level
- Provide 2 TV/IT sockets and 2 telephone sockets
- The main window should have its lower sill at 600mm above finished floor, with a transom at 1m above finished floor - the window head can be lowered from the standard 2.1m to 1.8m in order to reduce the size of the opening and cut costs.
- Plan for a possible connection with the bedroom (removable partition, sliding wall, folding doors)

4.2.3
Bedrooms

A bedroom should provide adequate space for a single bed arranged in peninsular fashion with provision for wheelchair manoeuvres on one of its sides and around its end. There should also be space for a possible second bed which could be placed against a wall. This requires a space measuring 3.6 x 3.2m or 11.5 sq.m. Additional space is needed to accommodate furniture and storage. It is therefore recommended that a bedroom should have a minimum area of 14 sq.m and a minimum cross dimension of 3.2m.

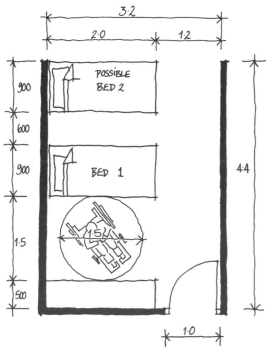

Fig. 4.2.3a: Space data for a bedroom

Fig. 4.2.3b: Connection between bedroom and bathroom

Checklist

- allow for a single bed, with space on at least one side for wheelchair access
- allow for wheelchair manoeuvres
- allow for the possibility of a second bed, possibly against a wall
- allow for other standard items of furniture: a bedside cupboard, a dressing table, a chest of drawers, a chair
- allow for easy access to the bathroom with the possibility to install a ceiling hoist
- allow for possible connection to the sitting room (sliding panels, removable partitions)
- provide one spacious built-in wardrobe with accessible hanging and storage facilities and lower shelves which can be removed to permit wheelchair access
- provide a suitable alarm call facility
- specify background temperatures in the range of 21-24°C
- provide two lighting connections in the ceiling with two-way switching between the bed position and the door
- provide an adequate number of electric sockets (at least 2 doubles, on opposite walls) 900mm above floor level
- provide a TV/IT socket and a telephone socket
- windows should be dimensioned to allow someone lying in bed to have a view to the outside: the lower sill should be 600mm above finished floor, and transom should be located to give minimum visual disruption; the window head can be lowered from the standard 2.1m to 1.8m in order to reduce the size of the opening and cut costs
- allow for the possibility of installing a remote control system for lighting, curtains etc.

4.2.4
Bathrooms

General Planning

Although many older people prefer baths to showers, it is generally accepted that showers are the more suitable option in Extra Care housing because they are more accessible, more hygienic, more economic and offer better temperature control. The basic equipment in a bathroom should include a shower, a WC, a washbasin, a storage cupboard and a mirror. These items should be disposed in such a way as to be accessible to fully mobile people, unassisted wheelchair users, assisted wheelchair users and people in hoists. There should be provision for a full wheelchair turning circle. A square cubicle measuring 2.2 x 2.2m internally provides sufficient space.

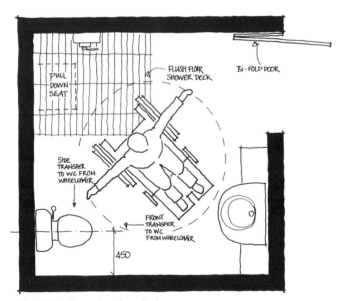

Fig. 4.2.4a: Space data for a bathroom

cantilevered basin

paddle handle

wheelchair access

sturdy shower

flush deck shower

floor drainage

Fig. 4.2.4b: Bathroom details

Checklist

- allow for a clear 1.5m diameter wheelchair turning circle at the centre of the bathroom
- provide an outward opening or double leaf door with minimum 800mm clear opening
- specify surfaces which are easy to clean: walls should be light in colour but not highly reflective; floors must be non-slip and fully sealed
- provide a drainage gully
- specify a constant background temperature of 24°C, with possible radiant boost
- specify a ventilation rate of 3 air changes per hour: the extract fan control should be linked to the lighting switch with a delayed overrun
- specify overall non-glare lighting to a level of 200 lux; highlight the main three activity zones
- provide an alarm call facility
- provide a level shower either as a fully integral floor laid to falls or as a suspended slatted shower deck
- shower controls should be simple to operate and give clear visual and tactile information; use a thermostatic valve to limit water temperature to 43°C; the shower head should be detachable; the folding seat should be self draining
- place the WC adjacent to a wall and leave a clear space for wheelchair transfer on its other side; specify a large paddle handle; provide a fixed grab rail on the wall side and allow for a retractable grab rail on the free side; specify a cantilevered WC bowl; wheelchair transfer should be possible from the front or the side, with or without assistance
- a cantilevered and adjustable height washbasin accommodates wheelchair users: provide adequate shelf space adjacent to the basin and a small cupboard and a mirror; taps should be simple to operate and give clear visual and tactile information; water temperature should be limited to 43°C by a thermostatic valve control
- heated towel rails should not be specified

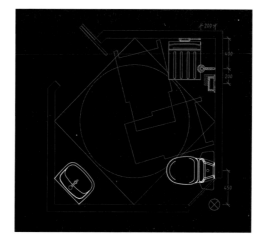

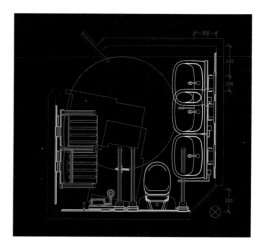

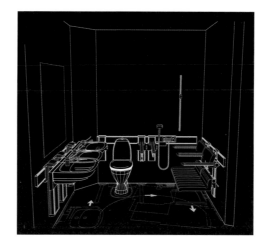

4.2.5
Kitchens

When planning a kitchen for Extra Care housing it should be borne in mind that older people are generally less likely to want to cook elaborate meals, that most kitchens will be providing food for a single individual, that frail people generally have smaller appetites and that in many instances residents may be provided with one cooked meal per day. The basic range of equipment should include a fridge and compact freezer, an electric hob, space and power supply for either a small electric work top oven or a microwave, adequate and accessible storage and a sink with draining board. Bearing in mind that most schemes will include a communal laundrette and will offer a laundry service, there seems to be little point in allowing space for a washing machine, particularly when the washing and drying of clothes produces undesirable humidity levels within the flat.

The kitchen can be planned as an enclosed compartment with a door or as an alcove which opens off the sitting room. A space of 2.2 x 2.5m is recommended as being adequate.

The ideal home kitchen of the magazines does not provide suitable conditions for older people and standard box construction kitchen units should not be specified. A design must take into account the fact that older people are generally less able to bend down or to reach up, and that people who are seated or in wheelchairs need leg-room below the worktop.

Finishes

- specify surfaces which are easy to clean, light in colour and non-reflecting
- floors should be non-slip
- use colour contrasts to highlight key elements

Fig. 4.2.5a: Seated people need leg-room

Layout

- allow for a clear 1.5m diameter wheelchair turning circle at the centre of the kitchen
- an 'L' shape arrangement with a continuous worktop is preferred
- space should be left under worktops to provide leg-room for people who are seated or in wheelchairs
- space should be allocated on the worktop for a mini oven or microwave, a kettle, a toaster and food preparation

Fittings

- standard 600mm tops are unnecessarily deep: provide a 500mm continuous worktop with a sequence of worktop - sink - worktop - hob - worktop - mini oven
- leave a space for one taller piece of equipment such as a fridge/freezer
- worktops should be divided into sections and mounted on adjustable brackets
- sinks should be fitted with flexible supply and waste pipes to enable their height to be altered
- specify a shallow sink with insulated base to improve leg room and assist reach
- a raised lip to the worktop will contain spills and reduce breakages
- worktop edges should be rounded to reduce injuries, and deep fascias should be avoided

Appliances

- provide a built-in electric hob: a flat hot plate is preferred; elements should glow when hot and cool down quickly; warning lights and bells should be specified; locate controls at the front of the unit for easier access
- allow space for a worktop mini oven or microwave
- allow space for a fridge/freezer

Fig. 4.2.5b: An accessible kitchen

Fig. 4.2.5c: Accessible controls

Fig. 4.2.5d: Awkward recessed strip handle

Storage

- cupboard doors should be lightly sprung and removable
- provide a set of open shelves from floor to ceiling
- provide storage under worktops in mobile consoles rather than fixed cupboards: drawers limit access for people who wish to sit at worktops
- provide shallow open shelves between the worktop and any upper storage units
- provide a pull-out rubbish bin on wheels

Controls

- controls, handles and power points should be highly visible and easy to reach; avoid fiddly buttons
- provide at least 4 switched double electric sockets as well as a cooker connection
- avoid recessed strip handles: 'D' handles are easiest to grip and manipulate
- provide swivel mixer taps with dual 'paddle ended' lever control (or specify infra-red sensors)
- a goose neck swivel tap will allow pans and kettles to be filled on the draining board
- water should be thermostatically mixed to a maximum temperature of 43°C to prevent scalding
- provide an alarm call facility and smoke detector (with visual and audible alarm)

Environment and Services

- specify a background temperature of 21°C
- specify a ventilation rate of 3 air changes per hour: the extract fan control should be linked to the lighting switch with a delayed overrun
- specify overall non-glare lighting to a level of 300 lux, with possible highlighting to give an illuminance of up to 500 lux at main activity points
- if possible provide a viewing window to the communal corridor (1/2 hour fire resistant)

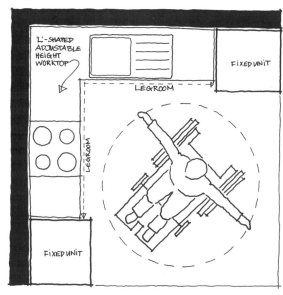

Fig. 4.2.5e: 'L' shaped kitchen layout

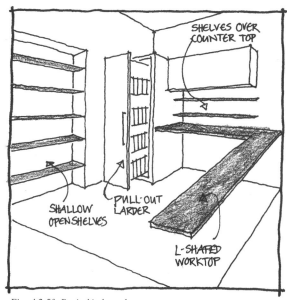

Fig. 4.2.5f: Basic kitchen elements

4.3 Openings

4.3.1
Doors

General Details

All too often doors create unnecessary barriers for older people. Doors which have been designed to promote security or to improve fire safety may have the effect of impeding safe passage. Fire safety and security are important issues which cannot be ignored, but careful design can ensure that secure doors are also 'user friendly'.

Checklist

- clear opening should be 800mm minimum, 850mm preferred, to allow wheelchairs to pass through
- all thresholds need to be flush, especially where there is a change in floor finish
- door surrounds should be fitted with seals to prevent the sound of 'slamming' and to improve sound reduction
- colour and tonal contrast on doors and architraves will increase their visibility
- limited force should be required to open a door and it should not close heavily
- doors should be positioned with adequate space for disabled people to reach the handle and allow space for manoeuvring on both sides of the opening
- doors should be positioned to avoid clashing of leaves
- door numbering should be raised or embossed and at a height where most people can reach or touch it
- glazed doors should be highlighted with patterns to avoid collision

Fig. 4.3.1a: Use of colour and contrast

Fig. 4.3.1b: A bi-fold door

Door Furniture

Handles should be easy to operate from a seated position and with a closed fist; lever operated 'D' handles with a return help to minimise catching clothing and should be located between 900-1000mm above finished floor level.

Fig. 4.3.1c: 'D' shaped handle   *Fig. 4.3.1d: Awkward catches*

Viewing panels should be low enough for a person in a wheelchair to see or be seen through.

Metal or plastic kick plates protect the lower parts of doors from wheelchair footrests.

Locks should be simple to operate and contrast with background; card keys and other electronic systems can replace small fiddly keys.

Electronic door openers can be fitted to any door and can be controlled either by a push button set at the side of the door or by remote control.

Electromagnetic door catches hold fire doors open; the doors are released and closed automatically when the fire alarm is activated. They prevent essential fire doors from being permanently propped open by occupants of the building, ensuring their effectiveness in fire containment. When used in corridors fire doors can be recessed into the wall thus reducing obstructions and visual clutter.

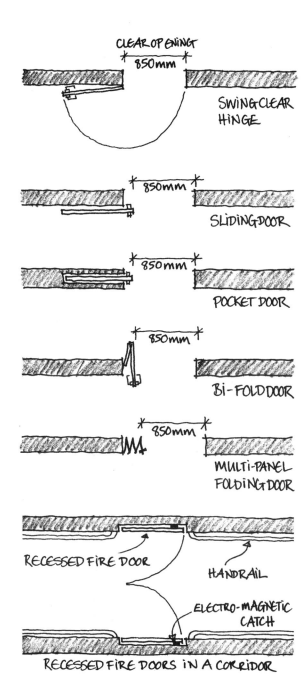

CLEAR OPENING
850mm

SWING CLEAR HINGE

850mm

SLIDING DOOR

850mm

POCKET DOOR

850mm

BI-FOLD DOOR

850mm

MULTI-PANEL FOLDING DOOR

RECESSED FIRE DOOR

HANDRAIL

ELECTRO-MAGNETIC CATCH

RECESSED FIRE DOORS IN A CORRIDOR

Fig. 4.3.1e: Door types

Door Types

Swing doors are easy to open but require a large amount of clear floor space. They can be heavy especially if they are solid fire doors or have glass set in them. 'Swing-clear' door hinges permit a door to swing all the way open and lay almost flat against the wall, increasing the clear opening of the doorway.

Sliding doors do not require clear floor space for a door swing but wall space is lost when the door is open. If they are lightweight and placed on a suitable tracking system they are easily opened from a wheelchair. Floor tracks should be avoided as they fill with dirt and if not recessed cause an obstruction. Sliding doors should be top hung with a bottom guide. Glass sliding doors are particularly difficult to use as they are very heavy.

Pocket doors slide into a wall cavity and have similar characteristics to sliding doors, but may require a thicker wall construction. The detailing of door handles must facilitate easy opening whilst permiting the door to recess.

Bi-fold doors are hinged a third of the way across their width. This reduces the effort required and the clear floor space needed to open them. The folded door leaf necessitates a wider structural opening.

Multiple panel folding doors are difficult to operate due to their flexible construction. They will also reduce the width of the clear opening.

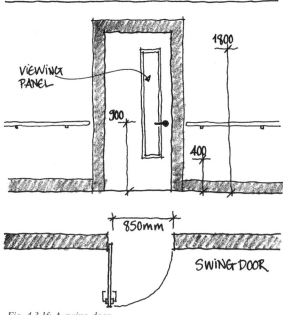

VIEWING PANEL

1800

900

400

850mm

SWING DOOR

Fig. 4.3.1f: A swing door

Fig. 4.3.1g: Excessively heavy doors

4.3.2
Windows

Windows are needed to provide adequate light and ventilation and to create a visual link with the outside world. They should be safe and secure and offer the means to maintain privacy. Controls must be accessible and easy to operate. The position and size of a window should be carefully determined in relation to the size of a room and the activities which it is expected to host.

A bay window   *A vertical pivot window*

A corner window   *A window sill*
Fig. 4.3.2a

Checklist

- main windows should provide views out for people who are sitting or lying down: sills should be at a maximum 600mm above finished floor
- locate horizontal mullions and safety rails carefully to give minimum disruption to any line of vision
- windows should be accessible: an openable window should not be placed above a worktop or sink
- ideally both sides of a window should be cleanable from within the room
- sills should be dimensioned to provide space for ornaments and flower pots
- handles and locks should be designed to be operable with one hand using minimum force and should be located at low level
- fit safety stays or restrainers to all opening windows; these can improve safety and security while allowing controlled ventilation
- the lower edge of any openable window should be at least 850mm above finished floor level
- position and size windows to avoid unnecessary cold radiation or draughts: lower window heads to 1.8m above finished floor to compensate for low sill heights
- position window openings to maximise the amount of light entering a room; excessive sunlight can be controlled by curtains or blinds
- use external shading devices and overhangs to minimise solar gain and glare through south and west facing windows
- specify double glazing to increase thermal insulation and to reduce cold radiation
- where outside noise is a problem specify double windows which incorporate a gap of 100mm-200mm between the panes of glass
- specify frames which incorporate controllable trickle vents
- a bay window allows lateral views of the world outside and acts as a light scoop

Window Fittings

Automatic Controls are a valuable aid for frail people. Remote controls for windows, curtains and blinds are easy to install but are only likely to be supplied on an individual basis according to need.

Espagnolette Security Bolts provide three point closing and locking from a single handle.

Safety Stays hold a window ajar and provide moderate ventilation while maintaining a degree of security and safety. The fact that they are designed to be impossible to open from the outside sometimes renders them difficult to open from the inside.

Handles and Locks should be easy to grip and manipulate. Handles should be located between 900mm and 1200mm above finished floor level.

Fig. 4.3.2b: Inappropriate window details

Types of Window

The following window types are ranked in order of their perceived suitability for Extra Care housing:

1. *Vertical Pivot Windows* have the advantage that they can be both opened and closed by pushing and are easy to clean from the inside. When fully open they offer a safe vertical barrier. They can be fitted with an espagnolette bolt with a single low level handle. The inward opening section interferes with curtains, and ornaments can only be placed on one side of the sill.

2. *Horizontal Pivot Windows* can be opened and closed by pushing, but the top surface is difficult to clean from the inside. Even when fully open they offer a horizontal barrier to prevent falls. They can be fitted with an espagnolette bolt with a single handle at low level. The upper inward opening section may interfere with curtains when fully open.

3. *Tilt and Turn Windows* open inwards and can be switched from side hanging to restricted bottom hanging. In the side hanging mode they take up a great deal of space and interfere with curtains. They can be heavy and difficult to open. Safety can be a problem if the window is opened fully and protection rails may need to be fitted.

4. *Casement Windows* can be hung from the top, bottom or side and can be fitted with an espagnolette bolt. They open outwards to give maximum weather protection. They cannot be cleaned from the inside and are sometimes difficult to open.

5. *Top Swing Fully Reversible Sash Windows* offer a restricted secure opening in one position but can be flipped over to allow cleaning from inside. This difficult manoeuvre requires two hands.

6. *Sliding Sash Windows* are not recommended. They can be difficult to open and are impossible to clean from the inside.

Balconies

Balconies provide a private outside sitting space. Economy, however, usually dictates that they are fairly small. They are also exposed to the elements and may often be too sunny or windy for older people. As a result they are often used only to support a few flower pots. Balconies have the added disadvantage that they take light away from the room and threaten security. Projecting windows in the form of either 'bays' or 'bows' have much more to recommend them. A projecting window allows lateral views and collects sunshine. It can also offer a number of the promised advantages of a balcony: in the summer with the window open it can feel like a protected balcony, while at other times it can be like a winter garden.

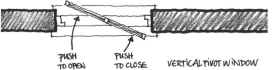

Fig. 4.3.2c: Vertical pivot window

Fig. 4.3.2d: Bay windows

Fig. 4.3.2e: A generous balcony

Fig. 4.3.2f: A balcony seat

4.4 Communal Facilities

4.4.1
Lounges and Sitting Rooms

The communal lounge serves as the focal point of the social and communal life in an Extra Care scheme. Its design requirements will be determined by the operating concept which is adopted for a particular scheme. In some schemes, particularly those in the private sector, only one main lounge area is provided; in others the main lounge might be backed up by a number of smaller lounges and specialised activity rooms.

The way in which a lounge is used will vary greatly from scheme to scheme and is very much determined by the scheme manager. In general it is said that active residents often avoid communal activities, while very frail residents are not able to participate; this implies that a lounge exists principally to serve the band which lies between these extremes.

The main lounge is likely to be used intermittently by individuals and small groups who are simply seeking a change of environment or a place in which to sit and chat with other residents. More formally it might also be used on a regular basis by groups who meet to play cards or to take part in some other shared activity. From time to time individual residents may book the lounge for private parties or 'functions'. Finally it will be used by the whole community for organised entertainments, concerts, keep fit classes, games evenings and tenants' meetings. It is therefore necessary to plan a room which is capable of accommodating all of the residents in some kind of formal arrangement and which can also function as the informal setting for a variety of happenings. The use of niches and alcoves can help to scale down the room and make it more inviting for individuals.

A space standard of 2 sq.m per resident was generally accepted in the past for communal lounges in public sector Category II sheltered housing schemes. In Extra Care schemes allowance should be made for the likelihood that a lower proportion of residents would be regular users, suggesting that 1.5 sq.m per resident could well be a suitable standard to adopt, particularly if secondary sitting rooms are provided.

It is quite common for a small residents' kitchen to be provided next to the lounge for tea-making, and in some schemes a licensed bar is provided for residents.

Fig. 4.4.1a: A residents' meeting

Checklist

- allow 1.5 sq.m per resident
- provide niches and alcoves which can serve as focuses for small groups
- if the lounge is adjacent to the dining room consider installing a sliding-folding partition between the two
- if the lounge is far removed from the main kitchen, consider providing a small tea kitchen
- provide visual and physical connection with a level garden terrace, possibly via a conservatory
- specify furniture which is comfortable, easy to clean, fairly light in weight and easy to move; use fabrics which hide stains and are easy to clean
- provide overall indirect lighting to give an illuminance of about 200 lux and provide for enhanced lighting in niches and alcoves
- design a colour scheme which is light and cheerful
- provide blackout facilities
- provide power sockets at appropriate points on each wall
- specify surface materials and furnishings which produce a fairly short reverberation time
- install an induction loop system to help people with hearing aids
- allow for a low level of background heating with rapid response 'top up'

Fig. 4.4.1b: A group sitting room with kitchenette

Fig. 4.4.1c: Informal groups

Fig. 4.4.1d: A fireside chat

Fig. 4.4.1e: A view to the garden

Sitting Rooms and Activity Rooms

A range of smaller secondary sitting rooms are provided in some Extra Care schemes. These may each be located in proximity to a cluster of flats and function as the focal point for a group of residents, or they may be located in a random manner to serve simply as occasional rooms for specific activities.

A secondary sitting room should have a domestic scale and be able to seat a group of up to eight people in comfort. As well as easy chairs there should be space for one or two tables with suitable chairs. An area of about 20 sq.m would normally be adequate - larger rooms can have an institutional feel and may not be used. Such rooms may come to be associated with particular groups of residents or may take on particular uses at particular times. A small sitting room might be used as a prayer room or a shrine, it might be used by card players, sewing groups, art classes, study groups etc.

Sitting rooms which are related to a particular cluster of flats are sometimes used as dining areas and are therefore equipped with small warming kitchens.

Other Communal Facilities

Other communal facilities which may be provided include a small shop selling basic foodstuffs and toiletries, a licensed bar and a room for religious observance.

Day Centre Facilities

In the future it seems likely that more and more Extra Care schemes might take on a dual role as day care centres. Where this happens the size of the main communal lounge will obviously need to reflect the activities which are expected to take place. In such instances it might be that two lounges would be provided, one being exclusively for the use of residents. The advantages of establishing day centres are obvious: older people in the community can take advantage of the facilities on offer and potential residents can get to know the scheme. The increased number of users makes it feasible to build extra facilities and to offer a much broader range of activities. These might include consultants' rooms, therapy rooms, an exercise gym, hydrotherapy facilities, a library, a craft room etc. However, the setting up of a day centre for non-residents can produce resentment among residents. The detailed design of day centres and the issues which they raise lie beyond the scope of this book.

Fig. 4.4.1f: Christmas decorations

4.4.2
Dining Rooms

General Planning

It is now common in Extra Care schemes for residents to be offered one cooked meal per day in a cafeteria restaurant. The system of meal provision varies from scheme to scheme: in some the service is optional and residents pay as they go; in others the residents are charged automatically for a 'meal plan'. Frail residents may have their meal delivered to their room, or they may be served their meal in a group sitting room.

The normal space allowance per diner for a cafeteria service restaurant with tables seating 4-6 people is about 1.2 sq.m. However, table spacing should take into account the needs of frail elderly residents and wheelchair users and a standard of between 1.5 and 2 sq.m per diner is recommended for Extra Care housing.

It is usual for restaurants to operate a mixture of cafeteria and waitress service: those residents who can are encouraged to serve themselves. The self-service counter should be well lit and the meal options clearly displayed. Trays should be easy to grip and have a non-slip surface and a substantial rim; crockery should be durable and stable; cutlery should easy to grip and manipulate.

Furniture

Tables would ideally vary in size to seat 2, 4 or 6 diners and should be square or rectangular with rounded corners. Circular tables are confusing for some residents. The table top should be cantilevered from a central pedestal so as to eliminate the need for legs at the corner and thus improve access for people in wheelchairs. Chamfered corners also improve accessibility. The table top can be lipped to prevent spillages and minimise the risk of upsets.

Chairs should be light and easy to move. They should be fitted with arms to help leverage. The body of the chair must be non-porous and easy to clean. The legs should be fitted with rubber ends to eliminate noise and prevent slipping.

Checklist

- allow 2 sq.m per diner or 1.2 sq.m per resident
- specify rectangular or square tables with rounded corners on pedestal legs in a variety of sizes to accommodate 2, 4 or 6 diners
- specify light-weight chairs with easy-to-clean bodies and non-slip feet
- floor surfaces should be sound absorbent and easy to clean
- overall lighting to be 150 lux with higher intensity lighting directed at the individual table tops
- design a colour scheme which is light and cheerful
- specify surface materials and furnishings which produce a fairly short reverberation time
- choose crockery which minimises noise disturbance
- specify a low background temperature with rapid response 'top up'

Fig. 4.4.2a: A wheelchair diner

Fig. 4.4.2b: A connected dining room and sitting room

Fig. 4.4.2c: A self-service cafeteria

Fig. 4.4.2d: Well designed furniture

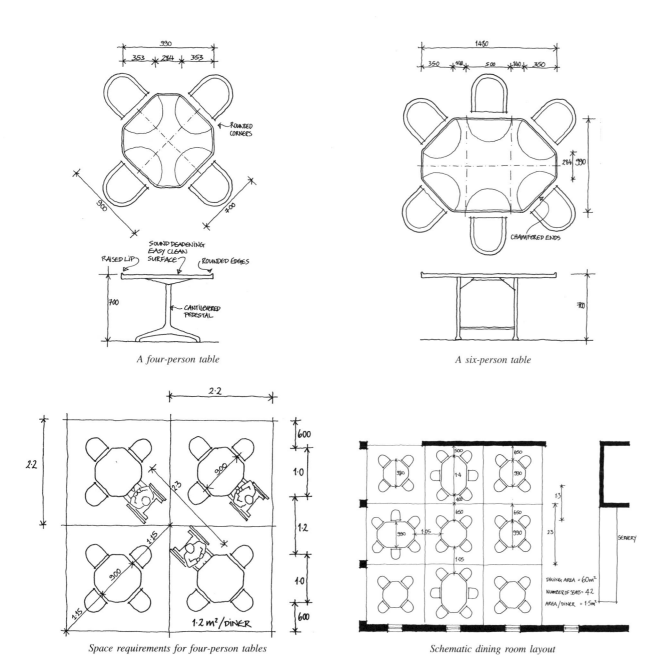

A four-person table

A six-person table

Space requirements for four-person tables

$1.2 \text{ m}^2/\text{DINER}$

Fig. 4.2e: Dining furniture

Schematic dining room layout

DINING AREA = 60m²
NUMBER OF SEATS = 42
AREA/DINER = 1.5m²

4.4.3
Kitchens

General Planning

The size and planning of a kitchen will be entirely dependent on the nature of the meal service which is provided. A kitchen which supplies a cafeteria service to forty residents in a dining room such as the one described in Fig. 4.4.2e would need a main cooking and preparation area of about 30 sq.m with additional stores and cold rooms. If the kitchen is required to provide a cafeteria service to non-resident day centre users as well as to ambulant residents and a delivery service to non-ambulant residents then it will need to be fairly large and well equipped. If cooked food is to be delivered to individual flats or to secondary dining rooms it is essential to make adequate provision for the storage and heating of delivery trolleys. The detailed design of kitchens is a matter for specialists and lies beyond the scope of this book.

The kitchen needs to be accessible from a service entrance which connects to a small screened service yard. Adequate provision should be made for refuse containers.

Kitchens are a source of noise and smell. If, as is often the case, they are to be located directly below flats special measures should be taken to contain any noise and to locate ventilation outlets above any neighbouring flats and well away from any windows.

4.5 Ancillary Accommodation

4.5.1
Staff Facilities

The Manager's Office

Traditional sheltered housing schemes were managed by live-in wardens whose umbrella role included everything from resident care to building maintenance. Such warden managers would typically have been allocated a flat in the scheme and would have occupied a poky office next to the main entry.

In many Extra Care schemes the live-in warden has been replaced by a non-resident scheme manager. The scheme manager is responsible for representing the interests both of the residents and of the association, for managing the facilities, for organising the daily life of the community and for co-ordinating care. The management and delivery of care is the responsibility of the leader of the care team.

However, some associations continue to employ resident managers who are responsible for both the premises and care provision. In such cases the manager's flat and office should be totally separate from each other and the flat should have its own private entrance.

For managers who are non-resident the office is their only base within the scheme. The design thus needs to balance the manager's needs for a private, secure and efficient working environment against the need to create a facility which is approachable and welcoming. Whilst a single office space of about 15 sq.m is probably adequate, it may be advisable to provide a suite of two rooms: an outer reception space and a private inner office.

Checklist

- provide a secure room with an area of 15-20 sq.m
- the office should be located next to the building's main entrance
- the manager should have a good view of the entrance to the site and the approach to the building as well as of the building entrance itself
- the office should be linked with the entrance hall by a counter and hatch: the hatch should offer the possibility of a view across the entrance foyer, though it should be possible to close it off completely when required

- allow space for a traditional desk with a computer table and provide adequate space for filing and records
- provide a set of pigeon holes for messages
- allow space for monitoring equipment, CCTV screens, alarms and controls
- provide a small safe
- provide a private corner with easy chairs where interviews and informal meetings can take place out of public view

Fig. 4.5.1a: An outer reception space

Fig. 4.5.1b: A carer at work

The Care Office

The concept of Extra Care housing embodies the idea that care will be delivered to residents according to their need. In some schemes care provision is organised by the association itself; in others it may be sub-contracted to private care organisations or it may be provided by the social services department of the local authority. Whichever is the case there is now a need to provide special accommodation for the care team.

The care office needs to be physically separate from the manager's office, though they should remain close to each other. The office provides a base for peripatetic staff with facilities for case meetings, interviews etc.

Checklist

- provide a secure room with an area of 15-20 sq.m
- allow space for a desk for the care team leader and one other 'hot desk' for members of the team
- provide a small conference table with space for about 6 people
- provide a private corner with easy chairs where interviews and informal meetings can take place
- provide a notice board and pigeon holes for messages
- provide a secure and cool store for drugs and medical supplies: this would ideally be a separate walk-in store room accessed from the care office

The Staff Room

The staff room should be a quiet and private space to which staff can retire during their breaks. Ideally it should offer a base for all staff including kitchen staff, service staff, carers and administrators. It might be provided with glass doors which open directly into a private staff patio or courtyard.

Checklist

- provide a room with an area of about 15 sq.m
- locate the room away from main circulation routes and ensure privacy
- provide a small tea kitchen
- provide space for easy chairs for 6-8 people
- provide secure lockers in an adjacent corridor for all permanent and semi-permanent staff
- provide at least two staff toilets and one changing/shower room

Sleep-over Accommodation

A self-contained flatlet should be provided for the use of staff on sleep-over duty. Normally one or two single bedrooms with a single bathroom will suffice.

Checklist

- provide one or two single bedrooms each with an area of about 10 sq.m
- provide a 5 sq.m bathroom with WC, basin and shower

Guest Accommodation

A self-contained flatlet should be available to offer overnight accommodation to relatives and friends of residents. The flat should be designed for full wheelchair accessibility. Such accommodation would be bookable in advance and would be charged at a nominal rate.

Checklist

- provide a 16 sq.m double bedroom
- provide an en-suite bathroom
- allow space for twin beds, built-in wardrobes, a table and chairs and two easy chairs

Fig. 4.5.1c: A carer at work

Fig. 4.5.1d: A guest room

4.5.2
Support Facilities

Assisted Bathrooms

Within the last few years showers have largely replaced baths as the preferred option for unassisted personal washing in sheltered flats: as a general rule baths are less hygienic than showers and they pose access problems for frail and semi-ambulant people. However there are still residents who prefer or who need to take baths: the very frail who are unable to take even an assisted shower and those with skin conditions which are relieved by immersion. For this reason it is usual to provide a small number of communal bathrooms of different types in an Extra Care scheme.

Simple Bathrooms would contain a free standing bath with suitable grab rails and poles, a WC, a washbasin and facilities for changing and storing clothes. The bath could be used in unassisted mode by ambulant residents, or as an assisted bath for frail residents using a fixed or mobile hoist. The room needs an area of about 12 sq.m.

Specialised Bathrooms would be fitted with one of the many proprietary baths which now exist: tilting baths, baths which can be raised and lowered, baths equipped with hydraulic swivel seats which lower the user gently into the water and baths used in conjunction with fixed ceiling-mounted hoists. Any of these baths can be fitted with whirlpool and hydrotherapy attachments. Again the room should contain a WC, a washbasin and a changing facility and needs an area of about 12 sq.m.

It is generally recommended that one bathroom should be provided for every 15-20 residents. If several bathrooms are provided these would ideally be of different types.

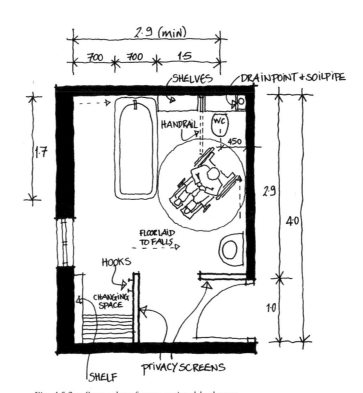

Fig. 4.5.2a: Space data for an assisted bathroom

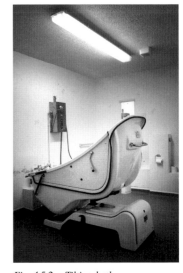

Fig. 4.5.2c: Tilting bath

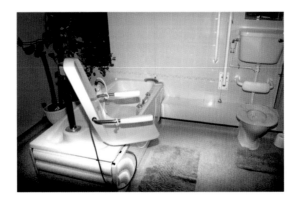

Fig. 4.5.2b: Standard bath with fixed hoist

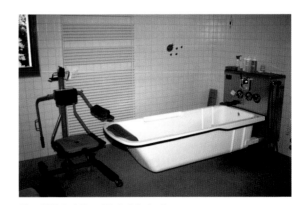

Fig. 4.5.2d: Adjustable height bath

Checklist

- provide a room of 12 sq.m minimum - 3 x 4m
- screen entry to prevent views in when door open
- adequate space is needed in which to turn or manoeuvre a wheelchair or a mobile hoist, or to transfer a resident from a wheelchair to a hoist
- standard baths should be mounted on legs without side panels to give access to mobile hoists
- provide a shower fitting
- provide a WC with fixed and folding grab rails
- provide a washbasin
- provide a seat with hooks and shelves for clothing
- provide convenient shelves for toiletries
- the floor should have a fully sealed non-slip surface with gentle falls to a drainage gully
- pipework should be enclosed
- walls should be tiled up to a minimum of 1.2m above finished floor using a matt tile to reduce glare
- make upper walls and ceiling acoustically absorptive to counter the effects of tiled walls and floors
- use colour and contrast to help partially sighted residents and to reduce any clinical ambience
- bathrooms should be lit to a general level of 200 lux to avoid glare from fittings or shiny wall surfaces
- bathrooms are used intermittently and can be maintained at fairly low background temperatures providing they can be quickly boosted to 24°C
- a ventilation rate of 3 air changes per hour should be maintained when the bathroom is in use, though higher rates can be used to clear humidity
- water should be supplied from thermostatically controlled mixer taps which limit the temperature to a maximum 43°C
- provide an alarm call facility.

Ancillary Rooms

Sluice Rooms are needed for cleaning equipment, bedpans etc. They are often located beside assisted bathrooms. Provide one fully tiled room of 5-10 sq.m on each floor.

Store Rooms are required for equipment and supplies. Provide one room of about 10 sq.m on each floor.

Communal Toilets should be provided on the ground floor close to the main communal facilities. One toilet should be located so that it is accessible from the garden. A toilet cubicle should have an area of about 5 sq.m and be fitted with an outward opening or split panel door. The WC should be placed beside a wall with sufficient space on its free side to allow transfer from a wheelchair. Grab rails should be provided.

Hairdressers

One room should be provided on the ground floor for the use of visiting consultants such as hairdressers and chiropodists. This should be a pleasant daylit room of about 15 sq.m and needs to be fitted with an adjustable basin with the usual shower attachments, mirrors and shelves.

Fig. 4.5.2e: A sluice room

Fig. 4.5.2f: Hairdressing facilities

Consultancy/Treatment

In most Extra Care schemes doctors and health workers examine and treat residents in their own rooms and there is no need to provide special consultation facilities. If such a facility is ever needed a room such as the hairdressing salon can be used. However, schemes which operate day centres require a range of consultation, therapy and treatment rooms.

Laundry

Most schemes provide a single laundry room for the joint use of staff and residents, though sometimes two separate laundries are provided. A residents' laundry should be located on the ground floor and give access to a screened drying court. A 15 sq.m room accommodates two washing machines and two spin dryers. These should be mounted on a plinth which serves the dual purpose of reducing the need to stoop and cutting down on structure borne sound transmission. The room should be well insulated to minimise sound transmission to any adjacent dwellings. A sink and ironing board should also be installed. The residents' laundry serves as a popular meeting point and comfortable seating should be provided.

Wheelchair Store

The use of powered buggies and wheelchairs is becoming increasingly common. As many of these are only intended for external use a room is needed for their storage and charging. This should be conveniently located in relation to the site entrance and the main building entrance. It requires a ramped approach to double external doors, and interior connection to the main entry system. Ideally doors would incorporate automatic opening systems and be operated by key or smart card. Space is needed to store and recharge wheelchairs when not in use. Each

wheelchair bay should include sufficient space for a resident to transfer from one wheelchair to another. A room 7 x 3m would provide 5 bays.

Plant and Store Rooms

- Main Plant Room
  The size of the main plant room will be determined by the nature of any heating and ventilating systems which are installed. The room should include space for standby systems and should be designed to enable large items of equipment to be replaced.

- General Store and Workshop
  A general purpose store room is required to house maintenance equipment, garden implements and disused furniture. It should ideally include basic workshop facilities.

Fig. 4.5.2h: A laundry

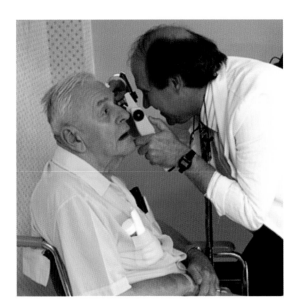

Fig. 4.5.2g: A consultation

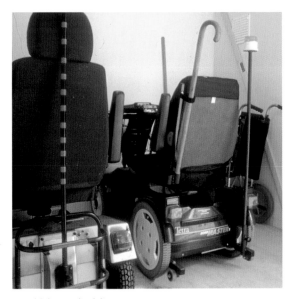

Fig. 4.5.2j: A wheelchair store

4.6 Circulation Spaces

4.6.1
Staircases

Although it is often assumed that most residents will normally use a lift, regular use of the stairs is considered beneficial and well designed stairs will encourage this.

Staircases are usually designed in either dog-leg or straight flight configurations. The dog-leg has two half-flights which connect to a half-landing and has the advantage of always returning to the same starting point on the plan. The half-landing provides a useful half-way resting place.

Straight flight stairs may seem to be more economical, but they usually require longer landings. A single straight flight will appear quite daunting to people who are frail, and should be divided into two separate half-flights.

Staircase Pitch

Conventional wisdom on staircase design suggests that as the height of the step or 'riser' increases so its net width or 'going' should decrease. The two are related in a rule of thumb which states:

$$2 \times riser + going = 550 \text{ to } 700mm.$$

Reducing the height of the riser results in an increased number of steps while, conversely, any reduction in the number of steps results in bigger risers. It is necessary to arrive at a compromise which balances the advantages of lower risers against the disadvantage of increasing the number of steps. Older people welcome a tread which is wide enough to stand on with some security.

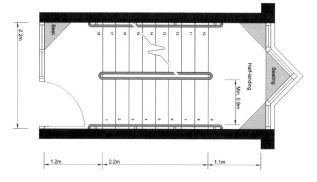

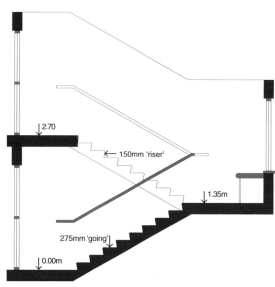

Fig. 4.6.1a: A dog-leg staircase

In Fig 4.6.1a the riser/going ratio is 150:275 which gives an angle of less than 29°. In this case $2 \times r + g = 575mm$. This is neither too steep nor too shallow, and the treads are deep enough to allow people to stand and take a breath.

The dog-leg staircase divides the storey height into half-flights allowing for regular pauses at landings and half-landings. Each half-flight has 9 steps, each with a rise of 150mm and a going of 275mm.

Glazed half-landings give a strong sense of contact with the outside, provide good lighting and can be fitted with corner seats. The stair width is nominally 1.1m to give a clear width of 900mm between handrails: this is wide enough to allow people to pass, but not so wide as to seem daunting. Treads should have non-slip surfaces with nosings picked out in a contrasting colour. The staircase should be well lit using indirect lighting which avoids glare and highlights the tread nosings.

Fig. 4.6.1b: Contrasting nosings and handrails

4.6.2
The Main Entrance

The main entrance to an Extra Care scheme needs to be located at a central point within the scheme to give direct access to the principal lift and staircase as well as to the main communal sitting room and dining room. The door itself should be situated next to the manager's office and should be fully surveyed, both directly and by CCTV. The entrance should be clearly visible from the public thoroughfare and should be accessible for taxis and ambulances as well as wheelchairs.

Fig. 4.6.2a: A sheltered entrance

Fig. 4.6.2b: A porte-cochère

The Forecourt

- the main entrance should be clearly visible from the entry to the site - this means, conversely, that the site entrance is surveyed from the entrance
- the entrance forecourt should be accessible to ambulances and taxis and should be protected by a canopy or porte-cochère to provide shelter for those alighting from vehicles
- the entrance forecourt needs to be lit to an intermediate level to provide a phased transition at night from outside to inside

Fig. 4.6.2c: A covered approach

Fig. 4.6.2d: A foyer

The Main Doorway

- the entrance doors should be glazed, but the glass needs to be given some distinctive marking and the entrance should be clearly distinguishable from any other glazed panels
- individual names and doorbells should be clearly displayed and bell pushes should be accessible to people in wheelchairs
- the entry phone system can be linked to CCTV for additional security
- access to the entrance should be level or gently ramped and the threshold should be flush
- the locking system should be 'user friendly' with key locks located at 1m above finished floor
- the main doors should be easy to open and automatic closers should be fitted with delays and dampers to avoid trapping or knocking people over
- automatic sliding doors are easy to negotiate and can be operated by smart card, pressure pad or infra-red control
- provide a generous flush fitted mat well to allow for wheelchairs to be drained and cleaned

The Entrance Foyer

- the entrance foyer should be well lit, ideally with indirect or concealed lamps, and should be brightly decorated to give a welcoming ambience
- the foyer should be heated to a background temperature of at least 20°C and the doorway should be designed and located so as to minimise cold draughts - frail people find draughty lobbies with two sets of doors difficult to negotiate
- the manager's office should be located next to the main entrance, ideally with a glass communicating screen
- the main lift and staircase should be immediately visible

- provide a well-lit information board to present necessary information for visitors along with clear and properly oriented plans of the building
- provide a well-lit notice board for the residents
- provide a small seating area: the entrance area is a popular place and residents may want to sit and wait for visitors, taxis, etc.

Fig. 4.6.2e: A reception desk

Fig. 4.6.3a: A corridor

4.6.3
Corridors

A development of Extra Care housing inevitably requires a system of corridors to connect the individual flats to each other and to communal facilities. Careful planning can reduce the length of corridors, thus reducing travel distances and minimising any sense of 'institution'. Breaking the scheme down into primary groups or clusters of flats can also help. As a general rule corridors should be limited to a maximum length of about 30m which is sufficient to serve about eight flats in a double banked system. The general arrangement of circulation spaces should be clear and 'rational' to assist people who are perhaps suffering from dementia or memory loss.

The residents in an Extra Care scheme will range from those who are active and mobile to those who are frail and rely on wheelchairs. A corridor should be wide enough to accommodate people in wheelchairs, people with zimmers, people walking with a helper, all moving in both directions. In addition it should be fitted with handrails to assist those who are unsteady and it should be free of obstructions such as projecting radiators or fire extinguishers. Ideally, the minimum width of a corridor should be 1.8m between handrails, or 2m between walls. However, some would argue that such a wide corridor is by definition 'institutional' and that it would appear daunting to the more frail. An alternative is to opt for a width of 1.2m and provide passing points at regular intervals.

Checklist

- limit corridor lengths to a maximum of 30m
- the recommended width for a corridor is 2m between walls or 1.8m between handrails, though uniform widths should be avoided
- continuous handrails should be fitted at 900mm above finished floor; these can be loaded with textural information to help the partially sighted
- a corridor should have contact with the outside at some point along its length: a window helps to orientate and provides some natural daylight
- alcoves can be used to vary the width of a corridor and relieve monotony: they can be fitted with seats where people can pause to take a breath or sit and chat with neighbours
- provide an alcove with a small seat at each flat entry to create a sense of arrival and threshold
- avoid placing a large window at the end of a corridor; this can produce disabling glare
- artificial lighting should be designed to achieve high levels of background lighting without glare: the actual light sources should be carefully screened from view
- each flat doorway should be highlighted
- walls should be light in colour with matt non-reflective surfaces
- floors should be darker than the walls to create a contrast, and should be non-reflective
- floor surfaces should be resilient, sound absorptive and non-slip
- each corridor can be given its own distinctive feel by designing distinctive colour schemes, by hanging the walls with 'themed' pictures, and by adding plants
- fire compartment doors should be maintained in an open position on magnetic links
- clear signs should be located at decision points to give clear and explicit information about the identity of the floor and the numbers of the flats.

Detailed Design

Chapter 5.0
Environmental Design

This chapter discusses some of the main environmental design issues which are specific to Extra Care housing.

5.1
Space Heating

The design of a space heating system for a sheltered housing scheme must address the special needs of older people. In particular it should take the following into account:

- Older people tend to be sedentary and have lower metabolic rates: they 'feel the cold' and generally prefer higher ambient temperatures.
- At least 80% of the accommodation in a sheltered housing scheme needs to be heated continuously.
- Older people are extremely vulnerable to scalding and must be protected from direct contact heat sources of more than 43°C.
- The need to promote individual independence has to be balanced against the need for an overall energy management and control system.

A wide variety of different space heating systems now exist, and each one can comprise a variety of different sub-systems and components. Choosing an overall system and its constituent components involves balancing a large number of often conflicting requirements. This section highlights those issues which relate specifically to sheltered housing.

A heating system cannot be considered in isolation from the building itself and the thermal performance of its envelope. The method of construction, the choice of building materials, the thermal mass and the amounts of insulation must all be taken into account because they will ultimately affect both the level of comfort which can be achieved and the amount of energy which will be consumed.

The key issues to be addressed in selecting an appropriate space heating system are:

- thermal performance of the building envelope
- target requirements for thermal comfort
- choice between central and local heat generation
- choice of heat emitters
- choice of fuel
- systems of control
- initial and running costs
- maintenance and replacement costs

5.1.1
Thermal Performance

A building loses heat mainly through its fabric and as a result of ventilation. Fabric losses are controlled by the insulation of the building envelope and are dependent upon the thermal transmission values of the individual building components and their surface areas. Ventilation losses are dependent upon the input rate of naturally and mechanically induced fresh air.

A building with good thermal performance will be more energy efficient, cheaper to run and less pollutive to the atmosphere. It is no longer sufficient simply to meet the minimum standards set out in the Building Regulations: new buildings should be designed to the highest feasible level of thermal specification. Energy Efficiency Office studies have shown that higher levels of thermal performance can be achieved at relatively low cost (EEO, 1993a). Slight increases in capital cost will be justified by savings in running cost.

A number of thermal performance scales are now in use. These include the Standard Assessment Procedure (SAP), which was introduced as part of the Approved Document L of the 1995 Building Regulations and which grades annual energy consumption on a scale of 1 to 100, the National Home Energy Rating (NHER), which grades consumption on a scale of 1 to 10, and the Building Energy Performance Index (BEPI).

5.1.2
Thermal Insulation and Heat Loss

The thermal transmission of a particular building element is indicated by its 'U-value'. U-values are expressed in watts per square metre per Kelvin or W/m^2K and define the amount of heat energy which will pass through 1 sq.m of an element in each second when the temperature difference between the inner and outer faces is 1°C. They are derived from the individual resistances and thicknesses of the materials which constitute an element. U-values can be used to calculate the expected heat losses of an entire building for any given combination of internal and external temperatures.

The most effective way to improve the thermal performance of a building is to lower the average U-value of its envelope, thus increasing the overall level of thermal insulation. Higher standards of thermal insulation, as well as cutting down on heat loss, also result in higher internal surface temperatures which improve thermal comfort.

Recent research has provided detailed comparisons of energy consumption and costs for different levels of insulation (e.g. EEO, 1993a; CIRIA, 1994) and it is generally accepted that it is both simple and cost effective to raise levels of thermal insulation above the currently accepted norms.

It is necessary to take into account the total amount of heat lost from every element of a building's envelope: the opaque walls, the windows, the roof and the floor. Savings resulting from highly insulated opaque walls can be squandered if there are large areas of poorly insulated and draughty glazing.

The current Building Regulation requirements should be regarded as an absolute maximum. For example, the requirement for opaque external walls is 0.45 W/m²K though conventional masonry construction with a 75mm filled cavity achieves a U-value of 0.37 W/m²K; the requirement for roofs is 0.25 W/m²K, though a roof insulated with 200mm of insulation achieves 0.18 W/m²K; the requirement for floors is 0.45 W/m²K, though a floor with 50mm of insulation achieves 0.35 W/m²K. Lower U-values substantially reduce the heat losses through the fabric and have a considerable impact on the building's energy requirements.

The window is the weakest thermal link in any building's external fabric. High rates of heat loss through glazing, as well as being costly to sustain, result in low internal surface temperatures. These cause discomfort and lead to condensation which in turn causes mould and bacteria growth. The use of single glazed windows in new developments is now considered to be unacceptable and double glazing of one form or another has become the norm.

Conventional double glazing systems can reduce direct heat losses by up to 50% while the use of low-emissivity coatings and gas-filled cavities can lead to even greater savings. Modern draught sealing can also substantially reduce heat loss from air infiltration around frames. All of these improvements, as well as leading to energy and cost savings, also raise thermal comfort by eliminating cold surfaces.

Until recently heating engineers urged designers to limit the size of window openings as much as possible in order to conserve energy, though there is now a growing appreciation of the solar energy gains which can result from suitably oriented windows.

5.1.3
Air Infiltration

Excessive levels of air infiltration or draught can result in serious heat losses and cause extreme discomfort to elderly occupants. An adequate supply of fresh air is necessary both for comfort and health, but air infiltration should be strictly controlled. If possible incoming air should be warmed, and extracted air should be passed through heat exchangers to conserve energy. The old adage: build tight and ventilate right still holds true.

5.1.4
Thermal Mass and Building Form

The thermal mass of a building is a measure of its ability to store heat. Thermal mass relates to the thermal capacities and masses of the various building elements. In general 'heavy buildings' will have higher thermal masses than 'light buildings'. Buildings of low thermal mass heat up and cool quickly; buildings of high thermal mass conserve heat and respond slowly to changes of temperature. Because sheltered housing is in constant occupation it requires a building of high thermal mass and slow thermal response.

The form of a building influences its thermal performance. For the same standards of insulation the most efficient form for a building is the one that encloses the maximum usable space with the minimum external surface area. It follows, therefore, that the ratio of surface area to volume provides one indicator of thermal efficiency. Although some heat loss does occur through the ground floor slab, mainly around its perimeter, most heat is lost through the walls and roof.

Fig. 5.1.4a compares the surface area of different plan forms for two-storey buildings with a footprint of 1,600 sq.m. Where a constant building depth is maintained variations in plan form do not have a very marked effect on surface area. Reductions in building depth produce corresponding increases in surface area.

If the design results in a complex building perimeter with many projections and recessions this can have a pronounced effect on surface area and heat loss. Fig. 5.1.4b shows the effect of 'tessellating' the perimeter wall: successive tessellations increase the perimeter by a factor of 1:√2.

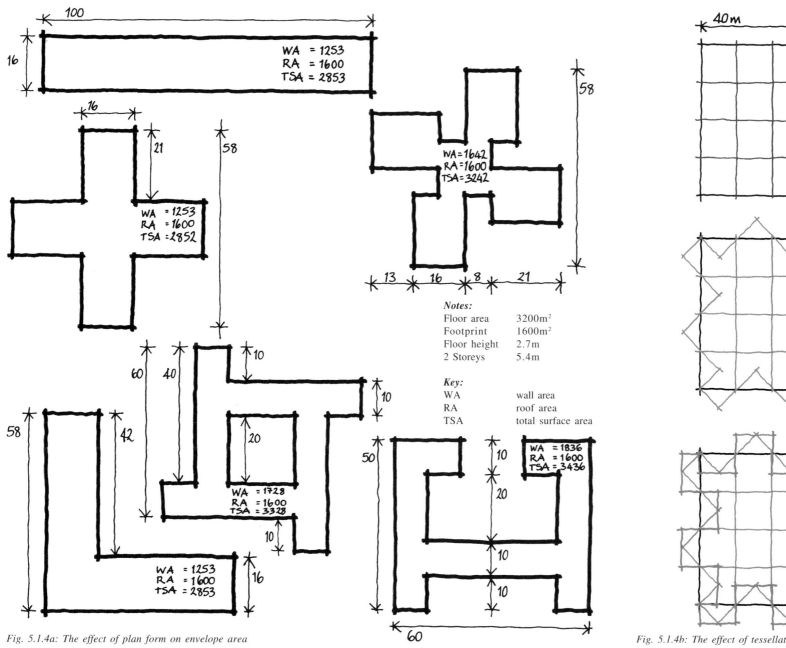

100

WA = 1253
RA = 1600
TSA = 2853

16

16

21

58

WA = 1253
RA = 1600
TSA = 2852

58

WA=1642
RA=1600
TSA=3242

13   16   8   21

Notes:
Floor area   3200m²
Footprint   1600m²
Floor height   2.7m
2 Storeys   5.4m

Key:
WA   wall area
RA   roof area
TSA   total surface area

10

60   40

10

20

58   42

WA = 1728
RA = 1600
TSA = 3328

WA = 1836
RA = 1600
TSA = 3436

50

10

20

10

10

10

WA = 1253
RA = 1600
tSA = 2853

16

60

Fig. 5.1.4a: The effect of plan form on envelope area

40m

perimeter
160m

perimeter
226.3m

perimeter
320m

Fig. 5.1.4b: The effect of tessellation on perimeter length

Increasing the number of storeys reduces the roof area but increases the area of vertical wall surfaces. Fig. 5.1.4c shows that the net effect of increasing floors is initially to produce a marked reduction in the total external envelope area, though beyond six storeys diminishing returns set in and there is a steady increase. Taller buildings also experience greater heat losses as a result of increased exposure.

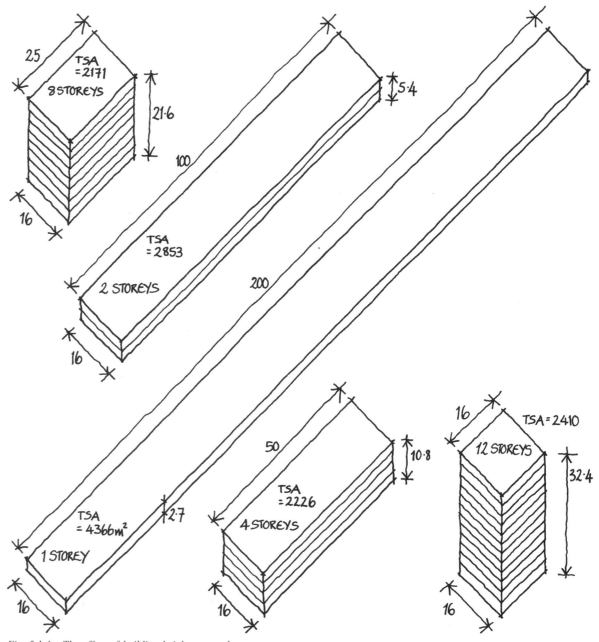

Fig. 5.1.4c: The effect of building height on envelope area

5.1.5
Patterns of Use

A sheltered housing scheme presents a variety of room types, room uses and patterns of occupation. The thermal response of the building fabric and the operation of the heating system must take this variety into account.

Individual flats are likely to be occupied continuously over 24 hours, day in and day out, by residents who are inactive and who have heightened thermal comfort requirements. This situation can be contrasted with that of a family home which is left empty during the day, or of an office which is left empty at night and at weekends. The need for continuous heating can best be satisfied by a building of high thermal mass which provides a slow thermal response and maintains steady conditions of thermal comfort over long periods of time. However, it is useful to be able to provide additional heat with a rapid response for those times when occupants are less active than usual or when the external climate is particularly severe.

The communal facilities may be subjected to intermittent and irregular patterns of use. In many schemes the dining room will only be used regularly at lunch-time, though its occasional use at other times would necessitate a quick response heating system. Other spaces which are used intermittently and which need quick response system are assisted bathrooms, sleep-over rooms and guest rooms. However, those elements which can be classified as having intermittent and irregular patterns of use may account for as little as 10% of the total accommodation.

5.1.6
Heat Sources

Space heating can be provided either from a 'local' source which is located within the room itself or it can be provided at a 'central' source from which heat is distributed to individual rooms through pipes or ducts. In sheltered housing a central heat source can be located within an individual flat, or a single central source can serve the whole scheme.

Local Sources

Local room sources include electric radiant fires, electric storage heaters and electric fan convectors. The choice of fuel for local heat generation is limited by concerns for the safety of older people which rule out the use of gas or coal. Electric installations are clean and safe, simple to use and control, easy to maintain and replace. Although initial installation costs are low, electricity remains a relatively expensive fuel.

Individual Central Heating

The use of a central system within each flat gives a high degree of individual control and can produce some economies of operation particularly if water and space heating are combined. Again gas is ruled out for reasons of safety, so that the favoured fuel source is likely to be electricity.

Scheme Heating

The use of a central system for the whole building produces further economies of scale. A single heating installation can supply both residential and communal spaces, though the needs of different zones must be evaluated. A scheme heating system utilises a single plant room and requires a single flue and combustion air intake. However it can involve the installation of complex and expensive heat distribution systems. A range of fuel types is

acceptable, though the final choice is likely to fall between gas and electricity.

Localised systems find favour in privately owned schemes where individual owners wish to take on the responsibility for the control and the cost of their own heating. Scheme heating systems offer economies of scale and are usually the preferred option in the voluntary sector.

5.1.7
Heat Emitters

Heat is emitted into a space either by convection or by radiation. Although heat emitters are commonly referred to as either 'convectors' or 'radiators' most provide a combination of both in differing proportions.

Convective heating systems heat the air within the room and have only an indirect effect on surface temperatures. High air temperatures affect the body's ability to dissipate heat by convection and can be uncomfortable.

Radiant heating systems heat the room's surfaces and have only an indirect effect on air temperature. Occupants receive radiant heat directly from the emitter and indirectly from the surrounding surfaces. Direct radiant heat can provoke a pleasant sensation on one side of the body, though it can provoke a reciprocal feeling of discomfort on the other side.

There is a high risk that older people will scald or burn themselves if they come in contact with high temperature heat sources and under current legislation estate owners may be liable for any accidents which occur in this way. The surface temperature of emitters should therefore be limited to a maximum of 43°C (NHS Estates, 1994). This can be achieved either by using low temperature emitters or by placing emitters within protective enclosures. All accessible hot water supply pipes must also be protected.

The positioning of heat emitters in rooms should be carefully considered. Bulky emitters need to be located so as to have as little effect as possible on furniture layout. Radiators placed under windows can counter the cold radiation effect of the glass surface and can be used to warm any incoming trickle ventilation.

The following is a brief review of some of the more common emission systems which are currently in use:

- Electric Panel Heaters

  An electric element warms the metal surface of a panel and heat is distributed by radiation and convection. Heat transfer is therefore dependent upon temperature and surface area: if unprotected surface temperatures are limited to 43°C the size of the panel must be increased. Running costs are high because the element uses on-peak electricity, but installation costs are low. Maintenance and replacement are relatively simple.

- Hot Water Natural Convector Heaters

  These are fitted with grilles at their top and bottom to encourage natural convection. Used as low surface temperature skirting heaters they ensure an even distribution of heat, though they limit the possibilities for arranging furniture. Running costs are low. Installation costs are quite high. Maintenance and replacement can be difficult.

- Hot Water Fan Convector Heaters

  A fan is used to increase the air flow rate across a heated element in order to increase heat output. Fan convectors are smaller than equivalent natural convectors. Output can be controlled by altering the fan setting either manually or by thermostat. Fans can be noisy. Running costs are low. Installation costs are quite high. Maintenance and replacement can be difficult.

- Electric Storage Heaters

  These use off-peak electricity to generate heat which is stored within material of high thermal mass. Heat is emitted mainly by convection, though surface temperatures can exceed the recommended limits and protective guards should be fitted. Modern storage heaters control the rate of heat emission by limiting the air flow across the thermal storage material though such controls are still fairly crude. Storage heaters are unresponsive and may emit insufficient heat at critical times in the cycle. They are bulky and unsightly. Running costs and installation costs are low. Maintenance and replacement are relatively simple.

- Electric Radiant Heaters

  A high temperature element is mounted in front of a reflector, and provides mainly radiant heat. Response is fast. There is a high risk of injury and fire unless effective guards are fitted. Running costs are high because the element uses on-peak electricity, but installation costs are low. Maintenance and replacement are simple. Radiant heaters can be used to provide top-up in conjunction with general background heating.

- Heated Ceilings

  Heated ceilings produce an inverted temperature gradient which discourages natural convection. They can produce feelings of stuffiness. They are generally unsuitable for Extra Care housing.

- Hot Water Radiators

  Hot water radiators are served by a central boiler and are usually sized to operate at 75°C. This means that they can only be used in sheltered housing if they are fully protected by guards. The name 'radiator' is misleading because heat is emitted partly by convection and partly by radiation, the proportion being dependent on the design of the panels. Some manufacturers now produce Low Surface Temperature (LST) radiators that operate within the 43°C limit, though these tend to be bulky. Running costs are low. Installation costs are quite high. Maintenance and replacement can be difficult and costly.

- Heated Floors

  Heat is emitted either from water pipes or electric cables embedded within the floor and is distributed evenly over the whole of the floor surface while the surrounding air is heated indirectly by convection. The feet are at a slightly higher temperature than the head which is an ideal condition, especially for older people. Surface temperatures are limited to 24°C in order to avoid a sensation of 'tired feet' and thus fall well within safety limits. There are no restrictions on furniture arrangements. A heated floor acts as a slow response system which utilises the thermal mass of the floor as a heat store and is thus ideal for sheltered housing. It provides background heating which can be topped up by a quick response heater. Running costs are reasonably low. Installation costs are quite high. Maintenance and replacement can be very difficult, though the use of dry suspended floors allows access to joints and manifolds and eases the problem of future replacement.

The final choice of heat delivery system may depend on such factors as the method of construction, the type of tenure and the pattern of use. Hot water radiators are cheap to run but need to be protected. Night storage heaters are cheap to install, but they are bulky, unsightly and unresponsive. Underfloor heating used in conjunction with a quick response top-up in the main living room meets most of the special requirements of the elderly though it is expensive to install and may be difficult to replace.

5.1.8
Control

Modern heating systems make it possible to control heat output and temperature levels in a wide range of separately identifiable zones and according to a variety of time patterns. They can offer a choice between individual and centralised control. Monitoring systems can be designed to adjust indoor temperatures to outdoor conditions and to take account of the particular needs of different individuals and different locations.

The use of a localised heat source rather than a central system simplifies control and enables each heat source to be timed and controlled separately by the individual resident. This places a degree of responsibility on the resident, responsibility which not all older people are willing or able to take on. It also requires that controls be easily understood and programmed.

Centralised systems make it possible for individual residents to control their own heating regimes as well as allowing individual flats to be monitored and controlled from a single central point. Individual heat emitters can be fitted with separate controls and each room can have its own thermostat and timer. Thermostats need to be carefully located so that they give an accurate indication of sentient temperatures.

Just as the communal areas of a scheme can be divided into independent zones, each capable of being separately monitored and controlled, so each flat can be subdivided. Sophisticated monitoring and control systems can lead to substantial energy savings and can ensure that residents are experiencing the appropriate temperatures in the appropriate places at the appropriate times.

All controls, whether they relate to a localised system or a centralised system need to be designed to take into account the special needs of the frail elderly. Controls must be designed in such a way that all those which are operated by the tenants themselves are easy to see, easy to reach, easy to manipulate, easy to read and easy to understand.

Fig. 5.1.8a: Awkward controls

5.1.9
Costs

The cost of a heating system ought to be evaluated in terms of initial capital costs, fuel costs, maintenance and running costs and recurrent capital costs. Ideally these should be considered together in order to arrive at comprehensive costs for the lifetime of the building. Such an approach is made difficult by the unpredictability of energy costs and uncertainty about the life expectancy and replacement costs of different systems.

Private developers are usually more concerned to minimise initial capital costs in order to keep down selling prices than to plan for reduced running costs. For this reason they favour localised systems such as electric storage heaters with individual electric emmersion heaters. Potential home purchasers are also attracted by lower initial costs and by systems which offer them the illusion of independence and control, and will rarely be swayed by arguments about long-term economies.

In the voluntary sector it is difficult to take a balanced view of full costs because initial and running costs may be paid from different budgets. The general preference however is for centralised scheme heating with gas as the favoured fuel. This choice offers economies of scale as well as savings on fuel costs.

The use of a centralised system can lead to difficulties with billing. Although metering of heat consumption is theoretically possible, it is difficult and costly to administer in practice. Private owners show a marked preference for localised heat sources because they like to think that they are in control of their energy consumption. However, they are quite willing to pay standard annual charges for the heating of the communal spaces which probably account for more than 40% of the area of a typical scheme. On the other hand tenants in the voluntary sector who pay fixed heating bills are offered little incentive to save energy, and can be seen opening windows in the middle of winter to regulate room temperatures.

A recent unpublished study produced by Gardner and Pozzoni for the Hanover Housing Association compared space and water heating costs for five alternative systems.

	system 1	system 2	system 3	system 4	system 5
a	£10.96	£16.18	£7.52	£12.20	£6.51
b	£41 K	£28 K	£46 K	£32 K	£61.5 K
c	£262 K	£412 K	£154 K	£288 K	£135 K
d	294	294	156	294	155

key:
a   weekly cost per flat
b   capital cost
c   whole life cost over 15 years
d CO_2 in tonnes/year
system 1   storage heaters in lounge and bedroom, fan heaters in bathroom and kitchen, individual hot water by electric immersion heater
system 2   electric panel heaters in lounge and bedroom, fan heaters in bathroom and kitchen, individual hot water by electric immersion heater
system 3   space heating from protected hot water radiators supplied from a single central gas boiler installation, individual hot water by electric immersion heater
system 4   electric underfloor background heating, panel heaters for boost, individual hot water by electric immersion heater
system 5   hot water radiator space heating and hot water supplied from a single central gas boiler installation

Fig. 5.1.9a: Costs of alternative heating systems compared (source: Hanover Housing Association)

Paradoxically the scheme with the lowest initial cost achieves the highest lifetime cost, while that with the highest initial costs achieves the lowest lifetime cost. On the basis of these figures alone scheme 5 would be the best buy in the long-term.

Fig. 5.1.9b: Windows left open at night to dissipate excess heat.

Fig. 5.1.9c: An over specified central boiler system

5.2
Ventilation

Many older people suffer from breathing difficulties and are highly sensitive to air quality. Adequate ventilation is needed to remove vitiated and polluted air, to replenish oxygen supplies, to remove unwanted heat and to control humidity levels. On the other hand, too much ventilation can allow the intrusion of unwanted sound, it can result in excessive heat losses and can produce uncomfortable draughts.

People often act to control those things which are directly apparent to them, ignoring the indirect consequences of their actions. It is quite common for them to block up every available source of ventilation in order to stem draughts and retain heat, though this can result in a stuffy atmosphere which can cause breathing difficulties and infections.

5.2.1
Requirements

The recommended ventilation rate for naturally ventilated dwellings is between 0.5 to 1 air changes per hour (BRE, 1993a). The Building Regulations refer to three types of ventilation - background ventilation, extract ventilation and rapid ventilation - and offer design options for combinations of fixed openings, extract fans, passive stack vents and opening windows.

A ventilation system should be designed to provide good indoor air quality and to achieve optimum energy efficiency. Air quality can be improved by preventing pollutants from entering a building, by removing them at source, or by diluting them with fresh air.

In Britain most domestic buildings use natural ventilation. This is inexpensive when compared with mechanical ventilation and avoids problems of noise and maintenance. However, natural ventilation is difficult to control, and may result in either excessive air intrusion or inadequate rates of air change. Full or partial mechanical systems may be necessary in places of high exposure or extreme atmospheric pollution and on sites where there are high noise levels.

5.2.2
Natural Ventilation

Most sheltered housing schemes rely on natural ventilation to ventilate habitable rooms and only use mechanical extract for kitchens and bathrooms. Natural background ventilation will be affected by external wind pressure and by the difference between indoor and outdoor temperatures. The use of mechanical extract in kitchens and bathrooms can draw the necessary background ventilation through a dwelling.

Uncontrolled infiltration of cold outside air in winter can cause a sudden drop in room temperature and induce cold draughts. It is important, therefore, to ensure that outside air used for background ventilation is well mixed with warm air and that it flows around occupants at controlled air velocities. Background ventilation can be provided by trickle vents placed in an outside wall. Inlets can be incorporated in window frames and are best located at high level to diffuse the incoming air. Incoming air can be preheated by locating inlets behind a wall mounted heat emitter such as a radiator.

The development of passive stack ventilation (PSV) has extended the possibilities for natural ventilation in homes. A vertical stack of 150mm diameter exploits temperature gradients to induce a steady trickle of ventilation and can be used to remove moist air from kitchens and bathrooms.

5.2.3
Mechanical Extract

Fans are used in mechanical extract systems to induce negative pressures and draw out vitiated air from the adjacent spaces. Supplies of fresh air are then drawn in to replace the air which has been extracted.

It is common for flats in sheltered housing to be planned with internal bathrooms and kitchens and some form of intermittent mechanical extract is thus necessary. Localised kitchen and bathroom extract fans are inexpensive to install and operate. Such fans can be controlled by humidistats or by linked light switches. It is advisable to provide fairly long overrun periods in bathrooms to ensure that all excess humidity has been removed after bathing.

Full mechanical extract systems are only likely to be installed in locations where high noise levels demand that the building envelope be sealed or in areas suffering from extreme exposure or high pollution. In such situations it may be necessary to install ducts for incoming fresh air as well as for extracted air. It then becomes advisable to incorporate some form of heat recovery system in order to reduce energy losses.

5.3
Water Supply

The provision of hot and cold water must be tailored to the specific needs of older people. The location and design of taps should be ergonomically correct, the temperature of all hot water supplies should be thermostatically limited to 43°C, and the water pressure from taps should be reduced. In addition the design of hot and cold water systems should comply with relevant regulations and guidelines including BS6700, the water supply bylaws and the Building Regulations.

5.3.1
Cold Water Systems

All drinking water should either be fed directly from the main or from properly constructed storage tanks which are sized to maintain high rates of replenishment. Cold water for other uses in dwellings can either be drawn directly from the main (direct cold water supply) or indirectly through water storage cisterns (indirect cold water supply).

Direct cold water supply systems have recently found favour amongst developers of new housing because, when water is supplied directly from the main, there is no need to install costly storage cisterns. Direct supply reduces the risk of contamination and provides the higher pressures necessary for instantaneous shower heaters. However, complete dependence on mains supplies can lead to problems.

Recent concern about the reliability of water supplies in the UK lends weight to arguments in favour of indirect supply systems. The use of storage cisterns can guarantee supplies for up to 24 hours and enables water pressures to be controlled more effectively. Lower water pressure makes it easier for older people to operate taps, it cuts down on noise in pipes, and it reduces water wastage.

In choosing between direct and indirect supply systems the designer needs to ascertain the probability of there being disruptions to water supplies and balance the advantages of installation cost against the wisdom of ensuring a back-up storage capacity.

5.3.2
Hot Water Systems

In blocks of flats hot water can be generated and stored centrally and then distributed to the individual flats, it can be generated and stored within each flat, or it can be generated instantaneously at the point of use. Instantaneous water heaters are not generally considered safe or suitable for older people and in sheltered housing the choice falls between generating and storing hot water centrally or locally. This choice may be linked to the choice of space heating system, though one does not necessarily follow from the other.

In designing the whole system it should not be forgotten that communal areas in most schemes include a central kitchen, a laundry, assisted bathrooms, sluice rooms and communal toilets, and that these together will account for a large proportion of total hot water consumption.

The adoption of a centralised system leads to obvious economies of scale and removes the need to accommodate tanks and boilers within individual flats.

Legionnaires' Disease

Water services for sheltered housing should be designed to minimise the risk of spreading Legionnaires' disease. This is a form of pneumonia to which older people, particularly men, are vulnerable and is caused by legionella bacteria which thrive in the hot water systems of large buildings. Infection is thought to result from the inhalation of infected water vapour or spray whilst bathing. Legionella bacteria remain dormant at temperatures below 20°C and cannot survive above 60°C. Thus, it is important to keep the temperature of cold water supplies below 20°C but to maintain hot water supplies above 60°C (CIBSE, 1991).

Hot water systems should be designed to minimise long distribution runs which produce static water at intermediate temperatures. Dead legs should be minimised and runs of blended water should be limited to 2m. Once installed systems should be subjected to periodic inspection and cleansing.

Scalding

Older people are particularly sensitive to temperature and are easily scalded. For this reason the temperature of draw-offs should be limited to 43°C. The risk of Legionnaires' disease makes it inadvisable to supply water at lower temperatures and mixing should only occur at the draw-off point. Mixer taps and showers must be fitted with thermostatically controlled valves.

Water Conservation

The growing scarcity of water coupled with rising demand have led to price increases and calls for

universal metering. Water meters favour older people, particularly those living in flats, because their consumption is well below average. New buildings should incorporate measures to limit water wastage. Modern WC cisterns can be limited to 6 litres and taps can be fitted with automatic time delays.

5.4
Lighting

'Generally, the older the eye is, the greater the amount of light required to perform tasks. As the eye ages, the lens tends to yellow. Also the adaptation process slows, so that moving from relatively bright areas to relatively dark areas can be problematic. Glare sensitivity increases with age... so older persons should be exposed to less harsh light sources...'

Gary R. Steffy (1990)

The fact that almost all older people suffer from some form of visual impairment underlines the importance of good lighting in sheltered housing. The basic problems which need to be addressed are the following:

- Older people may require twice or even three times as much light as normally sighted people in any given situation: they need relatively high levels of general diffused background lighting and they need localised directional lighting to focus on any particular task.
- Older people find it difficult to adapt quickly to changing levels of illumination: sudden contrasts, as for instance between a brightly lit lift and a dim corridor, must be avoided.
- Older people experience heightened sensitivity to glare: every effort should be made to shield bright light sources from direct view. Glare can be caused by a large window at the end of a long corridor, or by a bright unprotected light which falls at the edge of the field of vision.
- Older people suffer from a wide range of impairments and it is important to allow for flexibility and individual control. The use of adjustable light sources and dimmer switches should be considered.

5.4.1
Levels of Lighting

We see an object by virtue of the light which travels from that object to our eyes. The sources of the light which cause the object to be illuminated may be many: some light may have come directly from a primary source such as the sun or a light fitting, some may have been reflected more than once by surrounding surfaces. The following is a brief definition of the terms used in lighting:

- Light intensity is measured in lumens
- Illuminance is a measure of the light falling onto a surface and is measured in lux (lumens / sq.m)
- Luminance is a measure of the light reflected from a surface and is therefore a product of illuminance and reflection
- The standard unit of luminous intensity of a light source is the candela: a source of 1 candela emits a total of 4π lumens. This means that a plane of 1 sq.m at 1m distance from a source of 1 candela will have an illuminance of 1 lumen per sq.m or 1 lux.

The level of lighting which is needed to perform a particular task will depend on the nature of the task, the characteristics of the individual and the general level of background lighting. The inherent relativity which governs light perception makes it difficult to define lighting levels in absolute terms. For this reason design for natural lighting uses 'daylight factors' which relate target levels of illuminance within a room to the brightness of the sky outside.

The exact specification of lighting levels is a matter for specialists. The following list is based on CIBSE recommendations for standard illuminances in residential buildings (CIBSE, 1994), with recommended adjustments for people with impaired vision, and should only be treated as a general guide.

space/activity	standard maintained illuminance (lux)	adjusted illuminance for people with impaired vision (lux)
flats:		
entrance lobby	200	300
lounge	150	200
kitchen	150-300	300-500
bedroom	100	150
bathroom	150	200
communal areas:		
entrance lobby	200	300
corridor	20-100	100-150
staircases	100	150
lounges	100-300	150-500
dining rooms	150	200
laundries	300	300
treatment rooms	300	300

5.4.2
Daylight

Sheltered housing schemes tend to be designed as compact deep-plan buildings. As a consequence some rooms are windowless and rely totally on artificial lighting, while others need supplementary artificial lighting to augment natural daylight.

It is important to ensure that natural daylight is present in as much of a scheme as is possible. Visual contact with the outside is reassuring and views of distant objects provide an important opportunity for the muscles of the eye to relax. Sunshine brings psychological and physiological benefits and cues the passage of time.

It is likely that corridors will be artificially lit at all times. However it is important that there be some contact with the outside, particularly at the point of arrival from a lift or staircase and that some natural daylight

be admitted, if only as borrowed light from a staircase or communal sitting room. The use of clerestory lights or roof lights can be beneficial in appropriate locations.

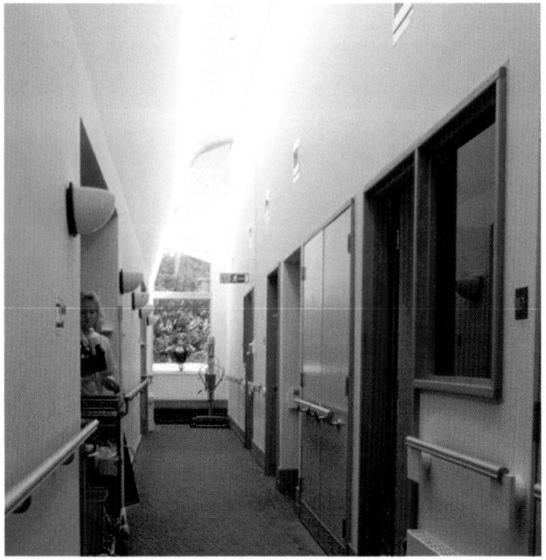

Many flats will depend on artificial lighting in certain areas: the entry, the bathroom and the kitchen. This makes it doubly important that bedrooms and sitting rooms should receive generous amounts of daylight and controlled amounts of direct sunshine. Windows to these rooms should be generous in size with low sills to allow views out for people who are sitting or lying down. Projecting windows can extend the field of vision and can scoop in sunshine from extreme angles.

Internal curtains, translucent drapes and louvres can be used to adjust the quality of daylight: these can be electrically operated if necessary. Translucent drapes and louvres have the effect of diffusing light to create an even distribution and also serve to protect privacy.

In some locations and for some orientations it may be necessary to fit external blinds, sun shades or louvres to limit solar gain and glare. These have the effect of trapping solar radiation before it is transmitted through the glazing. They can also be electrically operated. Such devices should be designed and located with the aid of a heliodon or sundial and should take account of trees and surrounding buildings. They can be designed so low level winter sun is admitted, while high level summer sun is excluded. It is a waste of resources to install sun shading on north facing windows, or on windows which are already shaded by trees.

5.4.3
Artificial Lighting

The design and specification of a lighting scheme involves the following stages:

- An overall lighting concept is developed
- Target illuminances are specified
- The main light source components are selected (lamps and luminaires)
- The luminance of the light sources is specified
- The locations of the light sources are determined
- Positioning of lighting controls
- A control system is specified (switches, dimmers, timers)

Lamps

A huge range of lamps now exist. These fall mainly into two principal categories: incandescent and discharge.

Incandescent filament lamps are the most common in general domestic use. Light is emitted from a glowing filament which is housed in a bulb of glass. Bulbs can be clear, diffusing or directional. They are popular because they are cheap to buy, and because

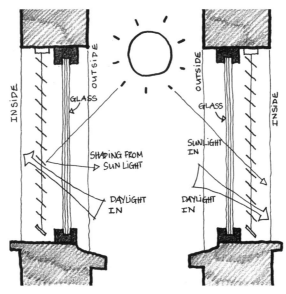

Fig. 5.4.2a: Clerestory lighting

Fig. 5.4.2b: Internal louvres to control daylight & sunlight

of their good colour rendering and flexibility. However, they are notoriously inefficient and produce far more heat than light, they are short lived and create glare. Recent developments include tungsten halide lamps which have better colour rendering and higher efficiency.

Discharge lamps produce light from a fluorescent coating on a glass tube through which an electric discharge is passed. They are efficient and cheap to run, have a long life and create relatively little glare. However, they can be difficult to dim and they suffer from high initial costs.

The choice of lamp will determine the:

- Colour of the light
- Intensity of the light and potential for focusing
- Efficiency of the system (output in lumens/watt)
- Economy of the system (longevity of lamps etc.)
- Potential for control (switching, dimming etc.)
- Ease of maintenance (re-lamping)

Lamps used within flats are generally of the incandescent type, though compact fluorescent lamps can be used successfully in kitchens, bathrooms and hallways. Fluorescent or compact fluorescent lamps are usually specified in communal areas for reasons of cost, efficiency and glare reduction.

Luminaires

The housing into which a lamp is placed is known as a luminaire. Luminaires provide support and electrical connection and modify the quality and direction of light. They are constructed from opaque or translucent materials with matt or reflective surfaces according to their precise function. Most lamps emit omnidirectional light, and a luminaire can redirect light in one or more preferred directions. A well designed

luminaire is capable of producing highly localised light with a minimum of glare.

Luminaires for communal spaces in sheltered housing will generally be selected to create even and diffuse general background lighting with a minimum of glare. This can be achieved using recessed battens with louvres.

5.4.4
Lighting in Flats

Kitchens, bathrooms and hallways are likely to receive little or no natural light and therefore depend mainly on artificial light. Kitchens and bathrooms should be provided with a moderate level of general diffuse background lighting supplemented by more intense task lighting focused on specific locations such as food preparation surfaces, washbasins and shower areas. The sources of any task lighting should not be directly visible. Hallways should be provided with a high level of overall diffuse lighting. Hallway and bathroom lighting can be activated by automatic sensors and switched off on a time delay.

The lighting fittings in living rooms and bedrooms are likely to be selected by the residents themselves. Dimmer switches with possible infra-red remote control should be specified for the main lighting controls. Pendant lamp fittings can be looped to allow for flexibility of location and height. There should be an adequate number of strategically placed sockets for table lamps, pedestal lamps and bedside lamps.

In specifying fittings for flats it should be borne in mind that residents will need to be able to change lamps themselves. Fittings which demand extremes of dexterity and agility should be avoided, as should obscure lamp types which are unlikely to be readily available from local shops.

Fig. 5.4.4a: No task lighting, difficult to see

Fig. 5.4.4b: Good task lighting in a kitchen

Fig. 5.4.4c: Bad task lighting in a private sitting room

Fig. 5.4.4d: Good task lighting in a private sitting room

5.4.5
Lighting in Circulation Spaces

Corridors need a moderate level of general diffuse background lighting. Lamps can be housed within luminaires which illuminate wall surfaces and floors and eliminate all glare. Alternatively a combination of wall-mounted high-level up-lighters and low-level down-lighters can be used to bounce light off the ceiling and illuminate the floor. The entrance to each flat should be picked out with more localised light of higher intensity to highlight name-plate, keyhole and handle. Staircases should be lit in such a way as to accentuate the treads.

A main entrance foyer needs a high level of general diffuse background lighting with localised lighting in the area of the front door, the lift and the notice board. At night, it is important to create an area of intermediate illuminance under the entrance canopy and in the lobby to serve as a transition between the inside and outside of a building. Route lighting at a scheme entrance and in circulation spaces will help people find their way around a building.

5.4.6
Lighting in Communal Spaces

Dining rooms need a moderate level of general diffuse background lighting with localised lighting directed down onto tables. This can be achieved by providing each table with its own lamp housed in a pendant luminaire which focuses the majority of light directly down towards the table and diffuses the balance upwards towards a light reflecting ceiling.

Sitting rooms should be provided with versatile lighting which can be altered to suit the occasion. Lighting for general use would comprise moderate level diffuse background lighting with more intense

localised lighting focused on small groups. Parties and meetings would require a higher level of general lighting. Entertainments would need a low level of background lighting with localised lighting focused on the performers.

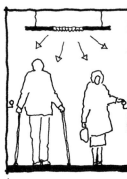 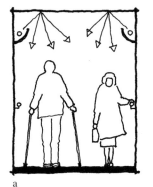

a   b

 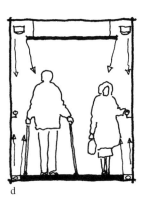

c   d

a Continuous strips of up-lighting, no glare, diffuse light
b Suspended ceiling with continuous strips of lighting from prismatic diffusers
c Lighting shelf with continuous concealed lighting, no glare, diffuse light
d Recessed continuous strip lighting in ceiling and floor, no glare, diffuse light

Fig. 5.4.5a: Lighting in corridors

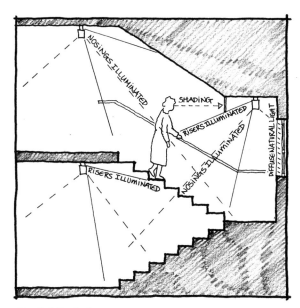

Fig. 5.4.5b: Lighting on a staircase

Fig. 5.4.5c: Transitional entrance lighting

5.5
Acoustics

People are more likely to suffer some form of hearing impairment as they become older. They also become much more sensitive to extraneous sound: the neighbour's TV, a door banging in the corridor, a passing ambulance. It is therefore important that the acoustic environment be designed to minimise the effects of impairments and to minimise unwanted sound intrusion.

5.5.1
The Nature of Sound

Sound is a form of energy which is transmitted as a standing wave through the air or as a vibration through solids. The pitch of a sound is determined by its frequency which is measured in hertz (Hz). The human ear distinguishes sounds in a range from 20 - 20,000 Hz, though the range 100 - 3,000 Hz is of principal interest to building acousticians. Each doubling of frequency is equivalent to a single musical octave. The level or intensity of a sound relates to the magnitude of the fluctuating air pressure within the standing wave and is measured in decibels (dB). The lower threshold of hearing for most people is about 5 dB, while a pneumatic drill emits a sound of about 120 dB. The intensity of a sound decays in proportion to the square of the distance from its source. Most naturally occurring sounds cover a range of frequencies with different sound levels at the different frequencies.

The behaviour of sound within an enclosed room is affected by the size and proportions of the room and by the absorptive qualities of its surfaces and contents. A room with highly reflective surfaces such as a swimming pool or coffee bar has a long reverberation time and is characterised by a confusion of overlapping sounds and echoes. A room with highly absorptive surfaces such as a hotel lounge has a short reverberation time and is characterised by muffled sounds which decay quickly.

People with normal hearing rarely experience total silence and are accustomed to hear a background hum of sounds which emanate from their immediate surroundings, from adjoining rooms or from the outside world. The normally acceptable level of background sound is about 30 dB in a bedroom and about 40 dB in a living room. Irritation or discomfort will result when the levels of extraneous sounds combine to exceed these acceptable background levels.

The designer's aim will generally be to enhance or modify purposeful sound through careful adjustment of reverberation times, and to reduce or limit the intrusion of extraneous sound.

5.5.2
Sound Quality

The communal spaces within a sheltered housing scheme should generally be designed with fairly short reverberation times in order to cut down on the general level of background noise. This makes it easier for most residents to take part in conversations.

The acoustic environment of a dining room can be enhanced by using absorptive materials on the walls and ceiling. Although a carpeted floor would also help to reduce the reverberation time and eliminate impact noises, carpets are difficult to clean and can harbour dust or harmful bacteria: foam-backed rubber or vinyl sheet offer a better alternative. Furniture should be fitted with rubber silencers, and crockery should be selected for its acoustic properties.

Corridors and staircases should also be fitted with sound deadening materials in order to reduce reverberation time and limit the effects of any impact sound. Corridor floors could be finished in rubber or vinyl sheet with a cushion underlay or in a hard-wearing fitted carpet. The walls and ceiling should incorporate absorptive finishes. Lower reverberation times in circulation spaces can help to eliminate any institutional ambience and can also reduce air-borne transmission to neighbouring flats.

5.5.3
Sound Intrusion

The extraneous sound which enters a dwelling will either be air-borne or structure-borne and may originate from a wide range of different sources. Air-borne sound from the exterior might be generated by traffic, by passing aeroplanes or by neighbouring buildings. It is transmitted through the outside walls of the dwelling and particularly through windows. Air-borne sound from within a scheme might originate in a neighbour's flat, in an adjoining corridor or in a communal space such as the main sitting room. It is transmitted through floors, ceilings and party walls and via service ducts. Structure-borne sound can result from the impact of feet on a floor or the vibration of a piece of machinery and is transmitted through the fabric of the building.

Extraneous sounds cause irritation or discomfort when they exceed the generally accepted level of background noise within a room. The effect of extraneous sounds can be reduced by removing or reducing them at source, by altering the relative positions of the room and the sound source, by erecting intermediate sound barriers, or by improving the sound insulation of the room's enclosing envelope.

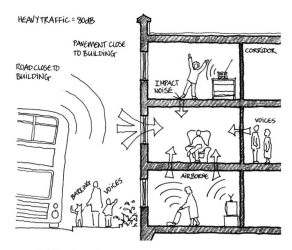

Fig. 5.5.3a: Sound transmission

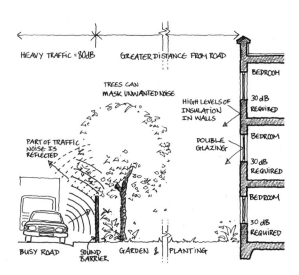

Fig. 5.5.3b: Reducing sounds from outside

The sound level at the kerbside of a busy road can be as high as 80 dB. The acceptable level of background noise within a bedroom is 30 dB. Thus, if a bedroom is to be located close to a busy road it will be necessary to reduce the effect of the traffic noise by a total of about 50 dB. This can be achieved in part by maximising the distance of the bedroom from the roadside, in part by introducing sound barriers between the building and the road, and in part by ensuring that the enclosing wall of the bedroom is constructed to achieve adequate levels of sound insulation.

5.5.4
Avoiding Problems

The intrusion of unwanted sound can sometimes be limited by removing or controlling the sound at its source:

- The problem illustrated in Fig. 5.5.3a could be solved by closing the road or restricting the traffic which it carries, though it has to be said that this is unlikely to be a practicable option.
- The neighbour who suffers from partial deafness might be persuaded to turn down the TV and use a hearing aid.
- Corridors can be fitted with cushioned floors to cut down on the generation of sound and with absorptive ceilings to reduce its propagation.
- Front doors to flats can be fitted with damped closing mechanisms and their frames can be fitted with a cushioning strip in order to eliminate the noise of banging, a common cause of complaint in sheltered housing.
- Noisy equipment such as pumps and lift motors can be fixed on resilient mountings and located within insulated enclosures.

Sound intrusion can also be controlled by planning:

- The problem illustrated in Fig. 5.5.3a could be solved by moving the scheme to another site, or by locating all bedrooms on the side of the building away from the road, or by pulling the building as far back from the road as possible.
- Flats can be carefully handed so that neighbouring living rooms do not occur next to bedrooms.

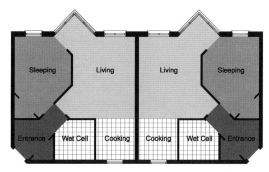

Fig. 5.5.4a: Handed pairs of flats

- Care can be taken to ensure that flats are not placed next to lifts or staircases, or above kitchens and plant rooms.

5.5.5
Controlling Sound Transmission

The final defence against sound intrusion is to use methods of construction which offer good sound insulating properties. The problem with sound insulation is that the performance of any wall or floor element is only as good as its weakest part. This can be illustrated by imagining a compartment which is enclosed by a thick concrete wall: it only requires one small hole to enable conversations to be conducted through it. Thus a wall may be designed to a theoretical target value, but its performance will be compromised by poor workmanship or by the penetration of service ducts.

Separating Walls and Floors

The requirements for air-borne and impact sound insulation in the separating floors and walls of multiple dwellings are given in the Building Regulations for England and Wales (1991). These state in brief that 'separating walls shall resist the transmission of air-borne sound' and 'separating floors and stairs shall resist the transmission of air-borne and impact sound'. The regulations set out a series of 'deemed to satisfy' construction details as well as laying down testing procedures for new forms of construction. Insulation values are defined for a range of frequencies, but in simplest terms the required mean values are as follows:

air-borne sound reduction in walls	53 dB
air-borne sound reduction in floors	52 dB
impact sound reduction in floors	61 dB

Generally the air-borne sound insulating properties of a wall or floor element depend either on mass or on isolation or on a combination of the two. Mass is achieved simply by increasing the thickness and density of the element. Isolation is achieved by forming a sandwich element from two or more separate membranes with intervening air gaps. In theory it is possible to achieve relatively high insulation values using light-weight sandwich construction though this is highly dependent on the quality of construction.

Party walls are usually formed with solid single leaf block construction which is plastered on each face. The 'deemed to satisfy' requirements for this form of construction stipulate 215mm blockwork to a density of 1840 kg/m³. The core thickness can be reduced to 150mm if the plaster is replaced by separate leaves of cellular plaster board with minimum 25mm cavities. Some 'deemed to satisfy' construction details are set out in Fig. 5.5.5a

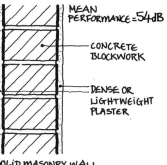

SOLID MASONRY WALL

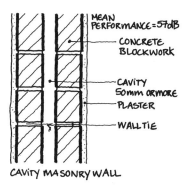

CAVITY MASONRY WALL

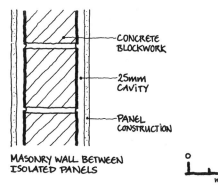

MASONRY WALL BETWEEN ISOLATED PANELS

Fig. 5.5.5a: Deemed to satisfy construction for separating walls - air-borne sound (Source: BRE, 1993b)

Separating floors are usually constructed of solid precast or in-situ concrete with an additional screed: in order to meet the deemed to satisfy standards the overall mass in such construction should be 365kg/m² for base plus screed (equivalent to 1840kg/m³ for a 200mm thick floor). Replacing a solid screed with a floating timber floor on spacer battens over a resilient quilt effects a marked improvement on impact sound reduction. This form of construction provides an accessible floor cavity which can be used for IT cabling as well as for some forms of underfloor heating.

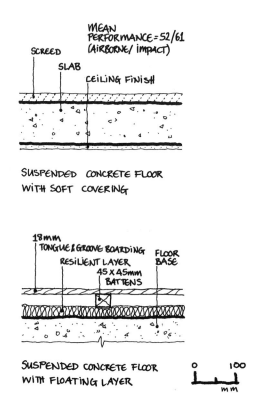

SCREED
MEAN PERFORMANCE = 52/61 (AIRBORNE/IMPACT)
SLAB
CEILING FINISH

SUSPENDED CONCRETE FLOOR WITH SOFT COVERING

18mm TONGUE & GROOVE BOARDING
RESILIENT LAYER
45 X 45mm BATTENS
FLOOR BASE

SUSPENDED CONCRETE FLOOR WITH FLOATING LAYER

0   100
mm

Fig. 5.5.5b: Deemed to satisfy construction for separating floors - air-borne and impact sound (Source: BRE,1993b)

Pipes and Ducts

The best defence systems against noise transmission can be breached by pipework and ducts which are badly designed or installed. Pipework can be both a source of noise and the means through which sounds are transmitted from one part of a building to another. Care should be taken to ensure that ducts and pipework do not pass directly through habitable rooms. Pipework should be securely fixed and all breaches through walls need to be carefully sleeved. Ducts should be adequately encased and properly sealed at all entry points.

External Walls

The Building Regulations make no stipulations for external wall construction. Here the influence of the window element is so great that in most cases the method of wall construction is of little consequence.

The sound reduction achieved by windows is largely influenced by their size and by the quality of their construction. Sealed double glazing units are reasonably effective in cutting sound transmission, though only if they are installed in well fitting and sealed frames. Opening lights need to be well sealed if they are to cut down sound transmission when closed - all sound reduction is lost when windows are open. Minimum requirements for ventilation can be met by installing trickle ventilators with sound absorbent baffles.

In critical situations where the level of extraneous sound at a point on the external envelope exceeds 60 dB it will be necessary to install double window construction: the pains of glass need to be set at least 150mm apart in separate frames with absorptive linings. This form of construction is capable of achieving a reduction in excess of 40 dB. Timber shutters can be used to achieve higher levels of reduction during the night for the purposes of sleeping. Mechanical ventilation will be required.

Internal Partitions

Most flats in sheltered housing schemes are occupied by single people and so there is no real need to achieve high levels of sound insulation for internal partitions. Ideally the enclosing wall of a bathroom would offer a degree of reduction particularly towards the sitting room, though this is likely to be compromised by the door opening. A target value of 40 dB could be achieved using 75mm dense blockwork plastered on both faces, or plaster board on 75mm studs with an insulating quilt.

Similar target values should be set for partitions in two-bedroom flats, particularly those between the living room and any bedroom or between adjacent bedrooms.

5.6
Special Equipment

As people become less mobile they come to depend more and more on aids of one sort or another and on assistance from friends, family and carers. Aids fall into two main categories: static and mechanical. Static aids include walking sticks, zimmer frames, transfer boards, grab rails, leg lifters and bed rope ladders. Mechanical aids include wheelchairs, powered mattresses, mobile hoists, ceiling hoists, stair lifts and passenger lifts.

The use of aids is often regarded by older people as being undignified because it implies an acceptance of frailty and highlights their loss of independence. However, as frailty increases necessity conquers diffidence and people soon realise the extent to which they can become re-empowered.

Beyond a certain point mechanical aids are employed as much to benefit the carer as the cared for. Carers and helpers often risk injuring themselves in attempting to lift people without aids. Back injuries are common amongst carers and it is now recommended that they should avoid manual lifting as much as possible. Although the capital cost of lifting equipment may be high it is far outweighed by the social and medical costs which result from injury. The interests of carers are now covered by legislation such as the 1974 Health and Safety at Work Act and the 1992 Manual Handling Operations Regulations.

The choice and specification of aids and equipment fall within the purview of professionals such as occupational therapists. They have detailed knowledge of what equipment is available and how it should be used. Much of it will be specific to the needs of individual residents and may have little bearing on building design. The following notes deal with two further categories of equipment which place special demands on space, construction and the environment: hoists and lifts. More detailed information can be obtained from a report published by the Disability Information Trust (Clevely, 1996).

5.6.1
Hoists

Three types of hoist are commonly used in sheltered housing: mobile hoists which are mounted on wheels and can be moved freely from place to place, ceiling hoists which move along fixed tracks and bath hoists which can be either mobile or fixed. All three are produced in manual and powered versions.

Most hoists employ some form of detachable seat or sling. It is important the correct type is chosen to suit the needs of a particular individual. Slings or seats which are used by more than one person can cause cross infection: it is therefore important to specify fittings which are washable or provide each user with their own fitting. Fittings should only be used with the type of hoist for which they were specifically manufactured.

The use of hoists brings a number of benefits:

- They reduce the risk of physical injury which may result from lifting, straining or handling
- They offer a greater degree of independence and freedom to people with mobility problems
- They give access to facilities that would otherwise be inaccessible such as baths, hydrotherapy pools, toilets; they reduce the need for bed pans or bed baths

- They are relatively easy to operate, and can be quickly mastered after simple instruction (some can be self-operated, some can be operated by friends and family, some require professional operators)
- They can be used in emergencies to lift people who have had an accident

There are currently over 60 hoists and at least 150 different types of sling and seat available on the market. It is therefore advisable to seek the advice of an occupational therapist before selecting a piece of equipment. Selection criteria should include safety, stability, comfort, bulk, lifting capacity, possibilities for cleaning, choice of seats and slings, manoeuvrability, battery specification and cost. The specific needs of the user and the carers should be considered as should the main spatial and structural characteristics of the rooms in which the equipment will be used.

Mobile Hoists

Mobile hoists are mounted on wheels or castors and can be used to carry someone from one place to another or to transfer them from one piece of equipment to another. They can be manually or power operated. Most  hoists can be operated within spaces designed to wheelchair standards, though undercarriages may need clearance under beds, baths and chairs. It is important to carry out a full trial on site before making a purchase. A typical Extra Care scheme might be equipped with two or three mobile hoists of different types and it is important to provide adequate storage facilities.

Mobile hoists offer a number of advantages within the context of an Extra Care scheme:

- A pool of two or three hoists is usually sufficient to serve a whole scheme
- Slings and chair attachments are interchangeable and can be allocated to regular users to prevent cross-infection
- They can be used in an emergency to assist someone who has fallen down
- They are flexible, versatile and relatively inexpensive
- They can easily be stored out of sight
- They can be used in assisted bathrooms: some sling attachments can be immersed in water

The possible disadvantages are:

- Very heavy people are difficult to propel and may need two carers, one to steady and one to push. Carers must be trained to manoeuvre correctly without risking injury to themselves or their passenger
- Small castors are difficult to operate on carpets, though larger castors will require greater clearance under furniture
- The fact that the sling is liable to swing can be disconcerting
- Mobile hoists are not intended to be used over long distances. For longer journeys it is advisable to transfer the passenger to a wheelchair

Ceiling Hoists

Ceiling hoists run along fixed overhead tracks, and connect pre-designated locations within a flat. Tracks must be fitted to ceilings and necessitate the adaptation of doorframes and removal of wall panels. They can negotiate curves and 90° corners and can be fitted with junctions to connect to more than one destination.

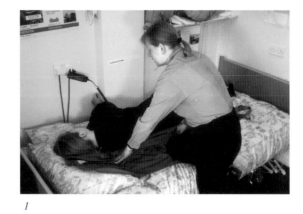

1

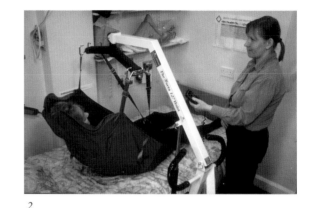

2

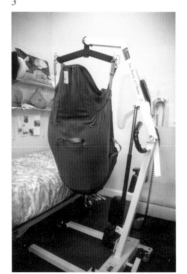

3

4

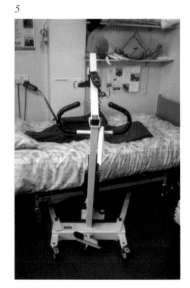

5

Fig. 5.6.1a: A mobile hoist in use

1

2

3

4

Fig. 5.6.1b: Using a ceiling hoist

Ceiling hoists are operated from a motor which is attached to the track. The sling is fixed to a rigid spreader bar which can be raised and lowered. The whole operation of lifting and moving is controlled by a hand-held console.

Manufacturers claim that ceiling hoists can be used without assistance. This may well hold true for young disabled people who have strong upper bodies and lots of determination, but not as a general rule for older people.

Ceiling hoists are usually used to connect the bedroom to the bathroom and for this reason it helps if there is a single door between the two. Such an 'en suite' arrangement may also be advantageous for wheelchair users. However it is quite impractical to omit the door which links a bathroom to the hallway and the rest of the flat and it can be difficult to plan a satisfactory arrangement of fittings in a bathroom with two doors.

The advantages of ceiling hoists are:

- They eliminate the need for lifting and reduce the risk of injury both to passenger and carer
- They are relatively easy to use and have the potential to be self-operated
- They do not require any additional floor space

In the context of Extra Care housing ceiling hoists have a number of possible disadvantages:

- They are expensive to install: a ceiling hoist can cost three times as much as a mobile hoist
- A ceiling hoist is fixed and only benefits one user along one predetermined track
- A ceiling hoist remains in full view and creates a clinical ambience
- Doors need to be full height and ceilings may need to be strengthened

On balance the use of ceiling hoists seems to be more appropriate to nursing homes and hospitals. Mobile hoists are a lower cost solution and offer the benefit of flexibility and versatility. It seems likely that future improvements to mobile hoist design will swing the balance even further in their favour.

Bath Hoists

At least one assisted bathroom will be provided in most Extra Care schemes. This will be particularly true of schemes which do not provide bath tubs in individual bathrooms. Not all assisted bathrooms are intended for disabled users, and there may be more than one category of bathroom in any scheme.

Of the many different types of assisted bath there are some which incorporate hoist equipment, some which, through their design, remove the need for hoists, and some which require the provision of separate hoists. Hoists which serve the latter category may be floor mounted or mobile.

Mobile hoists manoeuvre the user to either a seated or a lying position, in order to lift them directly into the bath. They are either manually or hydraulically operated. It is important that the hoist fits properly into the bath and that the sling allows the bather to be fully immersed. Adequate space should be provided in the bathroom to manoeuvre the hoist and there needs to be adequate clearance under the bath to accommodate the undercarriage.

Floor mounted hoists have a seat attachment which swivels out over the bath and lifts and lowers the user either hydraulically or manually. Some hoists are designed to be used without assistance but it is generally recommended that a carer be present. Adequate space should be provided beside the bath for the seat to swing out.

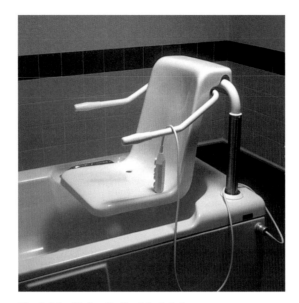
Fig. 5.6.1c: Hydraulic fitted bath hoist

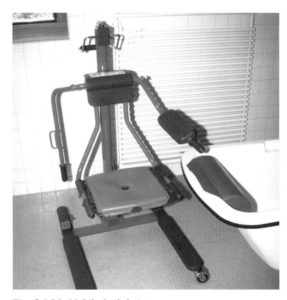
Fig. 5.6.1d: Mobile bath hoist

5.6.2
Lifts and Stair Lifts

Stair Lifts

Stair lifts are used as a means of helping disabled people to get from one floor to another in existing buildings where it is not possible to install lifts. They are also sometimes used to negotiate small changes of level which may occur between different parts of the same floor. Stair lifts are slow and cumbersome to use and rarely accommodate a wheelchair.

New Extra Care schemes should be designed to eliminate small changes of level and will in every case be fitted with conventional lifts to serve all floors. It is unlikely, therefore, that a stair lift would ever be needed and their use is not recommended.

Fig. 5.6.2a: Typical stair-lift installation

Lifts

It is accepted practice to install a lift in any Extra Care scheme of more than one storey. In larger schemes of three or more storeys it is advisable to install two lifts, partly in order to cut down on waiting time and partly to provide back up in the case of breakdown. Lifts should normally be placed in a central location and the scheme should be planned to cut down on travel distance. Where two lifts are provided, queuing theory would suggest that they be located in the same place, though in more extensive schemes it might be advantageous to separate them.

There are two main types of lift in common use: traction lifts and hydraulic lifts. Hydraulic lifts are slow but extremely smooth running. Although they are cheap to run, their high capital cost rules them out for sheltered housing. In specifying a normal traction lift it is necessary to decide between speed and comfort: slow lifts would seem to be better suited to the needs of older people. It is advisable to specify a lift car which can accommodate such things as a wheelchair, a hoist, a stretcher, a coffin, a food trolley, furniture etc.

The following general specifications are recommended:

- Car dimensions: 1.1m wide (minimum and ideal) by 1.4m minimum (2.1m ideal) deep with a clear door opening of 820mm minimum (900mm ideal)
- Carrying capacity: 8 persons or 630 kilos maximum; speed: 0.63 metres/second
- The car interior should be free from glare and well illuminated to levels which relate to the level of lighting at each landing
- The car should be fitted with a continuous hand-rail and a pull-down seat

- The car should be fitted with emergency alarm and a two way communication system
- Doors should be slow action and touch sensitive
- Controls both within and without should be clear, visible, tactile, easy to operate and located between 900mm and 1300mm above floor level
- Information should ideally be supplied in both visual and auditory form
- The car interior should be 'friendly' and 'reassuring'. Although mirrors can help people in wheelchairs they can also cause confusion to dementia sufferers and, on balance, should be omitted

Lift landing areas should be well lit and ideally should incorporate a window which gives a view to the outside to help with orientation. Each landing can incorporate special features or a specific colour scheme so as to distinguish it.

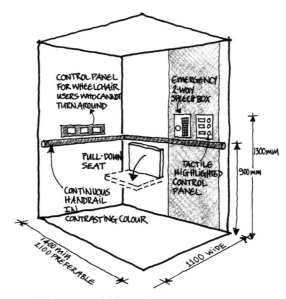

Fig 5.6.2b: A typical lift installation

If possible no flat should be located immediately adjacent to a lift shaft. Where this is unavoidable, steps should be taken to provide adequate sound insulation, and the flat should be planned so that its bedrooms are well away from the common wall.

Although lifts are usually immobilised in the case of a fire, the lift lobby in a sheltered housing scheme may be designated as a place of refuge and the lifts used by fire-fighters to evacuate any disabled people.

5.7 Smarter Homes

We are living through a technological revolution, the full implications of which have still to be appreciated by the majority of people. Although the new information technologies have had a considerable effect on the work place and on such specialised buildings as hospitals, their impact on the home remains limited. Sheltered housing may well prove to be one of the first types of residential building to be affected to any degree by information technology, partly because of its potential to enhance older people's capacity for self-care and partly because it can enable care by others to be delivered in a more effective and efficient way.

Many residents of sheltered housing were born during the first two decades of the twentieth century into homes in which the electric light and the radio set were still novelties and the private telephone was a rarity. Television became a universal form of mass communication during the 1950s when most of them were entering middle age and the personal computer arrived on the scene after they had reached retirement. It is quite ironic, therefore, that they should now find themselves in the vanguard of the drive to create 'smarter homes'.

Developments in the fields of telecommunications and

information technology could lead to the production of both 'low tech' and 'high tech' aids which would have an enormous potential to support older people in their day-to-day lives. Yet very few of the fittings which are currently produced for residential environments incorporate design features which are suited to people with impairments. Most domestic appliances are designed for the able-bodied market and do not offer features which would enable individuals with reduced physical, sensory or cognitive abilities to use them successfully (Valins & Salter, 1996). Equipment which is developed specifically for elderly or disabled people often has a prosthetic appearance and is usually very much more expensive than that which is marketed with the 'able-bodied' in mind.

Manufacturers of 'assistive technologies' compete by incorporating additional 'features' regardless of necessity or desirability. Their goal is to offer apparent versatility rather than to promote greater convenience or control. The addition of extra features and functions results in increased complexity but reduces the usability of a product.

'Smart homes technology' promises a whole Pandora's Box of innovations, though not all of what is possible is actually available or affordable at the moment. However, a building which is built today can expect to have a life of at least 25 years before it faces a major refit and it should be designed in such a way as to anticipate the likely developments of the next decades.

5.7.1
Yesterday's Technologies

Those innovations of the recent past which are now in common use might be described as 'yesterday's technologies'. They include the radio, TV and the telephone. Although they were developed yesterday, they are still important today and provision must be made for them.

Telecommunications

- Entry Phones
  Conventional entry phones run on wired systems, though recent developments use radio signals. They connect the main front door to the warden and to each

  of the residents. A resident can speak to a visitor via a handset and activate a door release. Sockets for the handset can be located in the bedroom and sitting room. The use of CCTV enables the warden to monitor visitors, and in some developments the images can be channelled to individual TV sets to enable residents to see their visitors on screen if they choose to.

- Television
  Television plays an important part in the lives of older people. Recent developments include the availability of new channels via satellite and cable, community based channels, in-house video channels and teletext systems. Residents in Extra Care should have the possibility to subscribe to new channels and new transmission systems as they become available. TV and power sockets should be located strategically at 900mm above floor level in both the living room and the bedroom.

- Telephone
  There have been very rapid advances in telephone systems during the past decade. Residents can now choose between competing companies and can elect to subscribe to

  a wide variety of services, including answering, paging, caller identification and fax. A variety of different types of handsets are now available. They include cordless phones which can operate over a fairly wide area and 'mobiles'. Handsets should be chosen with clear visual and tactile displays. Battery charging systems should be safe and simple to understand and use. Telephone sockets should be located 900mm above floor level at key locations and in proximity to power sockets.

- Computer
  Microchips and mini-computers are now installed as components in many items of domestic equipment such as microwaves and cookers. Facilities should be provided for personal computers and cabling should give access to 'e mail' and 'internet' services.

Alarms

- Personal Alarms

    Enormous strides have been made in the development of personal alarm systems during the past few years. Earlier 'pull-cord' systems are now being superseded by systems which are activated by either portable triggers or voice triggers. The alarm can raise the in-house manager, an alarm control centre, or a neighbour. Two way conversations are possible.

- Fire

    Smoke detectors have become a mandatory feature of sheltered housing and within flats are normally located in kitchens, living rooms and bedrooms. Fire alarms can be both auditory and visual. Alarm systems can be phased to avoid unnecessary panic and to ensure orderly evacuation.

- Security

    Older people live in great fear of burglars and intruders. Security systems are needed, not only to keep out traditional night-time burglars but also to deter day-time con-men.

    Traditional keys can now be replaced by swipe cards. These have the advantage of being easy to carry and use. They can also be reprogrammed from time to time.

    In certain localities ground floor accommodation may need to be fitted with additional window locks and alarm systems. Movement-sensitive security lighting should be installed in gardens and car parks.

    CCTV installations provide an effective deterrent to unwanted intruders and can also be used for monitoring residents' movements in corridors and staircases

Environmental Control

- Heating & Ventilation

    The scope for the control of heating systems is dependent on the type of heating system which is installed. Centralised scheme heating systems allow for three levels of control: control of the whole scheme which can be monitored and set by the scheme manager, control of a flat which can be monitored by the manager and set either by the manager or the tenant, and control of an individual space which can be monitored by the manager and set by either the manager or the resident. Monitoring and control can also be linked automatically to outside temperature sensors. All the evidence suggests that older people generally do not bother to adjust room or emitter thermostats, and that they prefer to adjust their heating either by opening a window, or by switching on a booster such as a radiant electric fire.

- Lighting

    The use of dimmer switches and infra-red remote control enable residents to adjust lighting levels to suit their activities and to respond to levels of daylight. Lighting can also be programme controlled, either in relation to time or to prevailing outside lighting conditions.

Physical Controls

Control systems can also be used to perform those physical tasks which frail people find difficult or irksome.

- Doors

    Systems for opening and closing doors using remote control are now widely available and can be of great assistance to wheelchair users. They are relatively expensive to install and would not be included in any standard specification package.

- Windows

    Remote control systems can be used to operate curtains and blinds, and can be programmed to respond to levels of daylight or to timers. These would be fitted by residents themselves.

- Furniture

    Recent developments in furniture include power operated reclining chairs and beds which can raise themselves or which provide massage.

5.7.2
Tomorrow's Technologies

The term 'smart home technology' refers to intelligent control systems which can be used to simplify the interface between people and their domestic environment. Smart home technology can bring together the various independent functions which have been described above as 'yesterday's technologies' and control them from a single system. Fire alarms, call systems, telephones, entry phones, pagers, door openers, thermostats, dimmers which today all require separate controls have the potential to be brought together in one intelligent system.

A smart home is one in which digital technologies have been installed to facilitate communication and control of a variety of functions. There is no precise definition of the technologies or functions involved, although the term implies the use of integrated and interactive systems within the home and between the home and external service providers. The control system is designed to make all tasks within the home easier to perform, thus encouraging greater independence of action and outlook. The control system makes it possible to operate doors and windows, to turn on heating or household appliances and switch lights on and off. It can be programmed to operate with push-button instructions, voice commands or even minimal head or eye movements.

Services and Benefits

The following is a list of a few of the services which smart home technology could make available:

- Tele-medicine
  This might include remote monitoring of general state of health.
- Remote monitoring
  A variety of physical indicators can be monitored: incontinence, sleep pattern, body temperature, etc.
- Tele-help
  Improved management of home care and domiciliary services
- Tele-rescue
  Improved alarm call systems
- Entertainment
- Tele-shopping
- Home banking
- Networks (friends, special interest groups etc.)
- Audio-navigation
  Operated by sensors and 'react card systems'

The benefits which are claimed for smart home technologies include:

- Improved medical and home care services
- A reduced need to use hospital facilities
- Improved access to modern information systems
- A reduced sense of isolation
- Greater independence, a reduced dependency on relatives and neighbours

The System

Smart systems include the following four components:

- basic 'node' technologies - the switches, sensors and actuators
- software to control applications
- the 'bus' - an infrastructure for linking different nodes into a network
- external information-based services

The 'node' can be a transponder or a transducer, an input or output device, a transmitter or receiver. Because each node is an intelligent unit, units can be joined without risk of central failure. Low cost sensors, instruments and sub-systems from different manufacturers can be integrated into one overall system. This principle is known as interoperability, the ability to 'plug and play' components from a variety of sources into one standard and compatible system in such a way as to exploit a wider choice of products with lower installation, maintenance and expansion costs.

A high frequency digital data transport network, the 'bus', carries control and feedback signals between nodes. The network runs on a small 'twisted pair' cable installed in conjunction with the mains cabling. Whereas in a conventional lighting installation the switch is directly wired to the lamp and makes the connection to the electricity supply, in a smart system the switch sends a coded message along the bus to all of the nodes in the network, though only the lamp which is programmed to react to the code is connected (Gann & Iwashita, 1995).

The bus system has the potential to offer the following:

- a powerful set of modular building blocks which enable the implementation of an interoperable control system
- an ability to mix and match products and systems from a variety of vendors
- an open infrastructure with common protocols
- a compatibility for systems to grow and be upgraded incrementally
- a simple user interface

There are already a number of competing bus systems in existence including the following: the European Installation Bus (EIB), an American system known as Echelon and the European Homes Systems (EHS). These are not mutually compatible and no single system has been adopted as the standard.

5.7.3
The Implications for Today

Accommodating Innovations

In order to anticipate the likely developments of the immediate future it will be necessary to incorporate ducts for bus cables, both within flats and in the scheme as a whole. However, it is difficult to persuade clients to invest in provisions for systems which do not exist, particularly if there is a strong possibility that any ducting which is provided may prove to be inappropriate when the time comes to use it.

Typical traditional construction uses concrete structural floors with wet screeds and blockwork walls with wet plaster and is not ideally suited to retro-fitting of cables. However, adaptable light-weight construction methods are not suitable for sheltered housing, particularly because of their acoustic performance.

The following are a few alternative methods of providing cabling ducts within flats.

- Floating Floors

    A floating floor can be substituted for a wet in-situ screed. A number of alternative construction systems can be employed: the simplest is to fix tongued and grooved chipboard to 19mm battens laid on a resilient layer over the structural concrete floor. The resilient layer can improve sound reduction and thermal insulation depending on its specification. The use of floating floors brings a number of advantages:

    - the floor void is reasonably accessible and can be used to install a wide variety of cabling
    - the floor void can be used to install underfloor heating
    - the isolated construction improves impact sound reduction
    - it removes a wet trade from the construction process

    The disadvantage is:

    - it is still necessary to run conduits up walls to serve wall-mounted sockets

- Ceiling Coves

    Ceiling coves offer a practical method to introduce a cabling duct into an existing flat. Their advantages are:

    - they are easy to install and access

- they offer continuous unbroken runs
- they are not unsightly

    Their disadvantage is:

    - it is still necessary to run conduits down the wall to serve wall-mounted sockets

- Skirtings

    Skirtings also offer a practical method to introduce a cabling duct into an existing flat. Their advantages are:

    - they are easy to install and access
    - they are not unsightly

    Their disadvantages are:

    - it is still necessary to run conduits up walls to serve wall-mounted sockets
    - they do not offer unbroken runs except at the perimeter

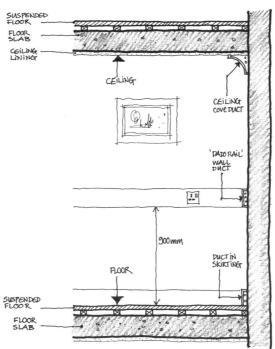

Fig. 5.7.3a Alternative duct positions

- Dado Rails

    Dado rails can be fitted as a cover to a wall duct at a height of approximately 900mm above finished floor, corresponding to the height recommended for sockets and switches. The cover can be almost flush with the wall and 'lost' or it can be expressed as a timber rail. Their advantages are:

    - they are easy to install and access
    - they need not be unsightly
    - they do not require additional vertical drops

    Their disadvantage is:

    - they do not offer unbroken runs except at the perimeter

5.7.4
Dilemmas

Smart home technology represents a vision which is driven by a sense of what is technically possible. However, the reality remains for the moment an array of disparate, fragmented stand-alone systems and semi-integrated services. The elderly population is being targeted as a potential market for assistive technologies, but the variety of their impairments demands a wide range of solutions, and the development of the other home building technologies - construction, furniture, equipment - has not kept pace with the development of new information technologies.

Smart home technology could well bring many advantages to older people, but its application to care provision raises important ethical questions. The use of remote monitoring may well improve the efficiency of care delivery but it may also dehumanise care and inflict greater isolation. It also threatens to erode privacy and encourage an ambience of 'Big Brother'. CCTV cameras and voice boxes can transmit images and sounds from within a private flat to a central monitoring system. While such transmission can be of enormous assistance in monitoring the care of older people and will undoubtedly help to save lives, it is clearly open to abuse. The use of remote monitoring must strike a balance between the advantages to health and welfare and the individual's right to lead an independent and dignified private life. In this respect it may be necessary to draw a line between sheltered housing and other forms of accommodation such as residential care homes and nursing homes.

5.8
Fire Safety

Older people in Extra Care housing are at risk because there is a higher probability that they might inadvertently be the cause of a fire and because, in the event of a fire breaking out there is a higher probability that they might not be able to move to a point of safety. However the implementation of a 'belt and braces' approach to fire safety can cause older people a number of problems in their daily lives.

5.8.1
The Principles of Fire Safety

The following are the main principles of fire safety:

- Prevention

    Everything should be done to ensure that a fire doesn't break out in the first place
- Detection

    If a fire does break out it should be detected immediately and the alarm raised. Extra Care schemes require a comprehensive system of smoke detection and fire alarm
- Containment

    Fire should be contained within the room of origin for as long as possible. Furnishings and fittings should be selected for low combustibility and spread of flame. Fire

compartmentalisation should be strictly enforced - fire doors held open on electro-magnetic catches are safer than fire doors which are propped open by fire extinguishers!
- Smoke Control

    Smoke should be prevented from reaching escape routes
- Extinguishment

    The fire should be extinguished as quickly as possible. Fire extinguishers should be properly located and well maintained. There should be adequate access for fire engines.
- Evacuation

    People should be able to move along protected routes to places of safety

Overall fire safety depends on how a building is designed and constructed, on finishes and furnishings, on the installation and proper maintenance of fire alarm and extinguishing systems and on the adoption of correct procedures. However, fire prevention is not an exact science and there are different opinions about what constitutes correct procedures. Although in most types of building evacuation is given a higher priority than extinguishment, where older people are involved evacuation may not be a practicable alternative. One school of thought maintains that every effort should be made to contain a fire and that residents should be encouraged to remain in the relative safety of their flats until the fire has been extinguished or they can be safely evacuated. An alternative theory argues for the creation of places of refuge on each floor next to a lift and a protected fire escape stair so that assisted evacuation can gradually take place.

5.8.2
The Causes of Fire

Fires may be caused in many different ways: an electrical fault, a falling candle, a burning chip pan. Two main preventable causes are lighted cigarettes and gas cookers.

A late night cigarette which slips down the side of an armchair or falls on to the bedclothes can lead quickly to a fatal fire. A total of forty two people died as a result of two such incidents in nursing homes:

'The fire was believed to have been started by an elderly and partially paralysed resident dropping a lighted cigarette after she had fallen asleep...Smoking was prohibited but it was known that the resident who was believed to have started the fire was addicted to smoking and in spite of her disabilities was quite capable of lighting her own cigarettes... One of the residents died of heart failure, the other seventeen died of carbon monoxide poisoning.'

'One patient was sitting up in a small day room at the end of the ward and it was believed that she dropped a lighted cigarette end onto the chair before going to bed... twenty four patients died as a result of asphyxiation.'

(Strother Smith, 1981)

Cigarette smoking is an addictive habit which is harmful to the health both of smokers and anyone in their vicinity. Although attempts have been made to write no-smoking clauses into leases it is difficult to ban smoking entirely from sheltered housing schemes.

Gas cookers present a serious fire hazard in sheltered housing. Older people can easily forget that they have left the gas on and the build up of gas can result in an explosion and subsequent fire. For this reason gas should not be used as a fuel within flats in Extra Care schemes.

5.8.3
The Building Regulations

Approved Document B of the 1991 Building Regulations which outlines fire safety is sub-divided into five sections:

1. Escape
2. Spread
3. Internal fire spread (linings)
4. External fire spread (structure)
5. Access facilities for the fire service

The main aim of the Building Regulations is to protect people at the origin of a fire. If the origin of a fire is within a person's flat protection can be provided in a number of ways:

- Fire doors can be installed within the flat to separate the various habitable rooms from each other and from the kitchen.
   In the case of a flat of 45 sq.m the effect of this can be to over-compartmentalise what is already a small enclosure and could lead to an inconvenient plethora of internal fire doors.
- The flat can be planned to ensure that the points of greatest risk such as the kitchen are located at the furthest point from the main exit and that escape routes are not compromised.
- Additional fire safety measures can be incorporated, e.g. quick response alarm systems.
   These can be used as trade offs against the need for internal fire doors.
- Provide a positive means to suppress a fire, e.g. sprinklers.

The use of sprinkler systems in residential buildings is not common in the UK and their practicalities are currently under review.

The Building Regulations relating to fire safety are subject to individual interpretations by building control and fire officers in different parts of the country. This is particularly true in the case of Extra Care housing which, though it should strictly be viewed as a residential building, is sometimes treated as if it were residential care accommodation. It is often forgotten that in an Extra Care scheme each resident is either the holder of a separate tenancy agreement or is the owner of a separate lease. Because confusion persists and because the regulations are subject to interpretation, designers should discuss their proposals with Building Control and Fire Safety officers as soon as possible in the early stages of a project. The aim of such discussions should not be to avoid compliance with important and necessary requirements, but rather to ensure that the correct and most up-to-date precautions are incorporated and that a balance is struck between the needs of fire safety and the everyday wellbeing of older people.

5.8.4
Fire Alarms and Smoke Detectors

The early detection of a fire may make it possible to limit the outbreak and to extinguish it before evacuation becomes necessary. For this to happen it is not sufficient for fire fighters simply to know that a fire has broken out: they also need to pin point its exact location. This requires the installation of an accurate and comprehensive warning system.

Fire detectors operate by sensing either smoke, flame or heat. The choice would depend largely on location and on the nature of the hazard. Detectors are usually fixed to ceilings in the vicinity of likely hazards, in

such a way as to minimise the risk of being tripped accidentally. They are connected to a central control system which is usually located in or near to the manager's office. When a fire is detected the system automatically alerts the local fire brigade and activates all necessary visual and auditory alarms and all safety devices such as electro-magnetic door restraints and extinguishing systems.

The control system can be programmed to activate alarms progressively according to need. If a fire breaks out in a flat it may only be necessary to alert the occupant of that flat in the first instance.

Fig. 5.8.4a: An audible and visual fire alarm

5.8.5
Compartmentalisation

Fire compartments divide a building into discrete entities and serve to limit the spread of a fire to other parts of a building. A compartment is only as effective as its weakest element: this might be a door, a duct or a false ceiling. Doors in compartment walls need to be self-closing and fire resistant, though they may be held open on electro-magnetic catches. Ducts and ceiling voids need to be effectively fire stopped.

In a sheltered housing scheme the individual flats constitute primary compartments: each flat is designed to contain a fire in order to protect both neighbouring flats and any adjacent corridor. Doors and windows which communicate with corridors must provide one hour resistance. Groups of flats together with their shared communal corridor then constitute larger compartments and serve to contain a fire which may have broken out of a primary compartment. Escape staircases and refuge areas can be considered as separate compartments within the overall system of compartmentalisation.

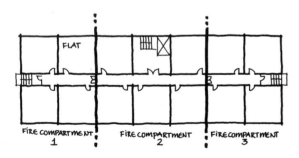

Fig. 5.8.5a: Fire compartments

5.8.6
Fire Doors

Fire doors are fitted with positive closing mechanisms which, when closed, offer a degree of fire resistance. They are an essential element in the creation of compartments to contain fire. Unfortunately they also form barriers which impede the free movement of people who are frail or in wheelchairs.

Fire Doors in Flats

It is not uncommon for flats in sheltered housing schemes to be fitted with internal self-closing fire doors. This may be seen by the scheme's designer as a worthwhile precaution or it may be a feature which is requested by the authorities. However, the current Building Regulations do not require internal fire doors to be fitted in any flat in which the furthermost point is less than 9m from the main entrance door, Fig. 5.8.6a. Regulation B1-2.12 states that one acceptable approach is.......'to plan the flat so that the travel distance from the entrance door to any point in any of the habitable rooms does not exceed 9m and the cooking facilities are remote from the entrance door and do not prejudice the escape route from any point in the flat'.

Heavy self-closing doors within flats causes enormous problems for the frail elderly, particularly those who are dependent on wheelchairs: powerful door-closers make doors difficult to open, they can trap hands or arms and they can even knock frail people over. To avoid these problems residents often permanently prop them open.

An example can serve to illustrate the dilemma facing the designer. In one scheme of bed-sitters the front door to each flat was a full fire door designed to wheelchair standards. The tiny cooking area had been treated as a

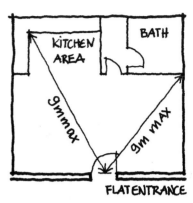

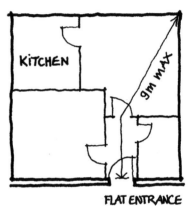

Fig. 5.8.6a: Flat with restricted travel distance.
Source: 1991 Building Regulations Part B

Fig. 5.8.6b: A fire door which has been propped open

separate compartment and was itself enclosed by a narrow self-closing fire door which was not wheelchair accessible. The result was a tiny, dark, cell-like kitchen with a heavy self-closing door which could barely be opened by the tenants. The kitchen had been rendered almost unusable even if the door was permanently propped open. The lesson is not that fire safety should be ignored but that design for fire safety must look at the whole problem. In the case of bed-sitter accommodation the solution might be to limit cooking equipment to kettles and microwaves and to ensure that these are located far away from the main exit door.

Fire Doors in Communal Corridors

Fire doors in corridors define compartments and serve to contain a fire and to prevent the spread of smoke. Like fire doors in flats they can impede the progress of people who are frail or in wheelchairs and are often propped open. Electro-magnetic catches can be installed to keep the doors open until such time as a fire breaks out. It is advisable to switch them off at night and leave the doors in a closed position. Electro-magnetic catches are not permitted for doors to protected fire escape stairs or designated points of refuge. Door closers should be adjusted to produce a slow and controlled action and to avoid any impact noise. In some situations it may be feasible to install automatic doors to help residents in wheelchairs.

5.8.7
Smoke Control

Smoke inhalation and asphyxiation are probably the most common causes of death and injury in domestic fires. There are two methods of smoke control in common use today: 'smoke dispersal' and 'smoke containment'. The two are largely incompatible.

Smoke Dispersal

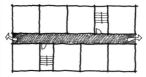

This method seeks to clear smoke from escape routes and relies on ventilation which is either natural or encouraged by mechanically induced positive pressure. It eliminates the need for compartment doors in corridors. For it to be effective corridors need to be open ended and directly ventilated by automatic louvres. Generally the dispersal method is not favoured by fire brigades because the rate of dispersal can be reduced by external wind pressure and the system relies entirely on mechanical pressurisation.

Smoke Containment

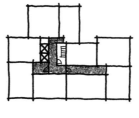

Discrete compartments are created in order to contain smoke and corridors are sub-divided by separating doors. Unfortunately doors are seldom wholly effective as smoke barriers and seepage occurs around frames. This can be eliminated by pressurising the corridors: air is drawn down from a roof vent by fans which are activated by the fire alarm. The containment method does little to help people who are already trapped within a smoke-filled compartment.

Neither method is without its drawbacks. The dispersal method eliminates the need for compartment doors, but may not be wholly effective under all conditions; the containment method does nothing to remove smoke from the compartment of origin.

5.8.8
Evacuation

'Evacuation of a building occupied by the elderly is fraught with problems, to which there are no final answers. It is possible that in time thinking on this subject will change, permitting or indeed encouraging the elderly to stay put in the event of fire.'

Weal & Weal, 1988

In the event of fire breaking out in a building most people's instinct is to try to escape towards the outside and most buildings are designed to create safe routes which help able-bodied people to escape. Problems occur in Extra Care housing when people are not able-bodied and are not able to move quickly and certainly towards a point of safety. For such people a number of alternatives exist:

- They can be encouraged to make every effort to evacuate themselves along designated routes. Here the risk is that they will become stuck in a corridor putting themselves at much greater risk. There is also a tendency for older people to move in a familiar direction towards the main lift and possibly towards danger, rather than in the recommended direction of escape.

- In modern buildings it is likely that compartmentalisation will offer sufficient protection until a fire is brought under control. Frail residents should be encouraged to remain in their flats and wait either until the fire is extinguished or assistance becomes available. However, this is a solution which in practice is very difficult to impose.

- Ambulant residents can be encouraged to move horizontally to a designated place of refuge to await assistance. Horizontal evacuation is less tiring both for residents and rescuers. A place of refuge should be established on each floor. Residents are moved progressively away from the fire from compartment to compartment towards the place of refuge. This should be an enclosure with minimum one hour fire resistance and should ideally communicate with both a lift and a protected staircase. Although lifts are always immobilised when a fire is detected, they can be re-activated under the supervision of the fire brigade.

It may well be that all three alternatives need to be adopted in Extra Care schemes. Active residents should be encouraged to evacuate themselves, immobile residents should be encouraged to stay put and the semi-ambulant residents should be encouraged to move to a place of refuge. What is clearly important is that there should be a very clear plan of evacuation which is clearly understood by staff and residents and which has been agreed by the fire brigade. This should be rehearsed in regular fire drills. It may also be useful to issue each resident with a 'Personal Evacuation Plan' which sets out clearly what they should do in the event of a fire breaking out or an alarm sounding.

For these systems to work it is important that all visual and auditory alarms are properly maintained, that signs and direction indicators are fully visible, that the building has effective and sufficient compartments, and that escape routes and staircases are kept clear of obstructions.

Emergency lighting such as that employed on-board an aircraft can be used to help people find an escape route. The RNIB are researching this concept within a domestic environment and with particular emphasis on lighting which can be seen by both sighted and visually impaired people.

5.8.9
Fire Fighting

A site must be planned to guarantee full access to fire fighting vehicles and equipment. Closed courtyards are not advisable and there should be a clear unobstructed route linking the main entrance to rear garden areas. On tight urban sites where full access can't be achieved it is necessary to install dry risers with outlets within a protected area at each floor level.

Fire fighting equipment should be distributed throughout the building in locations which have been agreed by local fire officers and should be kept in full working order. This should include hoses, fire extinguishers, fire blankets etc. Residents and staff should be instructed in how to use them.

Chapter 6
Generic Design

'We do not make very full value of the opportunities provided by technology because we prefer critical to constructive thinking, argument to design. The search for truth is like digging for gold... but if you are designing a house you have to design and construct the house. You are not going to 'discover' a house.'

Edward de Bono (1997)

6.1
A Design Tool

6.1.1
Introduction

A basic set of design criteria for Extra Care housing was defined in Chapter 2, while recommendations for the planning and design of the key elements which make up a typical Extra Care scheme were proposed in Chapters 3 and 4.

This chapter describes a simple design tool which can be used during the preliminary stages of a project to generate a whole range of alternative plan proposals. The tool consists of a modular planning system and a standard 'kit of parts'.

The kit of parts has been developed from a particular set of initial aims and assumptions. It is important to stress, therefore, that any designs which are generated from the kit of parts must be viewed, not as universal solutions or as blueprints for real buildings, but rather as generic forms which can be subjected to comparative analysis and which can serve eventually as generators of more specific proposals.

A series of generic building forms which have been developed from the kit of parts to suit sites of different shapes and sizes are described in some detail. The proposed forms have been identified after a detailed study of existing developments and vary in height between two and six storeys. Each proposal is based on a hypothetical brief for 40 flats with the usual range of communal facilities.

While a majority, if not all, of the flats would be of one-bedroom, the system allows bed-sitters and two-bedroom flats to be incorporated as required. The areas of the three principal flat types are 46.5 sq.m, 31 sq.m, and 62 sq.m respectively, in the ratio of 3:2:4. This makes it possible to vary the number of the different types of flats during the planning stage. Depending on the method of construction used, this flexibility could also be exploited during the life of a building.

6.1.2
Assumptions and Aims

The following are some of the basic assumptions and the design aims which have been incorporated into the planning tool and which have influenced the generic designs.

Assumptions

- A scheme which is built today can be expected to remain in use for at least 30 years, that is until the year 2025. It must be designed to adapt to changing circumstances.
- Residents might be young elderly or very old, they might be active or very frail, they might be alert or mentally impaired. The assessment criteria for admission - and for being 'moved on' - will vary from scheme to scheme and are likely to change over time.

- Sheltered housing schemes are often developed as deep floor plans with double loaded corridors in order to minimise circulation space and to improve energy efficiency. This means that a substantial proportion of flats will be single aspect.
- There will be an increasing tendency to build schemes on smaller urban sites, in order to locate them as close as possible to existing facilities.

Aims

- Planning must facilitate full wheelchair accessibility.
- Flats must be designed to offer maximum flexibility, both day-to-day and long-term. It should be possible to install a hoist, to accommodate a night-time carer, to connect a bedroom and sitting room, to remove or add doors as required.
- The entrance to a flat must act as a buffer space and must be big enough to accommodate a parked wheelchair. Front doors should be designed to create a sense of territory and threshold, maintaining privacy while inviting contact.
- Flats can be grouped into loosely defined clusters in order to break down the effects of scale and reduce the sense of institution. Each cluster could share a small open sitting room in which communal meals could be served if required.
- Corridors should be limited in length to cut down on walking distances and to avoid a sense of institution, and should be planned in a clear legible manner. They should be wide enough to allow for wheelchairs to pass, and be equipped with handrails and seats.
- Corridors should be well lit and enjoy some natural daylight and contact with the outside.
- Staircases should be designed and located in such a way as to encourage their use.

- Lift lobbies and staircases should be planned with a view to the outside to help with orientation and to provide daylight.
- The manager's office should be positioned to give maximum visual control over the approach and the main entrance spaces.
- Communal spaces should relate to the main entrance in such a way as to facilitate their use as day care facilities by non-residents. They should have a visual and physical connection with the garden.
- The form of the buildings should exploit the site in order to separate approach spaces from amenity spaces and to create intimately scaled outside areas which are sunny and shielded from the wind.

6.1.3
The Modular Planning System

The Tartan Grid

A basic grid has been derived from a study of relevant activities and the spaces which they generate. The following is a selection of such activities and their preferred dimensions:

- minimun width for a bedroom   3.2m
- minimum width for a sitting room   3.5m
- width for sitting + partition + bedroom   6.8m
- dimensions for a wheelchair-accessible
  bathroom cell   2.2m square
- a wheelchair-accessible kitchen   2.2m square
- width for a corridor, with side handrails,
  allowing wheelchairs to pass   2.0m
- width for a two-flight staircase (1.1m x 2)   2.2m

A study of these dimensions has led to the development of a 'tartan' design grid (Wachsman, 1961) with 2.2m square cells and stripes corresponding to 100mm, 200mm or 300mm wall thicknesses, see Fig. 6.1.3a.

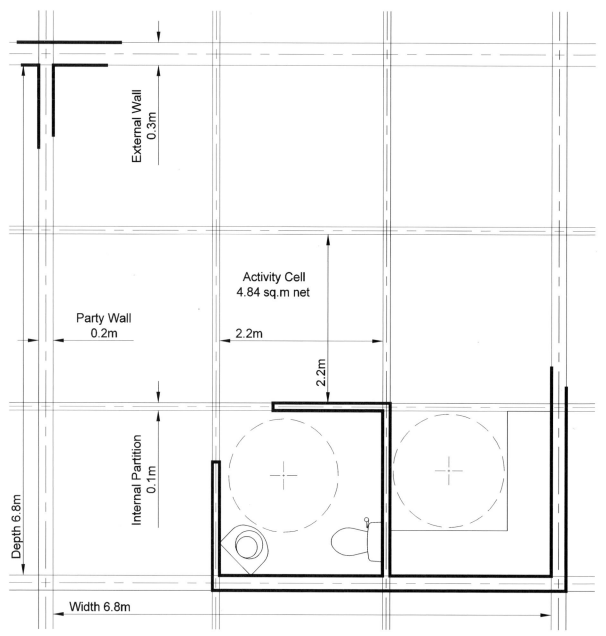

Fig. 6.1.3a: The tartan design grid

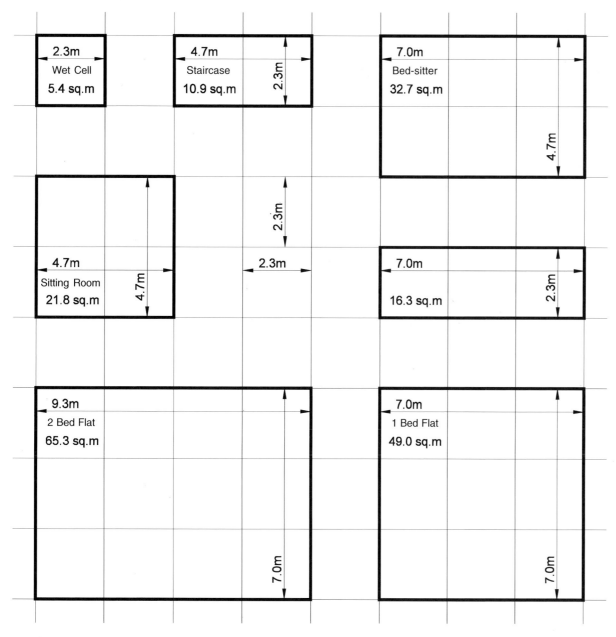

Fig. 6.1.3b: The centre-line planning grid

If the preferred width for a one-bedroom flat is 6.8m and the preferred area is 46.5 sq.m then the resultant depth will be 6.8m and the plan will be a perfect square. The dimension 6.8m can be broken down to 3 x 2.2m + 2 x 100mm, and the square can be represented as 3 x 3 rows of 2.2m square cells separated by 100mm tartan stripes. In the same way, using 6.8m as the standard plan depth the plan for a bed-sitter can be represented as 2 x 3 rows of cells giving 4.5m x 6.8m (30.6 sq.m), equivalent to 2/3 of the area of the one-bedroom flat. Similarly the two-bedroom flat can be derived from two bed-sitters plus a party wall thickness and represented as 4 x 3 rows of cells giving 9.2m x 6.8m (62.6 sq.m).

Using the tartan grid in this way it is possible to develop a 'family' of standard flat plans which, because they are related in the simple ratio of 2:3:4, are easy to interchange. A pair of one-bedroom flats can be replaced by a bed-sitter and a two-bedroom flat; a pair of two-bedroom flats can be replaced by a pair of one-bedroom flats and a bed-sitter; four one-bedroom flats can be replaced by three two-bedroom flats.

The Centre-Line Grid

Tartan grids are useful for the close-focus planning of actual rooms because they enable spaces to be fixed independently of varying wall thicknesses. In real buildings wall thicknesses vary according to whether they are external walls, party walls, room dividers etc. In the tartan grid system which has been described above it has been assumed that party walls are 200mm thick and that room dividers are 100mm; in reality these thicknesses could vary considerably according to specific circumstances. The careful use of tartan grids makes it possible to maintain the integrity of spaces while varying the thickness of the walls.

Such a level of accuracy is not required at the sketch design stage. For this reason the tartan grid has to be translated into a centre-line grid of 2.3m which is illustrated in Fig. 6.1.3b. This has been derived from the 7m dimension which is generated by the centre lines of 200mm thick partitions which define a 6.8m space. A 2.3m centre-line grid gives a good approximation to the 2.2m tartan grid which is illustrated in Fig. 6.1.3a: it produces a plan dimension for the one-bedroom flat of 7.0m square on centre lines and 6.8m between boundary wall surfaces.

The 2.3m grid equates with the overall gross dimensions of the three preferred flat shells, the preferred staircase and the preferred shared corridor. The half-grid dimension of 1.16m corresponds to the width of a domestic corridor, while the 'one-and-a-half-grid' dimension of 3.5m corresponds to preferred widths of such rooms as offices. The basic module of 2.3m has the advantage that it has been derived from spaces such as standard bathroom cells which are appropriate to the building type and which are easy to visualise. Interestingly the design of housing for general purposes is often based on a module of 900 mm: in this case the basic half-module of 1.16m reflects the increased dimensions which are preferable in sheltered housing.

Using squared paper, or its CAD equivalent, it is possible to generate a range of alternative plans in a short time. The fact that each grid square has a gross area of 5.4 sq.m, equivalent to a net area of approximately 5 sq.m makes it easy to calculate approximate areas for the whole or any part of a plan.

However, it is necessary to issue a number of caveats:

- The proposed grid has been derived from a study of activities and their spatial needs and does not relate to any system of preferred dimensions for building components
- The grid method can only generate approximate design solutions, and should not be used to produce final designs
- The slavish use of grids can lull a designer into adopting dimensions which are inappropriate

6.2
A Kit of Parts

6.2.1
A One-Bedroom Flat

Figs 6.2.1a & 6.2.1b show two versions of the proposed standard plan for a one-bedroom flat. The use of diagonally placed doors and walls allows smooth transitions between spaces and improves space-use efficiency. Observations of furnished flats show that residents often place items of furniture on diagonals across corners.

Living zones:

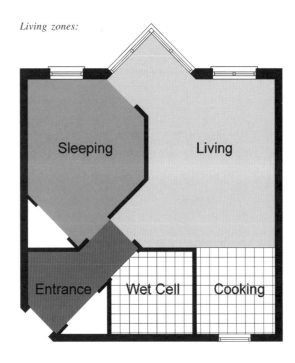

Fig. 6.2.1a: A one-bedroom flat with corner entry

Possible furniture layout:

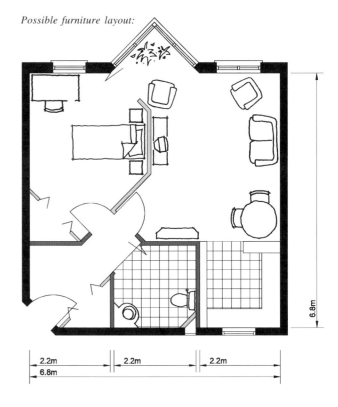

Fig. 6.2.1a shows a standard one-bedroom flat with corner entry. This has the advantage that it can be used to turn corners in cluster configurations and requires only single-stack drainage. The kitchen is remote from the entrance which aids escape in the event of a fire.

Fig. 6.2.1b shows a standard mid-run situation with a centralised hallway. It incorporates the following features:

- a recessed entrance with a delivery shelf overlooked via a small window from the kitchen
- a spacious hallway with a storage cupboard and space for a wheelchair or zimmer frame to be stored
- a standard wheelchair-accessible bathroom with split-leaf outward opening door
- door openings which are minimum 850mm clear and are placed to allow easy passage between the principal rooms - doors are on rising butt hinges and can easily be removed if necessary

- a bay window which is an extension of the sitting room but which can also be opened up to the bedroom - this scoops in sunlight, allows lateral views out and makes it possible to connect the bedroom with the sitting room
- a bedroom of 3.2m width with an area of 13 sq.m
- a sitting room of 3.5m width and area of 16 sq.m
- a compact wheelchair-accessible kitchen
- a partition wall between sitting room and bedroom which can easily be removed or replaced with a sliding-folding screen

Critical dimensions:

Possible furniture layout:

Living zones:

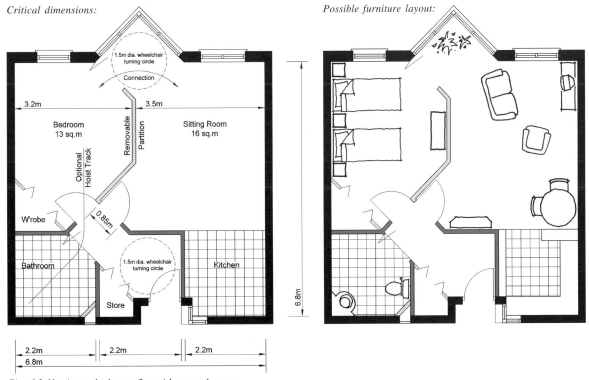

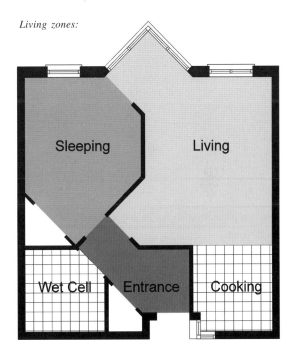

Fig. 6.2.1b: A one-bedroom flat with central entry

6.2.2
A Two-Bedroom Flat

Fig. 6.2.2a shows a standard two-bedroom flat for corner entry and Fig. 6.2.2b shows the central entry variant. The corner entry has the advantage that it can be used to turn corners in cluster configurations.

In both of these examples the two 'bedrooms' together occupy 5.6m and are nominally divided into rooms of width 3.2m and 2.3m. The dividing wall can, however, be moved to create two equal rooms or one very large room. The examples also show that the larger bedroom always has direct access to the bathroom. The bay window is shared between the sitting room and the bedroom/study adjoining it.

In space-use terms it should be possible to accommodate any of the following configurations by moving or removing a partition wall:

- one larger 'wheelchair' bedroom with one smaller bedroom
- one larger bedroom with a smaller room for a carer
- one large bedroom with a smaller multi-purpose room which can be used as a study or a guest room
- one large bedroom with double size lounge
- two bedrooms of equal size
- one very large bedroom

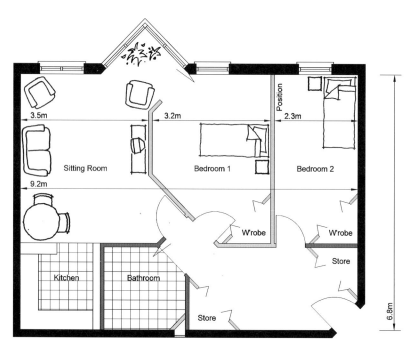

Fig. 6.2.2a: Two-bedroom flat with corner entry

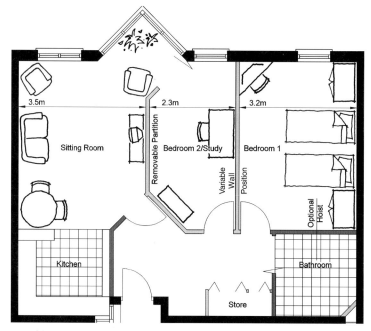

Fig. 6.2.2b: Two-bedroom flat with central entry

Generic Design

6.2.3
A Bed-sitter

The bed-sitter has been planned within a shell of 4.5m x 6.8m and incorporates a standard bathroom and hallway. A compact kitchen corner incorporates a small sink with a fridge and microwave and is intended only for the preparation of drinks and snacks. It could easily be removed or modified according to the needs of the occupant. Only one internal door is needed: that to the bathroom. The sleeping area can be screened off with a curtain.

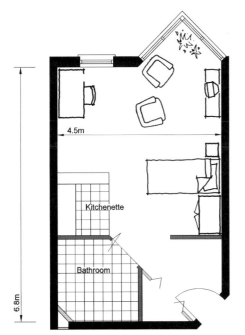

Fig. 6.2.3a: A bed-sitter unit

6.2.4
The Entrance Hall

The entrance hall in each of the standard flats is designed to give direct and easy access to each of the main rooms. The entrance itself is recessed and is provided with a small bench and a shelf for deliveries. The door incorporates a translucent viewing panel as well as attractive but manageable door furniture. In some cases the kitchen is linked to the corridor by a small viewing window. Within the hall there is a generous storage cupboard and adequate space to turn a wheelchair and to park it when not in use. There should not be any clashing door swings that could trap people or cause obstructions.

The spacious hall acts as a buffer zone between the circulation space and the rooms within the flat. It is a place to remove outdoor clothing and store mobility aids not used in the home and obscures views into the private spaces of the flat

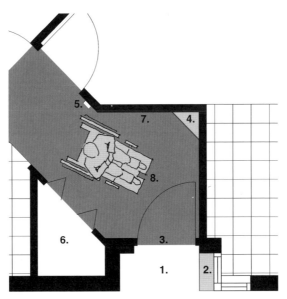

Fig. 6.2.4a: Entrance hall

Entrance and Hallway features, key to diagram:

1. ***Recessed doorway:***
    creates a semi-private zone
    offers opportunity to personalise entrance
    Wheelchair-accessible doorway:
    clear opening of 850mm
    minimum 200mm of wall space to the locking side of the door to enable people in wheelchairs to get near to the locks and handle
2. ***Delivery shelf:***
    for items such as milk and oversized parcels
    eliminates need for stooping
    Lighting in recess:
    illuminates doorway
    door numbers back-lit by a lightbox
3. ***Door furniture:***
    clearly visible and raised numbering
    simple and secure locks
    D-shaped door handles in contrasting colours
    Viewing panel in door:
    for recognising visitors
    placed between 1.1m and 1.6m from floor level
    Letter box and basket:
    to allow deliveries of post and eliminate need to pick up letters from the floor
    Flush threshold, with recessed entrance mat:
    avoids tripping
    easier access by wheelchair users
4. ***Internal shelf:***
    near to doorway 1.1m above floor level, for keys etc.
5. ***Door entry phone:***
    placed near to lounge and bedroom doorways
    1.1m above floor level so that wheelchair users can reach it
    Alarm pull cord and two way speech box:
    placed next to the door entry phone
6. ***Storage cupboard:***
    for bulky items and/or hot water cylinder
7. ***Space to stand a wheelchair/ zimmer frame/ shopping trolley***
8. ***Space for a wheelchair turning circle***

6.2.5
The Bathroom

The bathroom becomes increasingly important for people as they become more frail or unwell and must be designed for maximum convenience. In Extra Care homes all bathrooms should be fully accessible to unassisted wheelchair users, or to those who need one or even two carers to assist them; there should be room to operate a mobile hoist and, in the last resort, to install a fixed hoist linking through to the bedroom.

All of the generic flat plans incorporate a standard wet cell or bathroom unit. This consists of a square plan of side 2.2m with one corner removed to form a door. Such a cell could easily be prefabricated and delivered to site, complete with all fixtures and finishes.

Fig. 6.2.5a: Wheelchair-accessible wash basin

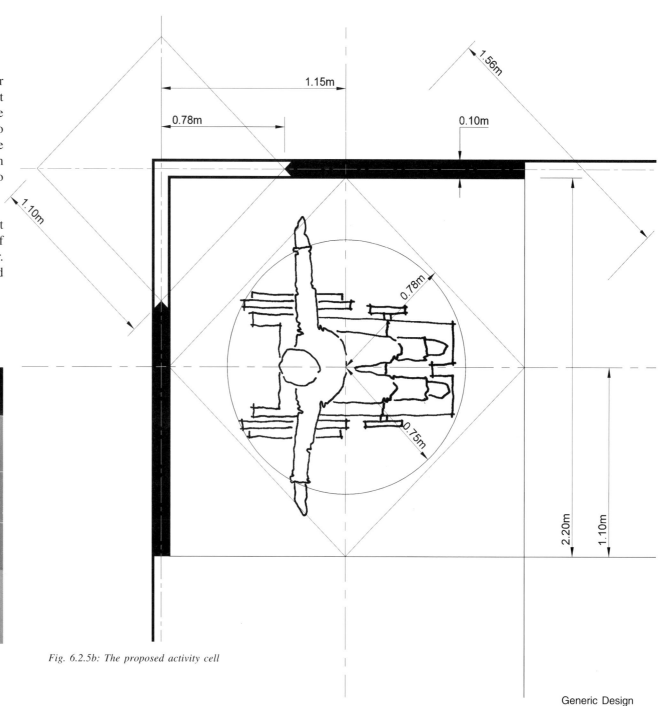

Fig. 6.2.5b: The proposed activity cell

Generic Design

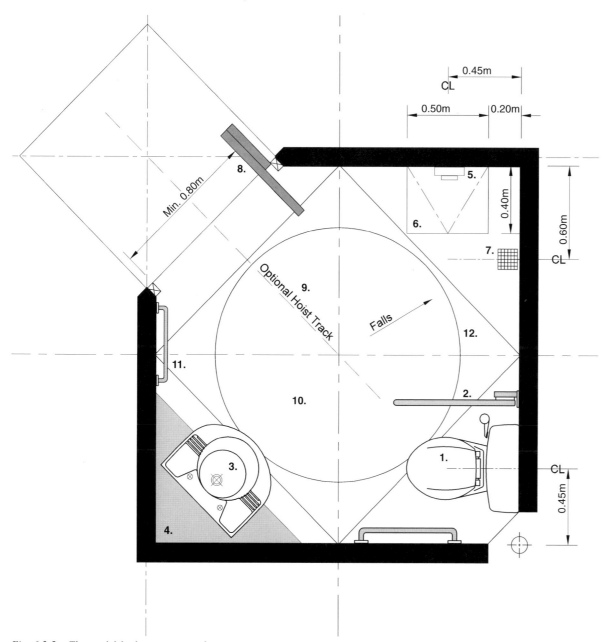

0.45m

CL

0.50m | 0.20m

8.

Min. 0.80m

5.

6.

0.40m

0.60m

7.

CL

Optional Hoist Track

9.

Falls

12.

11.

2.

10.

3.

CL

1.

0.45m

4.

Fig. 6.2.5c: The model bathroom proposal

Bathroom features and key to diagram:

1. **WC:**
   paddle shaped flush handle fitted to furthest side from the wall
   adjustable height seat
   accessible by a wheelchair both from front and side, with or without assistance

2. **Grab rails:**
   walls must be structurally able to take grab rails
   fixed grab rail on the wall at the side of the WC
   retractable grab rail at the open side of the WC

3. **Washbasin:**
   projecting, with leg-room to allow use by wheelchair users
   height adjustable with concealed brackets and supply pipes
   lever taps, safety temperature thermostat (43°C limit)
   surrounding worktop for toiletries

4. **Corner cupboard and mirror:**
   positioned over sink unit
   adjustable tilt mirror for different height users and those in wheelchairs

5. **Shower unit:**
   robust, substantial, clear and easy to use controls at a height that can be reached whilst sitting
   detachable shower head, variable water flow
   safety temperature thermostat (43°C limit)

6. **Folding shower seat with drain holes**

7. **Recessed shower deck in floor:**
   minimises spread of water across floor
   provides level surface

8. **Outward opening split-leaf door:**
   giving a clear opening of minimun 800mm
   D-shaped colour contrasting handle
   removable panel above door for possible provision of ceiling hoist track

9. **Direct route for hoist to link the bathroom and bedroom**

10. **Floor finish:**
    non-slip, non-reflective, sealed, with upstand at wall junctions
    falls to main shower drain
    additional emergency overflow drain pipe
    colour to be contrasting with bathroom fittings and walls

11. **Towel rail:**
    sturdy enough to be used as a grab rail in emergency
    if heated then it must be of low surface temperature

12. **Space for a wheelchair turning circle**
    Lighting:
    down-lighter fittings above shower, WC and washbasin
    Heat emitter:
    low surface temperature, quick response
    Alarm pull cord

6.2.6
The Standard Kitchen

Cooking can be a hazardous activity for the frail elderly and it is necessary to look beyond the 'modern' fitted kitchen with its fixed melamine veneered chipboard units, its fitted cupboards and natty recessed handles: the kitchen should be conceived more as a laboratory for food preparation. Traditional kitchens with their free standing tables and open dressers offer a more useful precedent than the dream kitchens of the magazines.

The kitchen in most of the standard flat plans fits within a 2.2m square cell which can be left open to the sitting room or closed off with a sliding door. The kitchen in Fig. 6.2.6c has been designed with a flexibility that allows both ambulant people and wheelchair users to adapt the space to their individual needs.

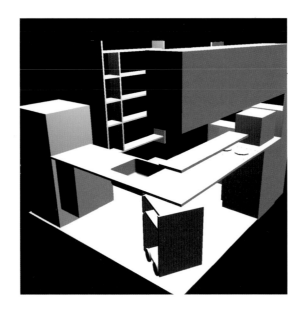

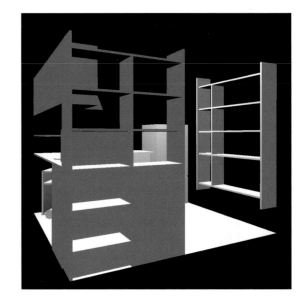

Fig. 6.2.6a: A wheelchair-accessible kitchen

Fig. 6.2.6b: The model kitchen proposal

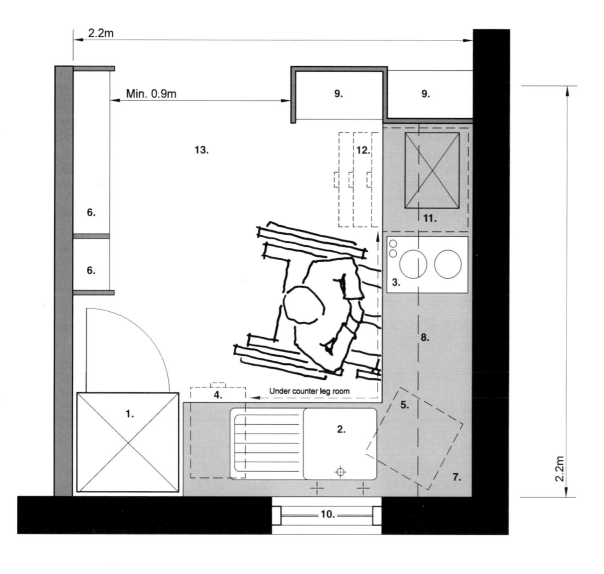

Kitchen components and key to diagram:

1. *Fridge-Freezer:*
   reduces need to visit shops
   useful for storing pre-prepared meals
2. *Sink unit:*
   mixer taps with lever handles
   shallow bowl to reduce amount of reach and give leg-room
   clear space below to allow leg-room
3. *Hob unit:*
   2 rings, overhead extractor with worktop level controls
   clear space below to allow leg room
4. *Rubbish bin:*
   fitted as a retractable unit under worktop
   (free standing bins can cause obstructions)
5. *Under counter mobile unit(s):*
   provides extra worktop, storage etc.
6. *Shallow open shelves:*
   200mm deep with safety rails
   avoids deep cupboards
   accessible to wheelchair users
   all items are visible
7. *Adjustable height worktop - sectioned, detachable and fitted on brackets:*
   500mm deep, facilitates reach
   non-reflective and colour contrasting
8. *Preparation area:*
   clear worktop space
   clear space below to allow leg-room
   room for preparation of food, toaster, kettle, microwave oven
9. *Dresser between lounge and kitchen:*
   open to kitchen and/or lounge (min. 300mm deep)
10. *Window to corridor:*
    allows views out and contact with neighbours
    fire resistant glass
    provision for fitting blinds or curtain for privacy
11. *Upper storage units:*
    open shelving (300mm deep)
    if doors fitted they should have baskets attached
12. *Other fittings - with D-handles, colour contrasted to surroundings:*
    cutlery drawer
    pull-out worktop
    large storage drawer
13. *Floor finish:*
    slip resistant
    water proof
    non-reflective and colour contrasted
    Lighting:
    individual recessed down-lighters for each activity area

Fig. 6.2.6c: The model kitchen proposal

6.2.7
The Sitting Room and Bedroom

People who are active and in good health are naturally concerned to have separate rooms in which to sleep and to live. One is a private room in which clothes are stored, in which dressing and undressing takes place; the other is a more public room for daytime activities where visitors are entertained. As people get older and more frail the distinction between the two rooms becomes less defined and during long periods of illness the bedroom becomes effectively the main living room.

The generic plans for the one-bedroom flat attempt to establish a special relationship between the bedroom and the sitting room. The bedroom has been designed to allow a single bed to be placed in a number of different positions. In a peninsular location it facilitates wheelchair access and can be linked by a fixed hoist track directly to the bathroom. The room will also accommodate a double bed or two single beds. The sitting room is conceived as a conventional room in which eating, televiewing and entertaining can take place. Adjacent to both is a bay window. While this is primarily a part of the sitting room it is also connected to the bedroom by a folding glazed screen. The bay window scoops in sunlight and affords lateral views to the outside. When the glazed screen is open it also acts as a connector between the two rooms. If the occupier is ill for a long period the central section of the dividing partition can also be removed so that the whole space becomes one.

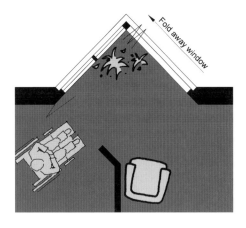

Bay window features:

- a connection between the living room and the bedroom
- space for a wheelchair turning circle
- glazed from 0.6m above the floor
- one side of the glazing is fixed, the other folds open
- lower section of glazing tilts inward for ventilation
- could be used as:
  conservatory, for plants and flowers; sitting and viewing bay; extension to bedroom; balcony

Wardrobe features:

- height adjustable hanging rail to suit individual needs
- flush entry for accessibility by wheelchair users
- side shelving for folded clothing etc.
- bi-fold doors, reducing space required when doors open

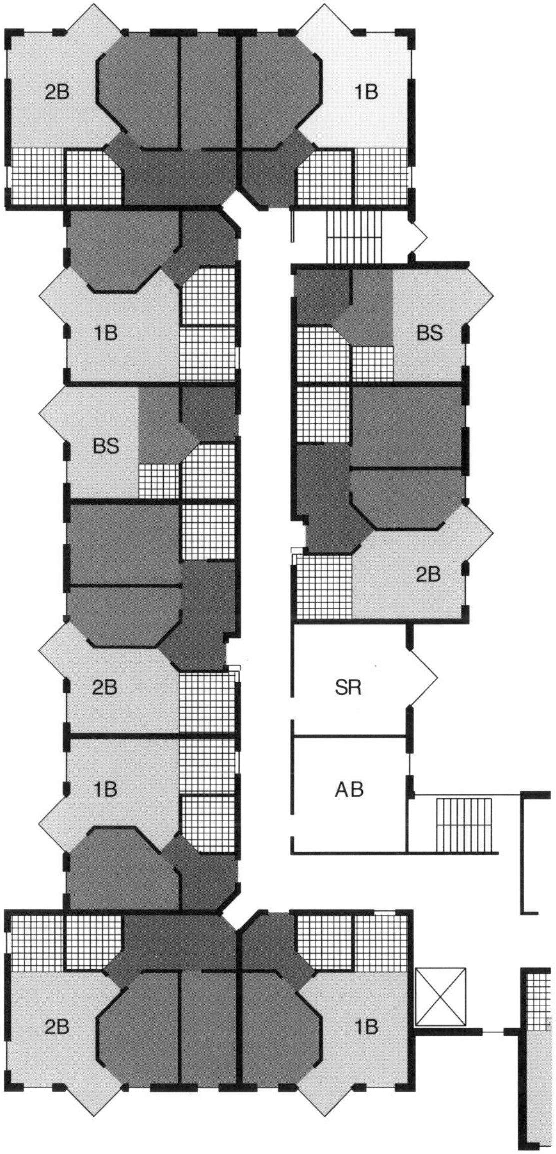

Fig. 6.2.8a: Alternative flat combination

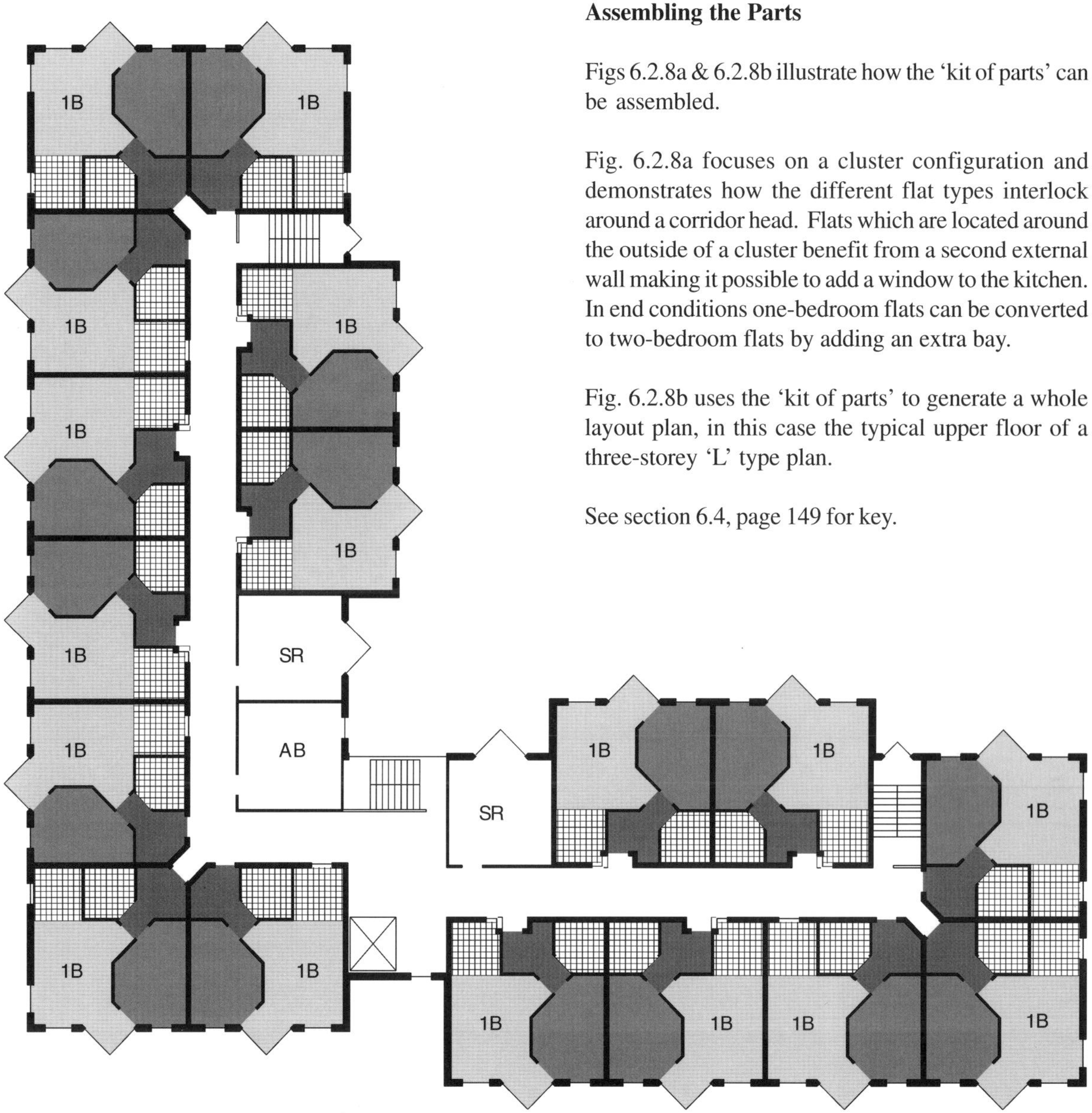

Fig. 6.2.8b: An 'L' shaped plan

6.2.8
Assembling the Parts

Figs 6.2.8a & 6.2.8b illustrate how the 'kit of parts' can be assembled.

Fig. 6.2.8a focuses on a cluster configuration and demonstrates how the different flat types interlock around a corridor head. Flats which are located around the outside of a cluster benefit from a second external wall making it possible to add a window to the kitchen. In end conditions one-bedroom flats can be converted to two-bedroom flats by adding an extra bay.

Fig. 6.2.8b uses the 'kit of parts' to generate a whole layout plan, in this case the typical upper floor of a three-storey 'L' type plan.

See section 6.4, page 149 for key.

6.3
A Taxonomy of Form

6.3.1
Methodology

Many different building forms are now employed in the development of sheltered housing (Goldenberg, 1981; Valins, 1988; Weal & Weal, 1988). These may have been generated by specific sets of client requirements, by particular site characteristics, by cultural imperatives or, indeed, by the whims of individual architects. A detailed study of the range of forms reveals the existence of recurring patterns. From these it is possible to identify a relatively small number of basic types and sub-types which, in turn, can be used to set up a general taxonomy. This process of classification is similar to that used, for instance, by biologists to classify different species within a genus.

Having identified a range of basic form-types the aim here is to subject them to comparative analysis in order to understand how they each perform in any given situation. What influence does a particular plan form have on the length of circulation, on the nature of circulation spaces, on fire safety, on building legibility, on the relationship between flats, on the disposition of external spaces?

6.3.2
The Taxonomy

- **Simple linear**
  Flats are arranged along a straight corridor with the circulation core at some mid point and fire escapes at the extremes. *(section 6.4.1)*

- **Offset linear**
  The simple linear form is offset at the circulation core to break down the scale of the central corridor and to articulate its relation to external spaces. *(section 6.4.2)*

- **'L' shape**
  Flats are arranged in two arms with the circulation core at the elbow. *(section 6.4.3)*

- **'T' shape**
  Flats are arranged in three arms with the circulation core at the meeting point. *(section 6.4.4)*

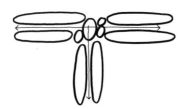

- **Cruciform**
  Flats are arranged in four arms with the circulation core at the meeting point. *(section 6.4.5)*

- **'U' shape**
  Two arms of flats are disposed on either side of a central court and are connected by a wing containing the communal elements. *(section 6.4.6)*

- **Atrium**
  The 'U' form is compressed and the external court becomes an enclosed atrium space under a glass roof. *(section 6.4.7)*

- **Cluster**
  Flats are arranged in compact clusters around a shared sitting room. *(section 6.4.8)*

- **Point block**
  A single cluster is arranged around the circulation core. *(section 6.4.9)*

Fig. 6.3.2a: Nine basic forms which comprise the proposed taxonomy

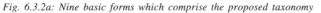

6.3.3
The Basic Brief

The 'kit of parts' has been used to generate a set of generic plans to correspond to the nine basic form-types of the taxonomy. Each one has been developed, so far as is possible, on the basis of the same aims and assumptions, see section 6.1.1, and in response to the same accommodation schedule, incorporating the same set of communal facilities.

Model Accommodation Schedule

Residential Areas:

• 40 flats @ average 46.5 sq.m net	1,860 sq.m	
	(60% of total)	

    for example:
    24 one-bedroom flats @ 46.5 sq.m
    8 bed-sitters @ 31 sq.m
    8 two-bedroom flats @ 62 sq.m

• shared sitting rooms, 4 @ 20 sq.m	80 sq.m
• assisted bathrooms, 3 @ 15 sq.m	45 sq.m
• sluice rooms etc., 3 @ 10 sq.m	30 sq.m
net total	2,000 sq.m
• circulation, lifts, stairs, walls @ 25% of net total	500 sq.m

gross total for residential areas	**2,500 sq.m**
	(80% of total)

Central Communal Areas:

• entrance space, reception	50 sq.m
• manager's office, meeting room	20 sq.m
• care staff: staff room, sleep-over room etc.	60 sq.m
• guest accommodation	30 sq.m
• activity rooms, 2 @ 20 sq.m	40 sq.m
• consulting room/hairdresser	30 sq.m
• main sitting room	60 sq.m
• dining room	60 sq.m
• kitchen, stores etc.	40 sq.m
• WCs, stores etc.	20 sq.m
• laundry	20 sq.m
• wheelchair room	30 sq.m
• plant, refuse etc.	40 sq.m
net total	500 sq.m
• circulation, lifts, stairs, walls @ 25% of net area	125 sq.m

gross total for communal areas	**625 sq.m**
	(20% of total)

TOTAL GROSS BUILDING AREA	**3,125 sq.m**

(equivalent to 78 sq.m gross per unit)

Site Amenities:

• parking for 20 cars	400 sq.m
• access roads and pathways	200 sq.m
• gardens and terraces	400 sq.m

total site area for specific amenities	**1,000 sq.m**

Note:

The areas allocated to the main sitting room, dining room and kitchen should be read in conjunction with the areas allocated to shared 'mini' sitting rooms. Different operating concepts will generate different space needs.

6.4
Generic Plans

The following is a set of nine generic plans relating to the nine form-types identified in the taxonomy. Each plan is accompanied by comparative analytical data and is illustrated with an actual example.

Key to abbreviations used on the plans:

1B	- one-bedroom flat
2B	- two-bedroom flat
AB	- assisted bathroom
AR	- activity room
BS	- bed-sitter
CO	- care office
CS	- chair store
CSR	- communal sitting room
D	- dining room
G	- guest room
HD	- hairdresser
K	- kitchen
L	- laundry
MO	- manager's office
P	- plant room
R	- refuse room
SH	- shop
SL	- sluice
SO	- sleep-over room
SR	- sitting room
ST	- store
TR	- treatment room
WC	- wheelchair-accessible toilet

6.4.1
Simple Linear

Fig. 6.4.1a: Typical linear layout

0   7m

The linear plan sits unhappily on a site and does very little to 'shape' external spaces. Generally only two sitings are possible: either the block runs longitudinally away from a narrow frontage or it runs laterally along a wide frontage. Inevitably gardens run in parallel strips along the facades and very little shelter or privacy is generated. In practice it would prove difficult to adjust the axis of the block to optimise on solar orientation, and in some locations half of all flats could well end up facing north.

Figs 6.4.1b & 6.4.1c illustrate a three-storey block which has total length of 70m and a maximum travel distance of 30m to the lift lobby. The corridors are long and potentially monotonous. It would be difficult to neutralise the sense of being in an institution. There is little or no sense of clustering, but the simple plan is highly legible.

A two-storey block would have a length of about 110m with a maximum travel distance of 45m. At six storeys eight flats would be arranged in two clusters of four on each of five floors and in theory only one staircase would be needed. The block length reduces to 33m and the maximum travel distance to 7m, but the total floor area remains constant at 3200 sq.m.

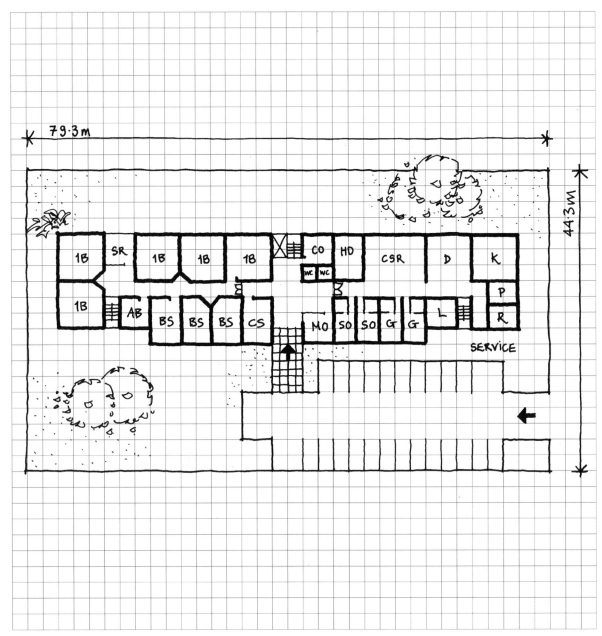

Fig. 6.4.1b: Ground floor

Generic Design

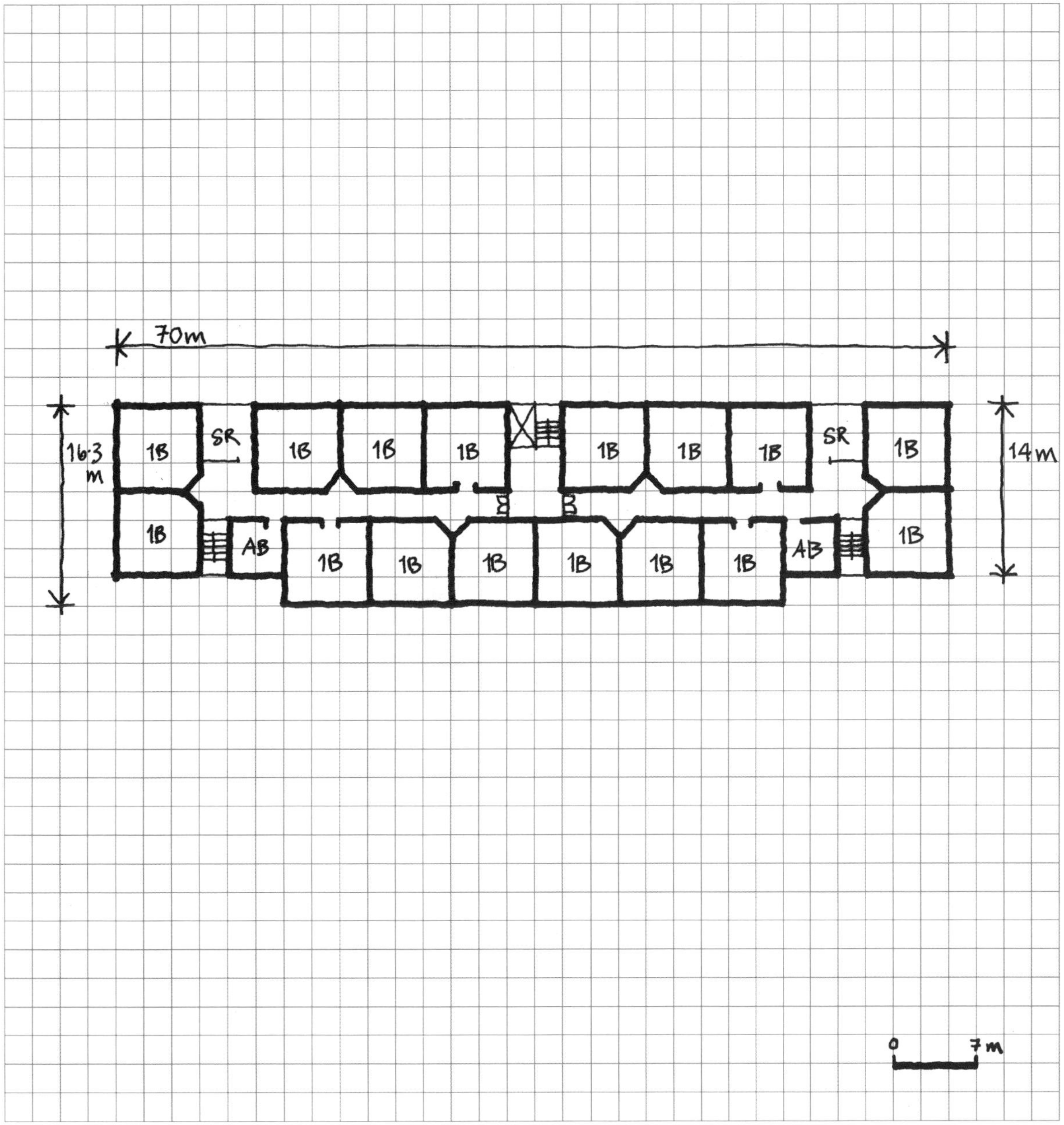
70m
16·3 m
14m
1B
SR
AB
0
7m

Fig. 6.4.1c: Typical upper floor

Simple Linear		
1	no. of floors	3
2	no. of units	40
3	footprint area	1,070 sq.m
4	communal facilities	600 sq.m
5	total area	3,200 sq.m
6	furthest distance from flat to lift lobby	30m
7	site area	3,500 sq.m
8	footprint ratio (3/7)	0.3:1
9	plot ratio (5/7)	0.9:1

Fig. 6.4.1d

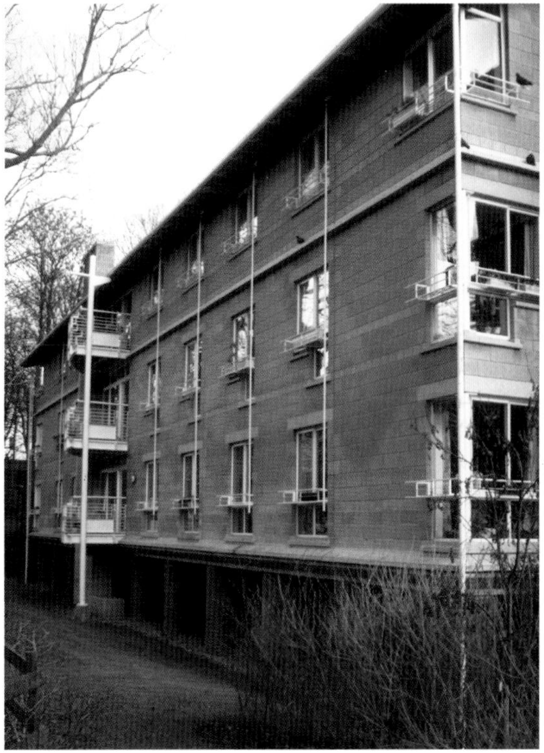

Fig. 6.4.1e: Linear development

6.4.2
Offset Linear

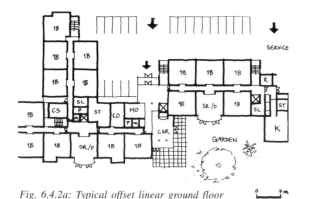

Fig. 6.4.2a: Typical offset linear ground floor

The offset linear type is more versatile than its straight progenitor. The cranked form of the block can be used to articulate the site: this form shows a clear differentiation between the entrance court and the more protected garden court. This type can be used on a wide range of sites, and, with handing and twisting, can be adapted to almost any orientation.

The plan defines five semi-autonomous clusters, each one containing eight flats. Each cluster shares a small common sitting room, and each pair of clusters shares an assisted bathroom and activity room. The communal facilities relate well both to the garden and to the service approach and could easily be used for non-resident day care.

The arrival point on each floor is linked visually to the outside and both the main stair and the lift arrive in the same lobby. The plan is both simple and legible and a clear choice of routes is offered at each floor.

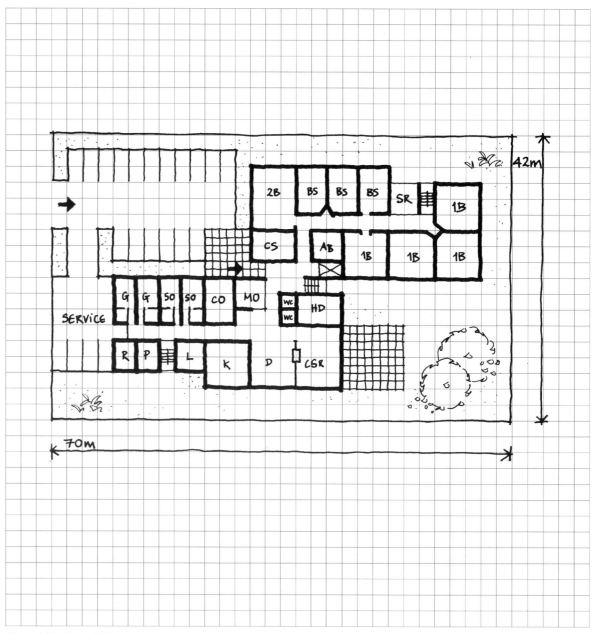

Fig. 6.4.2b: Ground floor

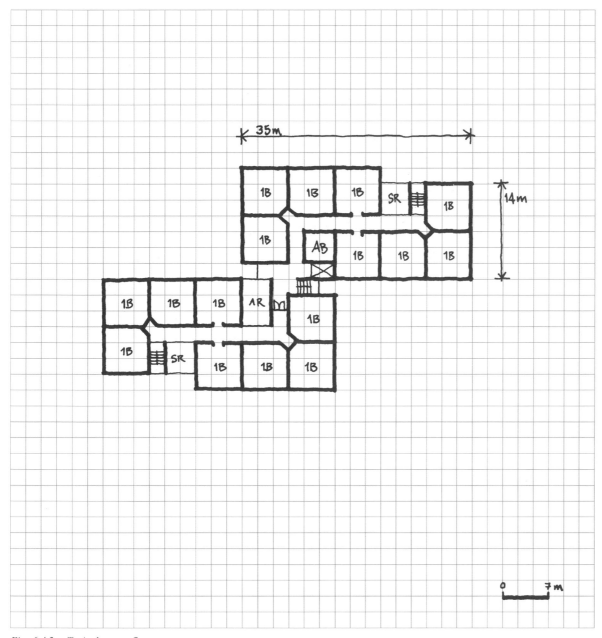

35m

14m

1B 1B 1B SR 1B
1B AB 1B 1B 1B
1B 1B 1B AR 1B
1B SR 1B 1B 1B

0   7 m

Fig. 6.4.2c: Typical upper floor

Offset Linear		
1	no. of floors	3
2	no. of units	40
3	footprint area	1,060 sq.m
4	communal facilities	560 sq.m
5	total area	3,170 sq.m
6	furthest distance from flat to lift lobby	25m
7	site area	2,940 sq.m
8	footprint ratio (3/7)	0.4:1
9	plot ratio (5/7)	1.1:1

Fig. 6.4.2d

Fig. 6.4.2e: Offset linear scheme

6.4.3
'L' Shape

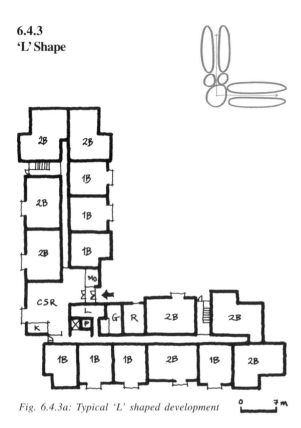

Fig. 6.4.3a: Typical 'L' shaped development

The 'L' type is one of the most common forms. It offers a very clear delineation between the outside world and an inner private world. It can fit on a site which is almost square, and by twisting or handing the plan almost any orientation can be accommodated.

The first version, Figs 6.4.3b & 6.4.3c, is on three storeys and provides for two unequal clusters on each floor. The lift and staircase lobby gives outside views, and the circulation pattern is legible. The communal facilities relate well both to the garden and to the service approach and could easily be used for non-resident day care.

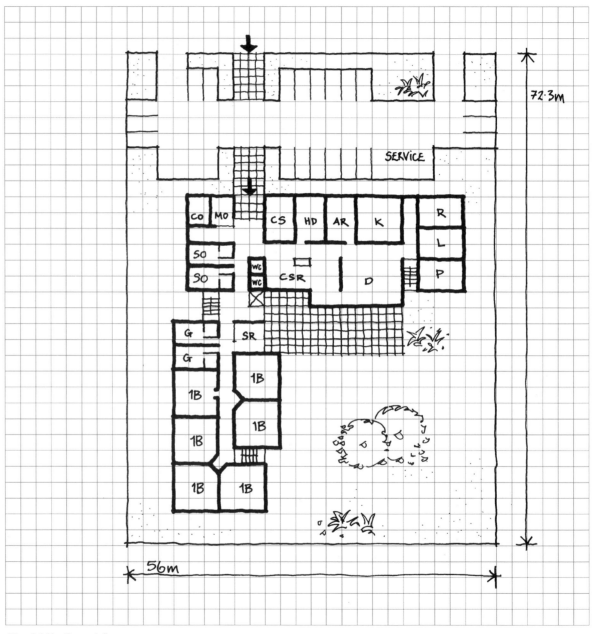

Fig. 6.4.3b: Ground floor

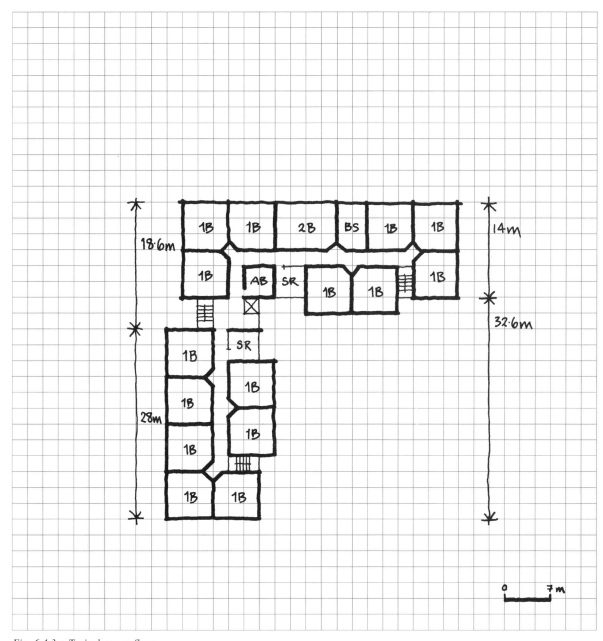

18·6m

14m

32·6m

28m

| 1B | 1B | 2B | BS | 1B | 1B |
| 1B | AB | SR | 1B | 1B | 1B |

1B	SR
1B	1B
1B	1B
1B	1B

0   7m

Fig. 6.4.3c: Typical upper floor

'L' Shape		
1	no. of floors	3
2	no. of units	40
3	footprint area	1,080 sq.m
4	communal facilities	660 sq.m
5	total area	3,240 sq.m
6	furthest distance from flat to lift lobby	35m
7	site area	4,050 sq.m
8	footprint ratio (3/7)	0.3:1
9	plot ratio (5/7)	0.8:1

Fig. 6.4.3d

Fig. 6.4.3e: 'L' shaped development

Compact 'L' Shape

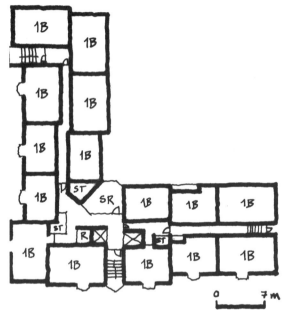

Fig. 6.4.3f: Typical compact 'L' shaped development

The compact 'L' occupies 5 storeys and has a footprint of 630 sq.m. It can be fitted on a site of as little as 1200 sq.m if basement car-parking is used. Each of its four residential floors can be viewed as a cluster of ten flats.

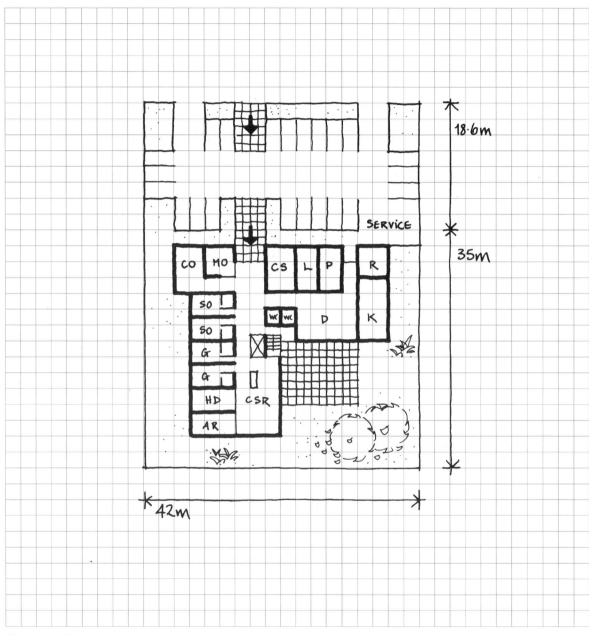

Fig. 6.4.3g: Ground floor

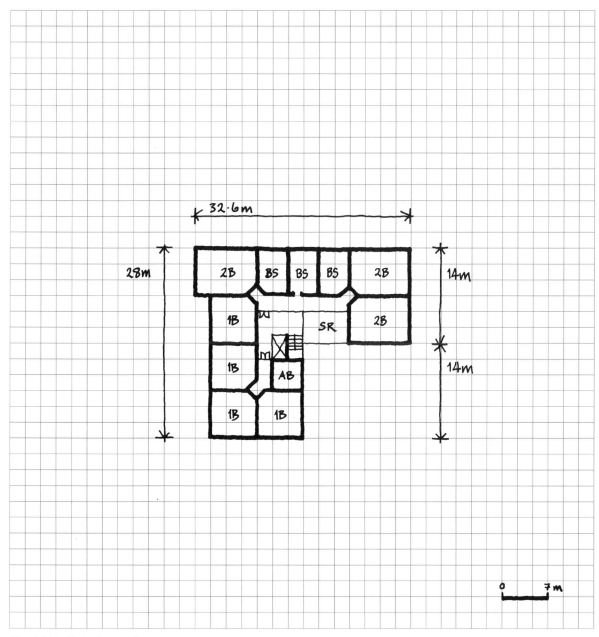

Fig. 6.4.3h: Typical upper floor

Compact 'L' Shape		
1	no. of floors	5
2	no. of units	40
3	footprint area	630 sq.m
4	communal facilities	630 sq.m
5	total area	3,160 sq.m
6	furthest distance from flat to lift lobby	10m
7	site area	1,500-2,250 sq.m*
8	footprint ratio (3/7)	0.4:1-0.3:1
9	plot ratio (5/7)	2.2:1-1.4:1

* smaller site area assumes basement car-parking
Fig. 6.4.3j

Fig. 6.4.3k: Compact 'L' shaped scheme

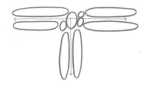

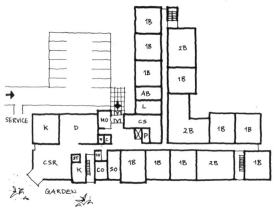

Fig. 6.4.4a: Typical 'T' shaped development

0   7m

The 'T' shape plan incorporates three arms and thus offers a compact circulation system even when planned on two storeys. The form can be arranged on a site in a number of ways, depending on site shape and orientation. Fig. 6.4.4b shows how the communal wing separates the entrance and service court from the communal garden. The communal facilities could easily be used for non-resident day care.

Although the 'T' shape offers a choice of three routes at each level, the stair and lift lobby have good visual links to the outside and orientation would be clear. Each arm contains a cluster of 8 flats and a small shared sitting room.

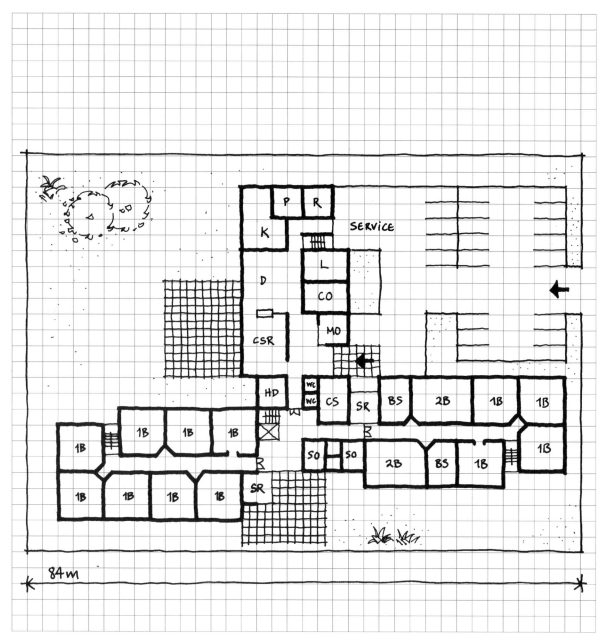

Fig. 6.4.4b: Ground floor

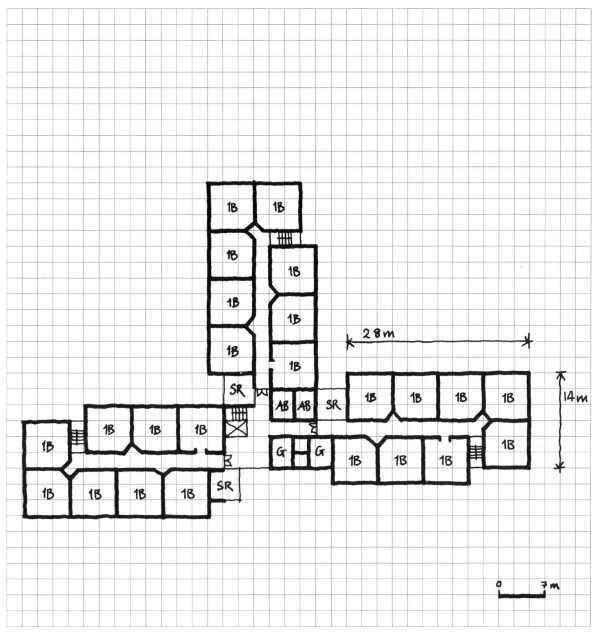

Fig. 6.4.4c: *Typical upper floor*

'T' Shape		
1	no. of floors	2
2	no. of units	40
3	footprint area	1,560 sq.m
4	communal facilities	540 sq.m
5	total area	3,130 sq.m
6	furthest distance from flat to lift lobby	25m
7	site area	4,895 sq.m
8	footprint ratio (3/7)	0.3:1
9	plot ratio (5/7)	0.6:1

Fig. 6.4.4d

Fig. 6.4.4e: *'T' shaped scheme*

6.4.5
Cruciform

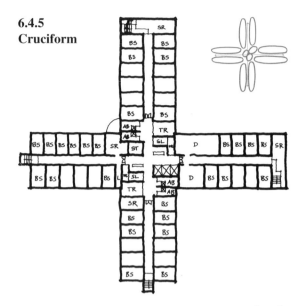

Fig. 6.4.5a: Typical cruciform development

0 ___ 7m

In theory the cruciform should offer the advantage of short routes within a low rise configuration, because all four arms take off from the main vertical core. In practice the central core is cut off from the external wall and is difficult to plan. The lift/stair core is necessarily large and the choice of four routes is likely to be very confusing.

With 40 units it is not practicable to plan a cruciform on more than two storeys: increasing height results in an ever greater proportion of the total plan area being locked within the core.

The form is easy to manipulate on a site and automatically produces four separate environmental areas. For any given orientation 25% of all flats will face north.

The built example, Fig. 6.4.5a, illustrates a cruciform with a large central core without the benefit of natural light.

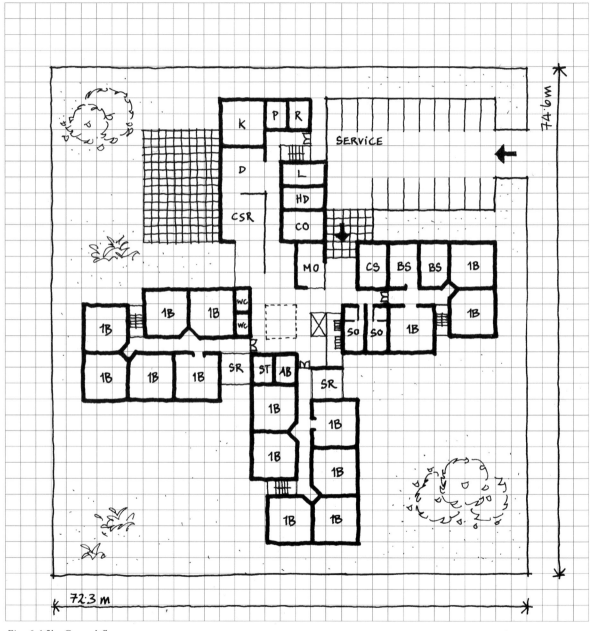

Fig. 6.4.5b: Ground floor

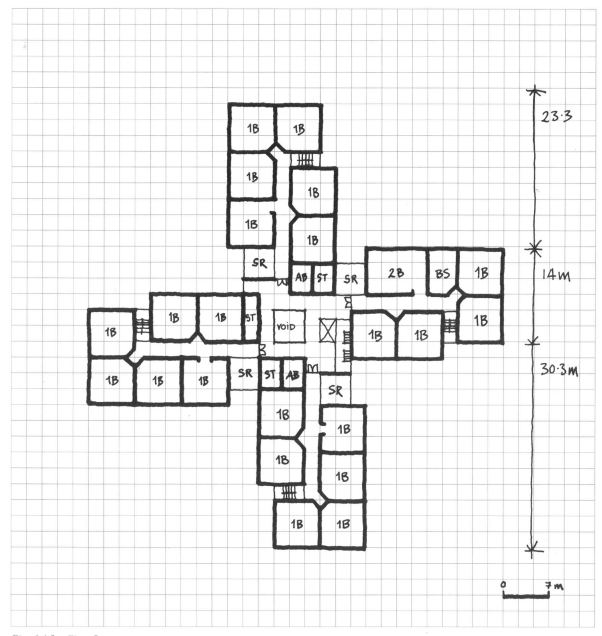

Fig. 6.4.5c: First floor

Cruciform		
1	no. of floors	2
2	no. of units	40
3	footprint area	1,700 sq.m
4	communal facilities	660 sq.m
5	total area	3,400 sq.m
6	furthest distance from flat to lift lobby	27m
7	site area	5,390 sq.m
8	footprint ratio (3/7)	0.3:1
9	plot ratio (5/7)	0.6:1

Fig. 6.4.5d

Fig. 6.4.5e: A cruciform development

6.4.6
'U' Shape Courtyard

At first sight the 'U' shape promises to be profligate in area, but with careful design an economic plan can be achieved. It is only feasible on two storeys and requires a fairly large site with access from the north or north-east.

The 'U' shape achieves a very strong sense of community: the whole arrangement is focused on the shared facilities and the garden, and the residents are in constant visual touch with these elements as they move around. The garden becomes a private and sheltered outside world which relates directly to the dining room and both the main and the subsidiary sitting rooms and acts as the heart of the scheme.

The very fact that this form seems to encourage a strong sense of community with highly integrated communal facilities could it make it unsuitable for use as a non-resident day care centre.

Figs 6.4.6a & 6.4.6b, show that each wing contains two clusters of ten flats each with its own small sitting room. The pattern of circulation is clear and legible, but the length of corridor could be a problem for very frail residents.

This form is only really suitable for two-storey development: a single-storey scheme would be too spread out, while at three storeys the central courtyard becomes too compressed.

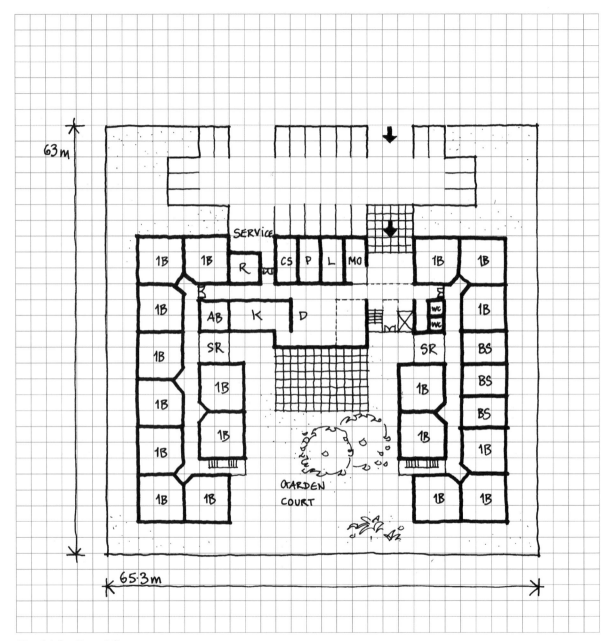

Fig. 6.4.6a: Ground floor

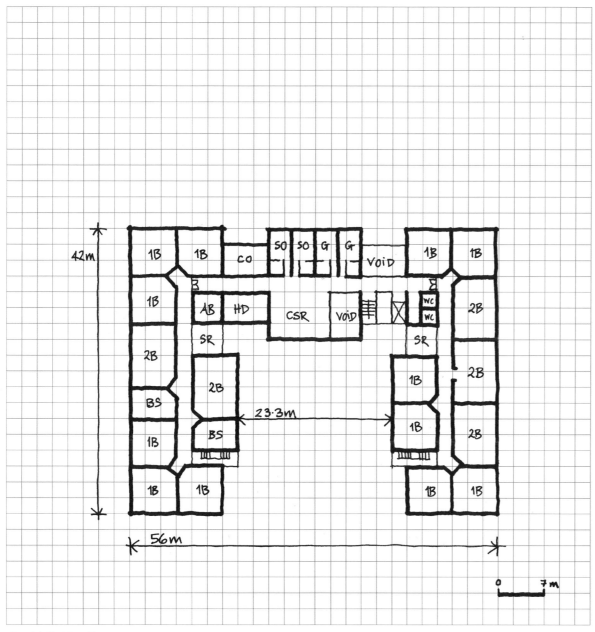

Fig. 6.4.6b: First floor

'U' Shape		
1	no. of floors	2
2	no. of units	40
3	footprint area	1,600 sq.m
4	communal facilities	700 sq.m
5	total area	3,175 sq.m
6	furthest distance from flat to lift lobby	55m
7	site area	4,110 sq.m
8	footprint ratio (3/7)	0.4:1
9	plot ratio (5/7)	0.8:1

Fig. 6.4.6c

Fig. 6.4.6d: Typical 'U' shaped plan

Fig. 6.4.6e: 'U' shaped courtyard development

6.4.7
Atrium

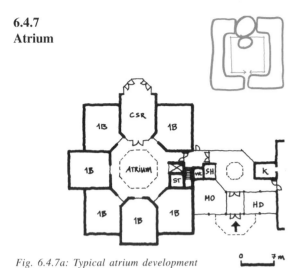

Fig. 6.4.7a: Typical atrium development

Modern 'atria' first appeared during the 1980s and offered interesting environmental possibilities for the design of public and commercial buildings on tight urban sites. A central glazed-over well acts as the central communication hub of the building. It links every floor together visually, and makes it possible to introduce natural daylight and ventilation into deep plans.

The application of atria to sheltered housing is a surprising development. In principle the atrium plan might be expected to reproduce some of the advantages of the 'U' type on a more compact plan. In reality it throws up a number of distinct disadvantages: problems with noise, privacy and fire-safety need to be solved. Worse still the atrium carries memories of institutional buildings like prisons and does not seem to hold out much promise of security and domesticity.

The atrium type incorporates single-sided balcony access and may require internal glazing. The total floor area is relatively high as would be the construction costs.

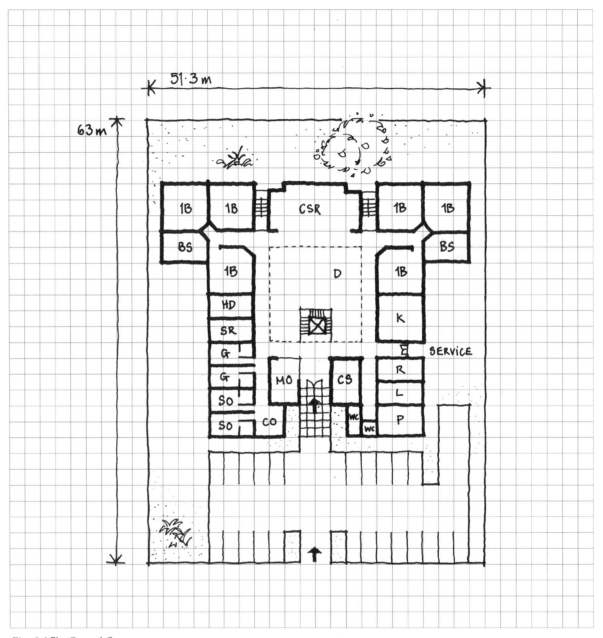

Fig. 6.4.7b: Ground floor

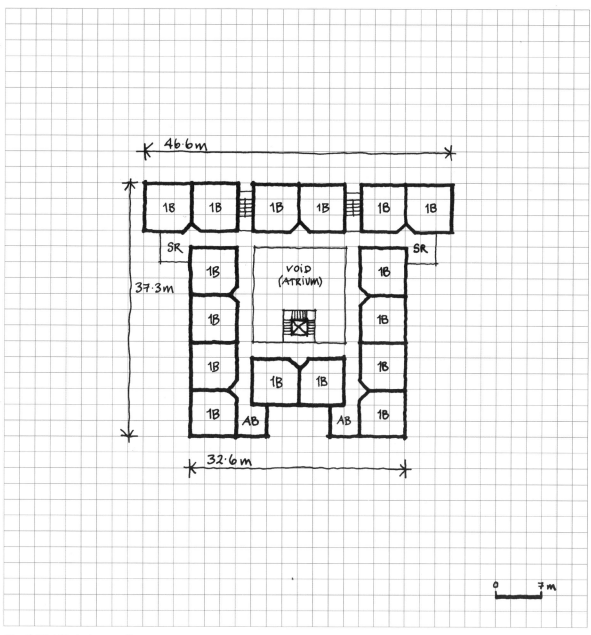

Fig. 6.4.7c: Typical upper floor

Atrium		
1	no. of floors	3
2	no. of units	40
3	footprint area	1,330 sq.m
4	communal facilities	620 sq.m
5	total area	3,530 sq.m*
6	furthest distance from flat to lift lobby	30m
7	site area	3,230 sq.m
8	footprint ratio (3/7)	0.4:1
9	plot ratio (5/7)	1.1:1

* smaller site area assumes basement car-parking

Fig. 6.4.7d

Fig. 6.4.7e: Typical atria

6.4.8
Cluster

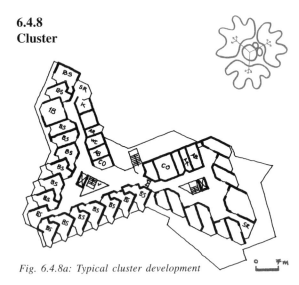

Fig. 6.4.8a: Typical cluster development

It is possible to develop relatively complex cluster forms in which individual flats are arranged in primary groups, which are sub-divided into secondary groups in order to create an artificial social hierarchy within the scheme. Whether or not such clustering is desirable is a matter for discussion. The example in Figs 6.4.8b & 6.4.8c has been simplified to illustrate the principle. It could also be classified as a compact version of the 'offset linear' type.

The four-storey version which is illustrated demonstrates that the plan form can be used quite successfully to articulate the site. The layout is compact and travel distances are kept to a minimum. The lift/stair lobby looks out towards the street. The ground floor plan would accommodate non-resident care activities.

Each floor is divided by the lift/stair lobby into two clusters of six flats which together share a small sitting room. The cluster of six is further broken down into two basic clusters of three flats. The twelve flats on each level share an assisted bathroom.

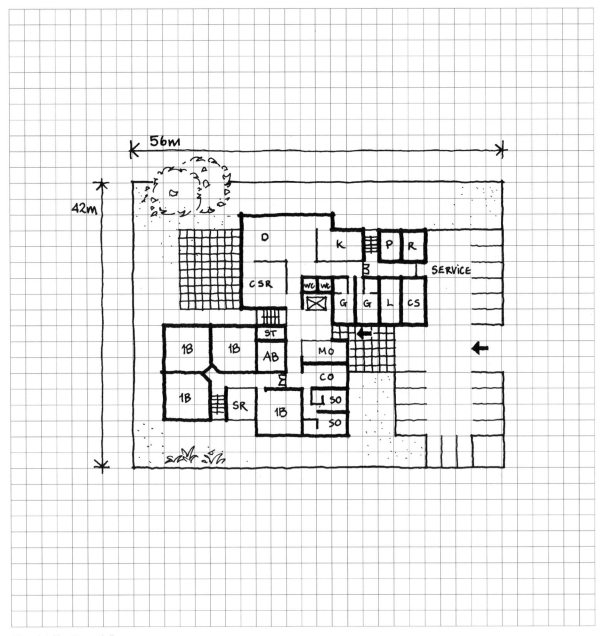

Fig. 6.4.8b: Ground floor

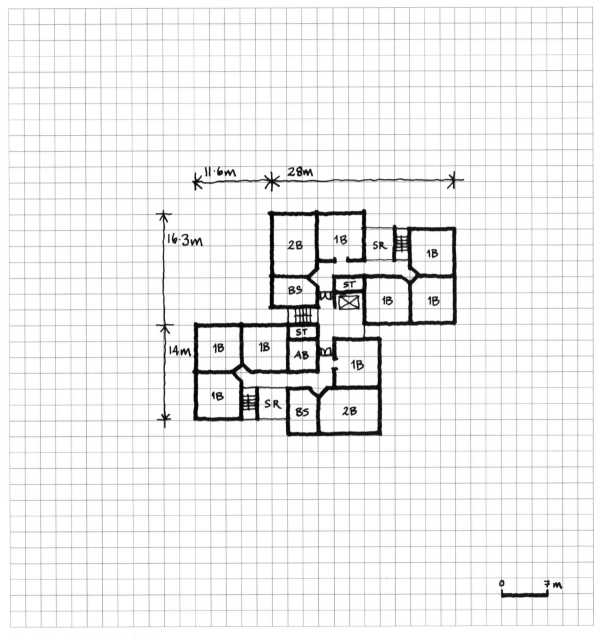

Cluster		
1	no. of floors	4
2	no. of units	40
3	footprint area	830 sq.m
4	communal facilities	540 sq.m
5	total area	3,320 sq.m*
6	furthest distance from flat to lift lobby	16m
7	site area	2,350 sq.m
8	footprint ratio (3/7)	0.4:1
9	plot ratio (5/7)	1.4:1

Fig. 6.4.8d

Fig. 6.4.8c: Typical upper floor

Fig. 6.4.8e: Interior of a cluster block

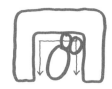

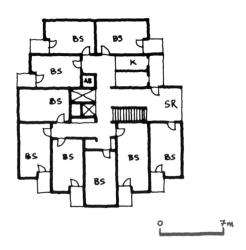

Fig. 6.4.9a: Typical point block development

Although there is a natural prejudice on the part of many older people against 'high-rise' buildings, this type offers a number of tangible advantages: it requires a relatively small site and would, therefore, be suitable for central urban locations, it has a compact plan with minimal travel distances and it can be easily oriented to suit local conditions.

Figs 6.4.9b & 6.4.9c illustrate a point block with five residential floors, each containing eight flats and a ground floor given over entirely to communal facilities. The flats on each floor are grouped in two clusters of four and share a small sitting room and assisted bathroom. No flat is more than 8m from the lift lobby.

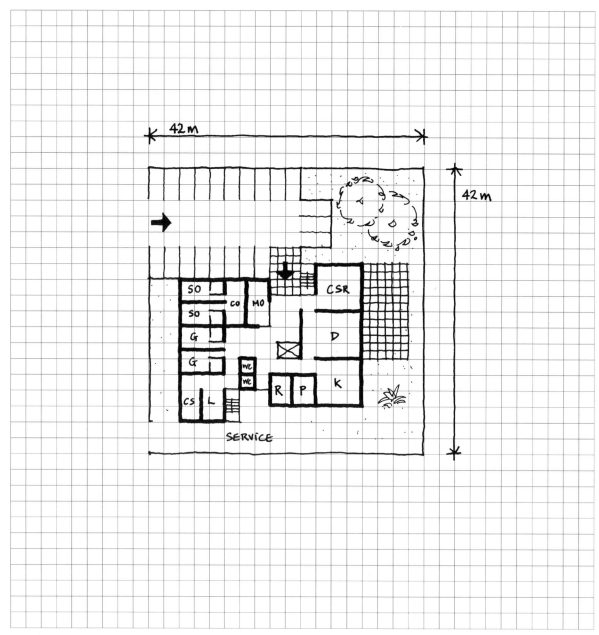

Fig. 6.4.9b: Ground floor

Generic Design

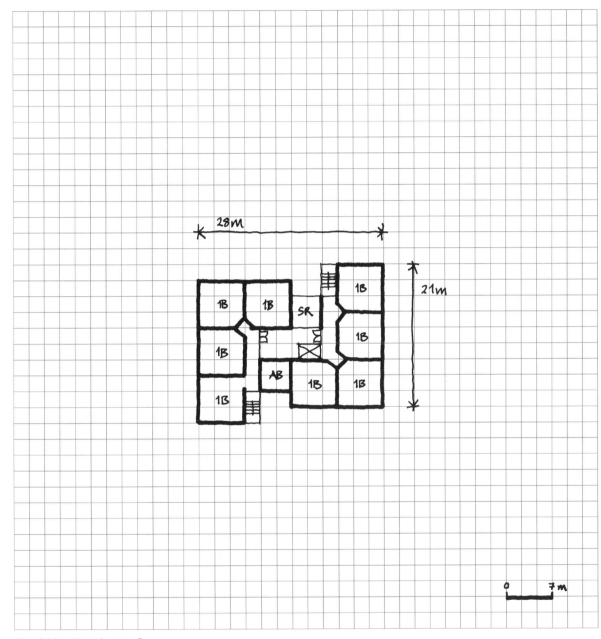

28m

21m

1B 1B SR 1B

1B 1B

1B AB 1B 1B

1B

0   7m

Fig. 6.4.9c: Typical upper floor

Point block		
1	no. of floors	6
2	no. of units	40
3	footprint area	540 sq.m
4	communal facilities	580 sq.m
5	total area	3,240 sq.m*
6	furthest distance from flat to lift lobby	10m
7	site area	1,400-1,760 sq.m*
8	footprint ratio (3/7)	0.4:1-0.3:1
9	plot ratio (5/7)	2.3:1-1.8:1

* smaller site area assumes basement car-parking
Fig. 6.4.8d

Fig. 6.4.9e: Point block

6.4.10
Comment

Although the general taxonomy is not exhaustive, experience has shown that most existing examples do correspond to one or other of the types, or can be classified as hybrids of two or more of the types.

Surprisingly the study reveals very little variation in total floor area between the examples: all but one fall within the range 3,130 sq.m to 3,320 sq.m. This suggests that the careful application of the planning tool to the standard room schedule can achieve almost the same degree of efficiency whatever the basic form.

However, floor area is only one criterion for comparison. Site areas range from 1,400 sq.m to 5,200 sq.m, and there is an obvious variation of footprint and roof area, depending on number of storeys. The study also illustrates the extent to which the different forms are able to shape the site and to create sheltered and private sitting areas.

It is interesting to compare the six-storey point block with the two-storey 'U' type. While both occupy almost identical floor areas, the foundation, external wall and roof areas vary considerably, see Fig. 6.4.10a. Although the external wall area of the 'U' type is smaller - because the plan is more continuous - the areas of the ground floor and roof are much greater, and the total envelope area is greater by 26%. These comparisons give some indication of relative heat losses and relative construction costs.

The study does not identify one single 'best buy': that was not its aim. It does provide a basis for comparing the different types and ought to be of some assistance to development managers and architects in identifying the appropriate type to adopt on any given site.

	'U' Type	Point Block
site area	4,110	1,760
total floor area	3,170	3,240
ground floor area	1,620	540
roof area (assume flat roof)	1,620	540
external wall area	1,1400	1,800
total envelope	3,640	2,880

Fig. 6.4.10a: 'U' type and point block: comparison of external envelop area (sq.m)

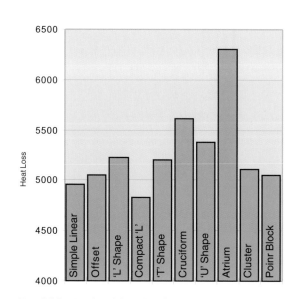

Fig. 6.5.1a: Predicted heat loss for taxonomy building forms

6.5
Building Form and Heat Loss

The effect of building form on heat loss was discussed in section 5.1.2, 'Thermal Insulation and Heat Loss'. The following is a comparison of predicted steady heat losses for the full range of generic plans which are described in 6.4, 'Generic Designs'.

6.5.1
The Generic Plans Compared

Fig. 6.5.1a lists the steady state heat losses for the complete range of generic plans which have been presented above. The heat losses have been calculated assuming that the fabric has been built to current Building Regulation standards for thermal insulation and that there is a ventilation rate of one air change per hour.

The figure shows that the most energy efficient building form is No. 4 the 'Compact L' with a specific heat loss of 4833W/K, whereas the least efficient is No. 8, the 'Atrium' with a loss of 6300W/K. On the basis of these figures it is predicted that the Atrium Type will require 30% more heat energy than the Compact L Type. This conclusion reflects the higher internal volume of the Atrium Type. The second highest consumer is the 'Cruciform' with a predicted loss of 5607W/K. The narrow bunching of the results reflects the fact that all of the generic types have been designed using the same basic plan depth of 16.3m.

Bibliography

Age Concern, *Building on Experience: a survey of older people's housing,* (London: 1996)

Baker S & Parry M, *Housing for Sale to the Elderly,* (London: The Housing Research Foundation, 3rd Report, 1986)

Barker Peter, Barrick Jon & Wilson Rod, *Building Sight,* (London: RNIB, 1995)

Bettyan, Boetticher & Raschko, *Housing Interiors for the Disabled & Elderly,* (New York: Van Nostrand Reinhold, 1991)

Bond J & Carstairs V, *Services for the Elderly,* (Scottish Home and Health Department, 1982)

BRE, *BRE Housing Design Handbook: Energy and Internal Layout,* (UK: BRE, 1993a)

BRE, *Sound Control for Homes,* (UK: BRE, 1993b)

BRE, *Continuous Mechanical Ventilation in Dwellings: Design, Installation and Operation* BRE Digest 398, (UK: BRE, 1994)

BRECSU, *Low Energy Design for Housing Associations,* (UK: BRE, 1995)

Bright Galba, *Caring for Diversity,* (London: Odu Dua Housing Association, 1996)

BS CP 342:Part 2, *Centralised Hot Water Supply: Buildings other than Individual Dwellings,* (London: BSI, 1974)

BSI, *Building Regulations Approved Documents 'F' Ventilation,* (London: BSI, 1995)

Burley Robin, *Towards a House Building Technology for the Adaptable Smarter Home*, (Norway: BESTA International Conference, 1994)

Butler Alan, Oldman Christine & Greve John, *Sheltered Housing for the Elderly - Policy, Practice and the Consumer,* (London: Allen & Unwin, 1983)

Cavanagh Sue, *Designing Housing for Older Women,* (London: Women's Design Service, 1992)

Cena K, Spotila J R & Avery H W, *Thermal Comfort of the Elderly,* (ASHRAE Transaction pp.329-342, 1986)

Cena K, Spotila J & Ryan E B, *Effect of Behavioural Strategies and Activity on Thermal Comfort of the Elderly,* (ASHRAE Transaction pp.83-103, 1988)

Chadderton D, *Building Services Engineering,* (London: E&FN Spon,1995)

CIBSE, *Installation and Equipment Data, CIBSE Guide B,* (London: CIBSE, 1986a)

CIBSE, *Environmental Criteria for Design ,CIBSE Guide A1,* (London: CIBSE, 1986b)

CIBSE, *Air Infiltration and Natural Ventilation, CIBSE Guide A4,* (London: CIBSE, 1986c)

CIBSE, *Water Services Systems, CIBSE Guide, Volume C Reference Data,* (London: CIBSE, 1988)

CIBSE, *Technical Memoranda 13 - Minimising the Risk of Legionnaires' Disease,* (London: CIBSE, 1991)

CIBSE, *Code for Interior Lighting, 1994,* (London: CIBSE, 1994)

CIRIA, *Environmental Handbook for Building and Civil Engineering Projects,* (London: CIRIA, 1994)

Clevely RC et al., *Hoists, Lifts and Transfers,* (Oxford: The Disability Information Trust, 1996)

Coleman David & Salt John, *The British Population: Patterns Trends and Processes,* (Oxford: OUP, 1992)

Collins K J & Hoinville E, *Temperature Requirements in Old Age,* (Building Services Engineering Research & Technology, vol. 1, no.4, 1980)

Collins KJ, Exton-Smith A N & Dore C, *Urban Hypothermia:* (British Medical Journal, vol. 282, pp.175-177, Jan 1981)

Collins K J, *Low Indoor Temperatures and Morbidity in the Elderly,* (Age and Aging, vol. 15, pp.212-220, 1986)

de Bono Edward, *Away with the Gang of Three,* (London: The Guardian 25 Jan 1997)

DHSS East Sussex SSD, *Growing Old in Brighton,* (London: HMSO, 1980)

DoE Circular 74/74 , Welsh Office Circular 120/74, Joint Circular 7 May 1974, *Housing for People who are Physically Handicapped,* (London: HMSO, 1974)

DoE, *The Building Regulations Approved Document L - Conservation of Fuel and Power,* (London: HMSO, 1990)

DoE, *The Building Regulations Approved Document B,* (London: HMSO, 1991)

EEO, *Energy Efficiency in New Housing: Future Practice R&D 2,* (London: Energy Efficiency Office,1992)

EEO, *Energy Efficiency in New Housing: Good Practice Guide 79,* (London: Energy Efficiency Office, 1993a)

EEO, *Domestic Ventilation General Information Leaflet 9,* (London: Energy Efficiency Office, 1993b)

Electricity Council, *Interior Lighting Design,* (London: The Electricity Council 1986)

Fich, Mortensen & Zahle, *Old People's Houses,* (Copenhagen: Kunstakademiets Forlag, 1995)

Fleetwood Hugh, *Designing Kitchens for the Elderly,* (Ormskirk: Thomas Lyster, 1990)

Gann David & Iwashita Shigeaki, *Housing and Home Automation for the Elderly and Disabled,* (SPRU, University of Sussex, 1995)

Garrett R H, *Hot and Cold Water Supply,* (Oxford: BSP Professional Books, 1991)

Goldenberg Leon, *Housing for the Elderly: New Trends in Europe,* (New York: Garland, 1981)

Goldsmith Selwyn, *Mobility Housing,* (HDD Occasional Paper 2/74, DoE, HMSO, 1980 - 1) (Reprinted from The Architects' Journal 3 July, 1974)

Goldsmith Selwyn, *Wheelchair Housing,* (HDD Occasional Paper 2/75, DoE, HMSO, 1980 - 2) (Reprinted from The Architects' Journal 25 June, 1975)

Goldsmith Selwyn, *Designing for the Disabled,* (London: RIBA publications, 3rd edition, 1976)

Hanover Housing Association, *Paying for Old Age, Conference Notes,* (UK: Hanover Housing Association, 1996a)

Hanover Housing Association, *Why Hanover Extra Care Housing?* (UK: Hanover Housing Association, 1996b)

Hanover Housing Association, *What is Hanover Extra Care Housing?* (UK: Hanover Housing Association, 1996c)

Harris Research Centre, *A Survey on Sheltered Housing,* (UK: McCarthy & Stone plc, 1989)

Health & Safety Executive, *Residential Care Homes,* (London: HMSO, 1993)

HMSO, *General Household Survey,* (London: HMSO, 1985)

HMSO, *Caring for People - Community Care in the Next Decade,* (London: HMSO, 1989)

Hoglund David, *Housing for the Elderly,* (New York: Van Nostrand Reinhold, 1985)

Holmes-Siedle James, *Barrier-free Design* , (Oxford: Butterworth, 1996)

Housing Corporation, *Good Practice Guide,* (London: Housing Corporation, 1989)

Housing Corporation, *Housing for Older People,* (London: Housing Corporation, 1996)

Housing Corporation, *Scheme Development Standards,* (London: Housing Corporation, 1995)

IOP, *Plumbing Engineering Services Design Guide,* (London: Institute of Plumbing, 1988)

Leibrock Cynthia, *Beautiful Barrier -Free*, (New York: Van Nostrand Reinhold, 1993)

Liddament M, *A Guide to Energy Efficient Ventilation*, (Coventry, UK: Air Infiltration and Ventilation Centre, 1996)

Lowe R, Bell M & Johnston D, *Directory of Energy Efficient Housing,* (UK: Chartered Institute of Housing, 1996)

Marshall Mary, *Designing for Disorientation,* (Access By Design No.58 pp.15-17)

Martin Frank, *Every House You'll Ever Need,* (Edinburgh: Edinvar, 1992)

Martin P L & Oughton D R, *Faber and Kell's Heating and Air Conditioning of Buildings,* (London, Butterworth-Heinemann,1995)

McCafferty Paul, *Living Independently,* (London: DoE / HMSO, 1994)

McGlone Francis, *Disability and Dependency in Old Age*, (London: Family Policy Studies Centre, 1992)

McIntyre D A, *Thermal environment: comfort - discomfort in air conditioning systems design for buildings, edited by Sherratt A* , (McGraw-Hill, 1983)

Medina John, *The Clock of Ages,* (Cambridge UP, 1996)

Meyer-Bohe Walter, *Bauen für alte und behinderte Menschen*, (Berlin: Bauverlag GMBH, 1996)

Micallef Marisa, *Difficult-to-let Sheltered Housing,* (Oxford: Anchor Housing Trust, 1994)

Moore F, *Environmental Control Systems - Heating, Cooling and Lighting,* (McGraw-Hill, 1993)

NFHA, *The Future of Housing: Who Cares? vols 1 & 2,* (London, National Federation of Housing Associations, 1991)

NFHA, *Challenging Times: the Changing Role of the Warden,* (London, National Federation of Housing Associations, 1996)

NHS Estates, *Safe Hot Water and Surface Temperatures*, (London: HMSO, 1994a)

NHS Estates, *Health Facilities Notes: Buildings for the Day Care of Older People*, (London: HMSO, 1994b)

Norman Alison, *Bricks & Mortals: design & lifestyle in old people's homes*, (London: Centre for Policy on Ageing, 1984)

OPCS, *English House Condition Survey 1991*, (HMSO, 1993)

Owen Hugh & O'Dwyer Phil, *Planning and Architecture Guide,* (Manchester: Guinness Trust, 1990)

Oxford Brookes University School of Architecture, *Buildings Design and the Delivery of Day Care Services to Elderly People,* (London: HMSO, 1994)

Palfreyman Tessa, *Designing for Accessibility,* (London: Centre for Accessible Environments, 1996)

Parkin P H & Humphreys H R, *Acoustics Noise and Buildings,* (London: Faber, 1958)

Parsons K C, *Thermal Comfort Standards: Past, Present and Future,* conference proceedings, (UK: BRE Garston, 1993)

Parsons K C, *ISO Standards and Thermal Comfort* edited by F. Nicol et al., (London: Chapman & Hall, 1995)

Penoyre and Prasad, *Accommodating Diversity* , (London: North Housing Trust, 1993)

Philips Derek, *Lighting,* (London: Macdonald, 1966)

Pilcher Jane, *Age Generation in Modern Britain*, (Oxford: OUP, 1995)

Randall Bill, *Staying Put - The Best Move I'll Never Make,* (Oxford: Anchor Housing Association, 1995)

Ranson R, *Healthy Housing - A Practical Guide,* (London: E & FN Spon, 1991)

Regnier Victor, *Assisted Living Housing for the Elderly*, (New York: Van Nostrand Reinhold, 1994)

Riseborough Moyra & Niner Pat, *I Didn't Know You Cared!*, (Oxford: Anchor Housing Trust, 1994a)

Riseborough Moyra & Niner Pat, *Who Wants Sheltered Housing?* (Oxford: Anchor Housing Trust, 1994b)

RNIB, *The Housing Needs of People with a Visual Impairment,* (London: The Housing Corporation, 1995)

Rohles F & Johnson M, *Thermal Comfort in the Elderly,* (ASHRAE Transactions, 1972)

Rostron Jack, *Housing the Physically Disabled,* (Aldershot: Arena, 1995)

Salmon Geoffrey, *Caring Environments for Frail Elderly People*, (London: Longman, 1993)

Scottish Development Department, *Housing for the Elderly,* (London: HMSO, 1980)

Scottish Homes, *The Design of Barrier Free Housing,* (Edinburgh: National Housing Agency, 1995)

Scottish Homes, *The Physical Quality of Housing: Housing for Older People and Disabled People,* (Edinburgh: National Housing Agency 1996)

Shearer Peter, *Ada's Story,* (Hanover Housing Association, 1996 unpublished)

Shields T J, *Fire & Disabled People in Buildings,* (UK: BRE, 1993)

Steffy Gary R, *Architectural Lighting Design,* (New York: Van Nostrand Reinhold, 1990)

Strother Smith N C, *Case Histories of Recent UK Fires* from *Fire Safety in Hospitals and Nursing Homes,* (London: FPA, 1981)

Thorpe Stephen, *Good Loo Design Guide,* (London: Centre on Environment for the Handicapped, 1988)

Thorpe Stephen, *Wheelchair Housing Design Guide,* (London: EMAP, 1997)

Tinker A, *Staying at Home: Helping Elderly People,* (London: HMSO, 1984)

Tinker A, *An Evaluation of Very Sheltered Housing,* (London: HMSO, 1989)

Tinker A, McCreadie C, Wright F & Salvage A, *The Care of Frail Elderly People in the UK,* (London: HMSO, 1994)

Tinker A, Wright F & Zeilug H, *Difficult-to-Let Sheltered Housing,* (London: HMSO, 1995)

Turner Janet, *Lighting,* (London: Batsford, 1994)

Valins Martin, *Housing for Elderly People,* (London: Architectural Press, 1988)

Valins Martin & Salter Derek, *Futurecare,* (Oxford: Blackwell, 1996)

Voutsadakis Stelios, *Housing for People with Disabilities,* (London: Islington Council, 1989)

Wachsman Konrad, *The Turning Point of Building,* (NewYork: Reinhold, 1961)

Wasch William K, *Home Planning for Your Later Years,* (USA: BCP, 1996)

Weal Francis & Weal Francesca, *Housing the Elderly ,* (London: Mitchell, 1988)

Wertheimer Alison, *Innovative Older People's Housing Projects,* (London: National Housing Federation, 1993)

WHO, *Indoor Environment: Health Aspects of Air Quality,* (World Health Organisation,1990)

Winstanley, Lorna, *Older People's Preferred Options,* (Hanover Housing Association, 1996 unpublished)

Index